Teaching Adult ESL

A Practical Introduction

Betsy Parrish
Hamline University

Consultants

Janet Isserlis
Brown University

Sylvia Ramirez
MiraCosta College

Teaching Adult ESL, 1st Edition

Published by McGraw-Hill ESL/ELT, a business unit of The McGraw-Hill Companies, Inc., 1221 Avenue of the Americas, New York, NY 10020.

This book is printed on recycled, acid-free paper containing 10% post-consumer waste.

1 2 3 4 5 6 7 8 9 QPD 9 8 7 6 5 4

ISBN: 0-07-285513-4

Editorial director: *Tina B. Carver*
Senior managing editor: *Erik Gundersen*
Developmental editor: *Louis Carrillo*
Production manager: *Juanita Thompson*
Interior designer: *Martini Graphic Services, Inc.*
Cover designer: *The Design Shop*
Illustration: *Martini Graphic Services, Inc.*
Indexer: *Do Mi Stauber Indexing Services*

McGraw-Hill ESL/ELT

Table of Contents

Dedication

To Jonas, Rémy and Sina—who were there for me with love and support during this more than year-long effort.

Acknowledgments

My deepest gratitude goes to Janet Isserlis, who has been with me from start to finish in the creation of this book. Her intellect, insightfulness, humor, and compassion have challenged and stretched me to write a book that is as responsive as possible to the needs of ESL learners and teachers working in diverse settings. The experience of collaborating with Janet enriched me professionally and personally. With her wealth of knowledge and experience, she directed me to resources, ideas, and experts in the field of adult ESL. She was exceptionally generous with her time and expertise (and patience!). Thanks, Janet.

I'm grateful to Erik Gundersen for his vision of the kind of book he felt was needed for teachers new to the field of adult ESL, and for giving me the opportunity to write such a book. Erik's trust, respect, professionalism, understanding, and guidance have made this journey a pleasant and rewarding one. I feel most fortunate to have had the chance to work with him.

My thanks also go to Sylvia Ramirez for the wealth of insightful feedback and suggestions she provided on the later draft of the book. She brought another very valuable perspective from working in contexts and with populations different from those Janet and I have experienced.

My thanks go Julia Reimer, Kathryn Heinze, Patsy Vinogradov, Janet Dixon, and Julie Pierce for reading and commenting on early drafts of many of the chapters. Julia was also kind enough to pilot a number of the chapters in her teacher education classes and workshops—and she was always there to listen as I talked through my plans or grappled with issues for many of the chapters.

Thanks to all of the teachers who welcomed me into their classrooms this year: Laura Lenz, Celeste Mazur, Beth Upton, Rosie Sharkey, Corinne Nash, Elizabeth Miller, Jeanne Specht, Tina Kush, Julie Hagen, Shayne Ernzer, and to the learners in all of those classes.

Thanks to Lyle Heikes, Beth Easter, Andy Nash, and Diana Pecoraro for giving so generously of their time and expertise during our lengthy conversations about text selection, assessment, accountability and standards—also to all those who responded to surveys and questionnaires, including Sylvia Ramirez, Donna Price-Machado, Barry Shaffer, Ellen Lowry, James Douglas, Suzanne Donsky, and Bonnie Olson.

Many thanks to my colleagues in the Graduate School of Education at Hamline University who supported this endeavor.

Foreword

Janet Isserlis

BACKGROUND — Why do we need this book? Why do we need it now?

Two years ago, Erik Gundersen invited reviewers to consider a prospectus for a book designed for novice teachers of adult ESL. It was huge in scope; a book you'd love to read but hate to have to write. The author's proposal addressed classroom practice, skills (speaking, reading, writing, listening), literacy and language development, classroom management, assessment, reporting and federal accountability guidelines.

I responded as thoroughly as I could to the prospectus, thinking all the while of how challenging it would be to develop the book and also wondering, really, do we need another handbook for adult ESL educators?

Betsy Parrish developed and accepted her own challenge to bring such a book to print. The text you're reading answers my question with an emphatic yes. Many of us tend to bookmark Websites, 'file' articles (to read later, to share with students, to get to someday), and otherwise not entirely take note of the fact that say, ten years have passed since we last saw a good book about teaching. While there are many timeless elements to good teaching practice that may well have been addressed in a text in the 1980s or 1990s, there are also many particular things about teaching adults that have changed over the last twenty years. By bringing together a guided set of readings and activities addressing sound educational practice, and providing detailed resource lists, all within a solid framework, the author has given new (and not so new) teachers a much-needed overview of what adult ESL instruction looks like, and, more importantly, what it looks like when done very well. Betsy brings her work as a teacher educator, her own international experience in learning and teaching languages, and her keen sense of what counts to this text so that the reader holds in her hands a complete introduction to the work we do when we work with adults learning English.

This work has grown out of an understanding of the general complexity of teaching well and the specific issues surrounding instruction for adults who possess a range of prior involvement with education, varied abilities to speak, read, hear, and write in their own languages and in English, and varied expectations of what school might look like in an English-speaking country. Beginning with an overview of who these learners might be, all the way through to an analysis of how they know and how we know what they've learned, this text provides teachers with a thorough overview of what learning looks like from intake to exit, who the stakeholders in the process are, and why it all matters in the first place.

Within the text, Betsy draws on examples of classroom practice and interaction gleaned from her own work and from that of colleagues. She describes processes through which to introduce and expand language development activities, considering the different contexts in which the work might occur, points to strengths and drawbacks of methodologies and consistently credits the reader with the sense to explore, reflect upon, and analyze the choices she or he makes in the classroom. She points to published student texts across a range of interests and perspectives, their potential usefulness and constraints. She offers an analysis of techniques and methodologies that work without condemning other approaches out of hand.

Betsy brings great integrity to this project. She believes in the primacy of learners' strengths and works against a deficit approach to teaching teachers—believing that ESL learners and educators possess skills and abilities, if not experience. Her aim here is to assist teachers in assisting learners as well as they can. She believes that teachers are constantly learning, and that they want to know what works for their learners. She believes that learning should occur in a safe and supportive environment and that teachers care about this learning deeply. With this text she provides both new, and more experienced, teachers with key points to (re)consider in undertaking teaching, and a wealth of resources for those who so choose, to dig more deeply.

Each chapter in this overview text contains sufficient information to enable educators to know what questions next to ask, what information next to seek. Betsy amply cites resources for further learning, as well, so that the text can function both as a linear guide to adult ESL teaching, as well as a useful reference for regular review and consultation. Each chapter provides an overview of standard terms and practice, resources for further learning, Web- and print-based materials, as well as references to others in the field knowledgeable in a given area. This compilation of resources makes the book especially valuable as knowledge grows, sources are scattered, and time for searching, reading, and reviewing is limited.

No work is neutral. As federal and state mandates increasingly drive and limit program possibilities, we need access to voices of reason to remind us of what good **teaching** practice is still all about—and that measurement alone does not improve instruction. Betsy walks readers through mandated frameworks and constraints incurred through those mandates while remaining aware of the realities inherent in daily classroom work. We learn how learners understand progress, how we can understand it, and how we can translate it to those outside our programs to whom we are accountable. The process is demystified because Betsy has made it transparent. This is no small feat at a time when accountability drives instruction in too many instances.

The Writing Process

Betsy and I first met at the International TESOL Convention in Salt Lake City, at what we'd thought would be a relatively brief breakfast meeting. Three hours later we emerged from the restaurant, having discussed a framework for the text, broad themes and specific resources, as well as having learned about one another's work, perspectives, and shared visions about language and literacy development. Over the following months we communicated by phone, met once in Minneapolis (where we spent an entire day working on the book, visiting, and sharing a brilliant meal), and met again in the spring of 2003 when the book was almost complete.

Our process evolved through a back and forth communication around each chapter as Betsy wrote. She would send the electronic version, I'd read it, respond in writing—and sometimes on the phone—and Betsy would rethink, revise, rewrite. Sometimes we'd push each other, always knowing that the other could push back. My classroom experience is largely rooted in very basic level ESOL literacy. Betsy has worked with more varied groups of learners. She taught me a lot about my own assumptions of what teaching 'should' look like, pushed my thinking and broadened my understanding, both of classroom practice and of teacher education.

Despite the fact that Betsy and I talked through our decisions carefully—*how to sequence material? what should we emphasize?*—I worried that the book might reflect my own biases too much. Because our experience felt somewhat limited by the kinds of programs we'd worked in, we sought the perspective and voice that Sylvia Ramirez brought to the work as our third reader and critical friend. Her experience as an administrator running a large program in California compels her to think long and hard about the implications of standards-based practice and its demands on teachers and students; that thinking shaped this work and strengthened it immeasurably. We are grateful to her for reminding us of points we hadn't considered—usually because our contexts differed from those she knows well, and are grateful, too, for the support she gave us when Betsy's text was, after all, moving in the right directions.

Throughout the process, we were always glad for, and cheered by Erik Gundersen's endless goodwill and support.

Audience

I see this book serving multiple audiences. As an overview text for teacher education within higher education, it brings together points that other authors may cover in greater detail, but not always within the broader contexts that this text addresses. It also lends itself quite well to independent reading and exploration, and would be a useful vehicle for program-wide professional development. Betsy addresses an ongoing need for educators with a thirst for learning but limited time and resources for gathering information scattered across various media, including print, Web-based, and video. She frames her intentions clearly, lays out each chapter carefully and in the end has created a text that welcomes educators into acknowledging the joys and challenges of the work we do by informing us all of what's come before, what's possible, and what has to be done.

Introduction

Betsy Parrish

In the foreword, Janet Isserlis shared the process involved in creating this book, our shared philosophy, as well as some ideas as to how this text might best be used. A fundamental aspect of our collaboration was a shared vision of what teaching and learning should look like. I would like you, the reader, to have a sense of what beliefs shaped the work I completed over the past year and a half, and then invite you to reflect on your own beliefs about teaching and learning as a means of framing how you read, interact with, and understand the teaching principles and practices presented in the coming chapters.

It is my belief that learning starts from within. Every ESL learner as well as every ESL teacher experiences what we do in the classroom differently. Everything that happens is shaped by experiences, culture, expectations, strengths, and needs. Each of you will experience this text differently. Some of you may have spent a considerable amount time in an ESL classroom already and will draw on those experiences to shape and understand the principles and practices covered in this book. Those of you who are new to teaching ESL will draw on your experience learning other things. It is because of this belief that every chapter is interspersed with tasks that allow you to preview content, explore your ideas and practice and, finally, apply what you've learned in your own class, or through observing and talking with others.

I also believe that learning is cyclical and that it takes time. While I have chosen to organize the content of this book in a particular order, there may be some topics that you'll revisit as you read the book, particularly those of you new to ESL. Chapters 1 and 2 provide a broad context for you as a reader, examining issues of ESL learner life circumstances, second language acquisition, a broad overview of teaching approaches, and program options. Chapters 3 through 5 focus on the tools of classroom teaching—presenting and practicing language, developing listening, speaking, reading, and writing skills. Chapters 6 and 7 look at planning for and managing teaching and learning. Chapter 8 points to materials selection and the use of technology in the classroom. The last two chapters provide an overview of assessment, accountability, and standards. While you may work through these topics in a linear fashion, they should be viewed as interconnected and as a starting point for further exploration.

Finally, I believe that the best learning and teaching are collaborative. Collaboration is what makes my work as teacher, learner, and colleague rich and rewarding. I had the opportunity to collaborate with many people as I developed this book. My collaboration with Janet had a tremendous impact on the structure and content of this book. My collaboration with learners and teachers throughout my career has given me myriad examples to draw on, which I hope provide you, the reader, with vivid examples of learning and teaching in action. The activities in this book serve to promote collaboration between you and your classmates or colleagues, and the teaching principles presented in these chapters are grounded in the belief that good teaching is based on a genuine collaboration with learners.

Before you begin reading, take some time to think about your own beliefs about teaching and learning. You will be invited to reflect on these beliefs again at the end of the book, but continue to think about how your views evolve and change throughout the process of learning more about teaching ESL to adult learners.

Looking Forward

Complete these statements with your current beliefs about teaching and learning in adult ESL contexts. Work with a group of classmates or colleagues, or write your reflections in a journal.

1 Strengths and challenges adult learners bring to the ESL classroom are. . .

2 Some common purposes for learning English are. . .

3 Learning a second language involves. . .

4 If I walked into an adult ESL classroom, I'd like to see. . .

5 Learners' roles and responsibilities in class are. . .

6 My responsibilities as an ESL teacher are. . .

1 Working with Adult ESL Learners

Part I ◆ Making the Adjustment to a New Culture

1.1.1 Introduction

Adult ESL learners come to communities and classrooms for a variety of reasons and with a variety of backgrounds. The transition from one culture to the other is far easier for some than it is for others. There are a number of factors that contribute to one's ability to adjust to a new culture and to acquire the skills (linguistic and nonlinguistic) to survive and thrive in that new culture. These factors include everything from the reason one has emigrated from his or her country to access to transportation in the new culture. In Part I of this chapter, we examine the challenges immigrants and refugees face as they make the adjustment to a new culture. We also consider principles of learner-centered teaching that are responsive to learners' diverse strengths and needs, which may help ease the transition to a new culture. Next, we turn to the issue of second language acquisition. What do we know about the process of learning a second language? How do age and previous educational experience affect the ability to learn a second language? These are among the questions and issues explored in Part II.

Checklist

After reading this chapter and completing the activities, you should be able to

- enumerate factors that contribute to successful cultural adjustment.
- describe the characteristics of the learner-centered classroom.
- define communicative competence.
- discuss developments in second language acquisition theory that have influenced current teaching approaches.

Getting Started

Task 1.1

There is no question that the primary goal of learners in ESL classes is to acquire the English skills needed to thrive in a new culture, but why does meeting that goal come more easily for some people than for others? Read the following stories of two immigrants and decide who faces the greatest challenges as an immigrant to the United States. Identify the advantages and disadvantages each may have and complete the table below:

Yurie is a 44-year-old Russian immigrant who came to the U.S. with his family in 1995. He completed an advanced degree in Russia and worked as a researcher at a prominent university. His son, Gregor, was born in the U.S. and has been going to school here since kindergarten. As a family, they always speak Russian at home, and Gregor is completely bilingual. Upon completing the highest level of ESL courses in the adult education program in his district, Yurie found a position as a researcher at a local university. While he is satisfied with his professional situation in the U.S., he misses the professional status and respect he had gained in Russia. Yurie and his family take part in sports, go to the YMCA, and are involved in Gregor's school. They return to Russia regularly and have family visit them every year.

Thida is a 39-year-old Cambodian widow and mother of four. She and her family came to the U.S. in 1985 from a refugee camp in Thailand, escaping from the Khmer Rouge regime in Cambodia. She came from a family of rural farmers, so she has no formal education and no literacy in her first language. Two of her children were born in the refugee camp, and the other two were born in the United States. Thida's husband died after the birth of her fourth child. Her two younger children seem to be learning English and adopting American ways very quickly. Her culture expects extreme respect for elders, which she doesn't see her children extending to her. As a widow, she would like her children to stay with her, but her daughters want to live and work away from home. Thida has been on and off public assistance through the years, but she has held the same job as a line operator in manufacturing for the past three years.

Complete this chart with information from Yurie's and Thida's stories:

Yurie's advantages	**Yurie's disadvantages**
Came to the U.S. with an advanced degree.	
Thida's advantages	**Thida's disadvantages**
Is currently employed.	

Follow-up Compare and discuss your answers with a classmate. If you are working on your own, you may want to start a journal with responses to the questions in the book. What did you notice about Yurie's and Thida's lives? Differences in education, connection to family, and involvement in the community are all factors that would most certainly influence their chances of success in a new culture. These variables have a tremendous impact on teaching and learning, and, while you cannot possibly know everything about every learner in class, understanding students' situations can help teachers become more responsive to learner needs and more understanding of what learners are going through as they adjust to a new life.

1.1.2 A Process for Understanding Adult ESL Learners

As ESL professionals, we can only imagine what it must be like for our learners as they come into a new culture, which entails learning new systems of education, government, and commerce. At the same time, they have left behind family, jobs, and the country they probably lived in their entire lives. What can help educators begin to understand the challenges they face?

Laurie Olsen (1988) has suggested factors that serve to predict how successfully one is able to acculturate. **Acculturation** means the ability for **minority cultures** to adapt to the **dominant culture**, which involves an understanding of the beliefs, emotions, and behaviors of the new culture, without letting go of the first culture (Scarcella 1990). Schumann (1986) has suggested that acculturation aids language acquisition, enabling adult immigrants to become active members of their communities. Acculturation is very different from **assimilation,** which implies complete absorption of the second culture practices, beliefs, and norms. While assimilation may be the goal for new immigrants, we'll see that it isn't always easy to do and may actually cause some problems. An immigrant's or refugee's ability to acculturate is not, for the most part, based on conscious choices, but rather on his or her life circumstances. Understanding those circumstances can help guide ESL teachers in the choices they make in their classrooms.

Factors Affecting Cultural Adjustment

To help you understand your learners' life circumstances, you can use the following cultural adjustment checklist (Table 1.1). On the left are the various factors that can affect a person's ability to adjust to a new culture. On the right are the things you can consider and the questions you can ask yourself about your learners.

TABLE 1.1 Cultural Adjustment Checklist

Factors	Things to consider/Questions you need to ask yourself
1 Country of origin	Are there any similarities between life in the first and second cultures (shared religions, customs)? Have there been waves of immigration from that country at earlier times?
2 Reasons for coming to the U.S.	Is your learner an immigrant or a refugee? Has she or he come by choice, or due to war or other trauma? Was she or he forced to leave because of political circumstances? Does immigration mean improved economic conditions? Many refugees may feel 'unsettled' in the new country because they may have hopes of some day returning to their country if the political or social conditions there change.
3 Age at which the person emigrated	As you will see later in this chapter, the ability to acquire a second language can be affected by the age at which one begins learning that language. The ability to adjust to differing cultural norms can be easier for younger people as well.
4 Financial resources/ Changes in status	Immigration may bring an extreme change in economic conditions or social status (Scarcella 1990). Many immigrants and refugees come with few resources and find themselves with no work or in low paying jobs, even after a number of years in the new country.
5 Difficulties in the journey/Extent of life disruption and upheaval during war	Did the student escape his or her country? Has she or he spent time in a refugee camp? Many learners may have been victims of torture or may have experienced the trauma and atrocities of war. The result may be post-traumatic stress disorder, depression or, at the very least, feelings of insecurity. It can be extremely difficult for these learners to concentrate and attend to the task of learning language.

6 Immigration status (official refugee, legal or undocumented)	As an undocumented worker, is there fear of arrest? Even those who are here legally can be uncertain of immigration laws. A distrust of government and authority may result in immigrants not taking advantage of social and government services from which they could benefit (health, education, etc.).
7 Education and level of literacy in first language/ Previous exposure to English and other languages	Is the learner preliterate? Has she or he had any formal education and, if so, are the educational conventions in his or her country similar to or very different from those practiced in the United States? As you will see throughout the book, education and level of literacy in the first language have an enormous impact on one's ability to acquire literacy and other skills in the second language. Knowledge of English will facilitate the process of cultural adjustment tremendously. Even knowing other languages will facilitate the process of learning English.
8 Extent of family separation	Did the person come alone or with family? Is the extended family in the new culture, or have they been left behind? Whether or not family members have opportunities to reunite or visit one another can have an impact on cultural adjustment.
9 Experience living in another country	Has the person been through the experience of navigating new systems (education, government, etc.)?
10 Status of cultural group/Amount of discrimination they face (Scarcella 1990)	There may be groups that hold more status, perhaps due to history, familiarity of the immigrants' culture (e.g., North Americans are more familiar with Chinese culture than they are with Sudanese culture). Do immigrants face discrimination? There may be limited job possibilities due to educational background, literacy, and different life experiences.

(List of factors from Olsen 1988:18)

Now we can use this checklist to examine Yurie's and Thida's stories. As you will see in Table 1.2, this checklist can provide a detailed description of the journey taken by any immigrant or refugee.

Table 1.2

Factors	Yurie	Thida
1 Country of origin	There are some shared holidays and religious practices between the U.S. and Russia. There were earlier waves of Russian immigrants, particularly at the beginning of the 1900s.	Cambodia and the U.S. are very dissimilar in terms of religion, cultural beliefs, and practices. Thida came with the first wave (which started more than 20 years ago) of immigrants from her culture. There are many Cambodians residing in her city in the U.S.
2 Reasons for coming to the U.S.	Yurie is an immigrant. He came by choice to continue education and then chose to apply for residency.	Thida is a refugee. She came as a result of war in her country.
3 Age at which the person emigrated	Yurie came as an adult, but his son certainly has the advantage of youth.	Came as a young adult; two of her children came at a young age and have acquired language skills very quickly and have tried to assimilate into the second culture. This has caused a rift between Thida and her children.

4 Financial resources/ Changes in status	Yurie could afford to move to the U.S. and has sufficient funds to return to his country. Perhaps some change in his status; he was well-known in his field in Russia, and now needs to reestablish a reputation in his field.	Clear economic deprivation—on and off public assistance. She's a single parent. Continued employment in past few years is positive.
5 Difficulties in the journey/Extent of life disruption and trauma during war	No particular difficulty.	Extreme disruption and likely trauma during the war in Southest Asia and during her escape. She has gone from living in a rural setting to living in an urban area unlike anything she's ever experienced.
6 Immigration status	Legal resident	U.S. citizen
7 Education and level of literacy in first language/Previous exposure to English and other languages	Highly educated; was fluent enough in English to pursue graduate study; has studied other foreign languages as well.	No formal education; not literate in her first language; no experience learning other languages.
8 Experience living in another country	Had never lived in another culture, but had traveled extensively.	None
9 Extent of family separation	Separated from extended family, but sees them twice a year.	Many of Thida's family members are in the United States. While there may not be physical separation, there appears to be emotional separation with her children.
10 Status of cultural group/Amount of discrimination they face (Scarcella 1990)	Highly regarded within the academic circle within which he works, though he feels some loss of status here as compared to that which he held in Russia. Difficult to judge the extent to which he experiences discrimination; many immigrants, regardless of their country of origin, feel some degree of discrimination by the majority culture.	Part of a group that is not well understood by many in the community. For Thida, this may come in the form of discrimination at work because of her limited education.

Through reading and thinking about Yurie's and Thida's lives in great detail, we can begin to answer the question: What *exactly* is it that helps or hinders an immigrant's ability to thrive in the new culture? By considering your students' lives in this way, you can have a more profound understanding of their circumstances and then take steps within your instruction and interactions that take these factors into consideration.

Some Other Considerations

Many of your learners may be holding down more than one job or working split shifts due to family needs and obligations. Very few of your students will want to leave their children in the care of strangers, preferring to leave them in the care of relatives. This means that they may have to work and take ESL classes at times that allow for other family members to care for their children. This can result in sporadic attendance and fatigue in class, both of which are understandable. Lack of reliable transportation is another factor affecting a learner's ability to access ESL programming.

Another challenge for new immigrants is **intergenerational tension** that may occur within the nuclear family. Children of immigrants will most likely adapt to the new culture and acquire the new language very quickly. They may attempt to assimilate in order to fit in with their peer group, resulting in the rejection of their parents' values and beliefs. In *Crossing the Schoolhouse Border*, Laurie Olsen (1991:31) cites the view of Carlos Cordova, a lecturer in the Raza Studies Department, San Francisco State University:

> There is an increasing sense of separation between the parents and the children, where the parents are still having some trouble adjusting to the culture, to the language, the students themselves are moving forward which sometimes includes losing their sense of their roots. There's a clash in terms of the language, the values, the backgrounds. As a result, children ask 'Why don't my parents understand what I am feeling, what my values are?' and the parents ask 'Where have my children gone wrong, why don't they understand my values and my language any longer?'

This rift between parents and children can add to the stress learners are encountering in a new culture.

Legislative measures can have an impact on learners' commitment to attending ESL classes. Recent welfare-to-work legislation has meant that many immigrants have left the classroom for the workplace as positions become available before having adequate language skills for the job. Unemployment rates can also have an impact on how long students stay with a program. As the unemployment rate fell to record lows in Minnesota, many immigrants and refugees found themselves in the workplace within two weeks of their arrival in the U.S. These realities can have an enormous impact on *what* you need to be teaching your students if they manage to get to classes at all. Let me share a scenario I recently encountered in a plant that manufactures plastic containers and screwdriver shafts:

> Five line workers from Russia had recently been hired at the plant. They had all been here a very short time and had minimal oral language skills. The plant floor was very noisy and hectic, so it was hard to hear people. The workers' job consisted of filling molds and operating presses. One day a supervisor noticed a problem with a piece of equipment that could have caused severe injury to the employee using it. He made a frantic gesture of cutting his throat (meaning that the employee needed to shut off the machine immediately). The employee took great offense, interpreting the message to mean: You're fired!

Typically, in a class for new immigrants, you might think of starting with basic introductions and greetings, language needed to find their way around their communities, etc. But were you to have these five immigrants in your class, they may have the more immediate need of understanding gestures used on a noisy shop floor. We'll look at the process of assessing your learners' needs as well as the most prevalent types of programs in greater detail in Chapter 2. The point here is that there are always variables to consider that will differ with any group of learners and these variables will affect the choices you make as a teacher.

1.1.3 Implications for the ESL Classroom

Of all groups of ESL learners, adult immigrants and refugees probably have the greatest number of obstacles to overcome in order to become proficient users of English. Personal factors that affect learning include educational background, level of literacy in the first language (**L1**), financial status, and family and job responsibilities, just to name a few. Societal factors may include pressure to move into the workplace before having adequate language skills. Most adult immigrant learners have precious little time to attend ESL classes and practice outside of the classroom. That is why it is paramount that adult ESL instruction be highly customized, accessible, and **learner-centered,** giving learners an optimal setting for acquiring the language skills they need to function within our communities.

What does learner-centered mean?

- Learners' knowledge and experiences are validated.
- Learners have active roles in the classroom.
- Learners make choices about content and classroom activities.
- Learners control the direction of activities.
- The content of instruction is relevant to the students' needs and interests and draws on their experiences and knowledge.
- Classroom interactions and tasks are authentic.
- Teachers use authentic language in their interactions with learners.
- Learners acquire strategies that help them learn inside and outside of the classroom without the help of a teacher.
- Teachers listen actively for themes that emerge from learners.
- Teachers constantly assess teaching and learning in relation to learners' needs.

A learner-centered view of teaching acknowledges that adult learners come to your class with a wealth of knowledge and experience. Because of their limited ability to communicate and express themselves in English, that knowledge and experience may feel locked inside of them. In the words of Susan Ferguson:

> Questions of who the students are and what they want become the basis for learning. The point of my instruction is to help students label and give voice in a new language to their own life experiences and needs. Immigrants come as students to the program with widely different levels of formal education and first language literacy. Students start their language learning with who they are. My instruction starts with that. The students are the instructor's manual. The language is the text (Ferguson 1998:5).

The knowledge and strategies needed to provide this kind of learning environment are the foundation of this book. As we examine different program options as well as approaches and strategies for teaching ESL to adult learners, we will look at numerous means of connecting instruction to learners' lives. Connections can be made through the questions we ask, the materials learners choose, the direction activities take, or even an entire curriculum based on your learners' lives and experiences (Weinstein 1999). Let's first turn to what the profession has to say about what it means to *know a language* and *how* it is that learners can achieve some level of competence in a second (or, in many cases, third, fourth. . .) language.

Part II ◆ What Does It Mean to Know a Language?

1.2.1 INTRODUCTION

In order to understand language instruction overall, it's important to first understand what it means to *know* a language. Is it a question of conjugating verbs correctly, using intelligible pronunciation, or knowing how to ask someone for help or offer an opinion? Clearly, the answer to this is dependent on the needs and strengths of the learner. There are, however, a number of areas of language that you can draw on when developing your lessons for adult learners.

Getting Started

Task 1.2

What do the following areas of language have in common and what are the differences? See if you can sort the following examples of language into four categories.

Grammar	Appropriate intonation
Using gestures to demonstrate meaning	Pronunciation
Guessing meaning of new words	Vocabulary
Writing for different purposes	Body language
Formal/informal language	Asking for definitions
Language functions (e.g., making complaints, greetings, and introductions)	Reading for different purposes
Using colloquial language appropriately	Spelling
Asking someone to speak more slowly	Listening only for the information you need

FOUR DIFFERENT AREAS OF LANGUAGE Sort the examples of language into these four categories. If you're doing this in class, work with a partner:

Category 1: Language Forms	Category 2: Social Interactions

Category 3: Language Skills	Category 4: Learning How to Learn

Follow-up Compare your answers with another group. Can you add one more example of your own to each box? Our goal as language teachers is to help learners attain some level of proficiency in *all* of these areas. We want them to attain communicative competence, which goes far beyond the traditional focus on learning vocabulary and grammar.

1.2.2 Helping Learners Attain Communicative Competence

Communicative competence describes the ability to use language in a variety of settings (at work, at a store, at home) with varying degrees of formality (with a friend vs. with a boss). In order to achieve communicative competence, a learner needs to become proficient in a number of areas, including language forms, social interactions, language skills, and learning strategies. In other words, the ability to convey your intended message and make yourself understood are equally, if not more important, than the ability to produce grammatically correct sentences. The four areas of competence are outlined in Table 1.3.

Table 1.3 Areas of Language That Can Lead to Communicative Competence

Language Forms (Linguistic Competence)	Knowledge of grammatical forms, spelling, vocabulary, and pronunciation.
Social Interactions (Sociolinguistic Competence)	Ability to use language, both verbal and nonverbal, appropriately in social contexts.
Language Skills (Discourse Competence)	Ability to read, write, understand, and use spoken language.
Learning Strategies (Strategic Competence)	Ability to use strategies to make yourself understood; how to learn on your own outside of the classroom.

Regardless of the focus of instruction, for example, English for work or family literacy, attaining a degree of competence in all of the areas above should be the goal of any second language instruction. Drawing from all of these areas of language helps shape and inform the choices that adult ESL teachers make about their curricula, materials, and classroom practices. The following chart represents the four areas of language competence along with the examples that you sorted into categories in Task 1.2. How does this chart compare to yours?

Category 1: Language Forms	**Category 2: Social Interactions**
Grammar	Formal/informal language
Pronunciation	Language functions
Spelling	Polite intonation
Vocabulary	Using colloquial language appropriately
	Body language
Category 3: Language Skills	**Category 4: Learning How to Learn**
Writing for different purposes	Using gestures to demonstrate meaning
Reading for different purposes	Asking for definitions
Listening only for the information you need	Asking someone to speak more slowly
	Guessing meaning of new words

In order to understand better how these concepts help to shape instruction in ways that are appropriate for learners, look at two teachers' objectives for their lesson plans on "Asking Questions." What areas of language does each teacher include? Which lesson do you think would provide more opportunities to develop some degree of communicative competence in the area of asking questions?

TABLE 1.4 Sample Lesson Plan Objectives for Two Lessons on Asking Questions

Teacher	Objectives
Teacher A Question Formation	Students will be able to use the DO-support rule correctly in questions. Students will choose the correct question word (*who, what, when, where, how*). Students will use falling intonation for *wh-* questions; rising intonation for *yes-no* questions.
Teacher B Asking Questions at Work	Students will be able to interrupt co-workers appropriately. Students will be able to ask co-workers for help. Students will be able to ask for clarification. Students will use appropriate polite intonation when interrupting and asking for assistance. Students will be able to use the DO-support rule correctly in questions. Students will choose the correct question word (*who, what, when, where, how*). Students will use falling intonation for *wh-* questions; rising intonation for *yes-no* questions.

Everything in Teacher A's lesson focuses on language forms: rules and patterns for question formation, and rising or falling intonation. Teacher B, however, has taken a broader view of the language of questions. She includes the following:

- *Social Interaction:* interrupting co-workers politely; using polite intonation when asking for assistance
- *Learning Strategies:* learning how to ask for help at work
- *Language Forms:* learning appropriate forms to ask questions

Teacher B's lesson goes further in addressing a variety of language outcomes and will address a broader range of learner needs. Lesson B is more authentic as well, including communicative purposes for using language.

1.2.3 How Do Learners Attain Competence in a Second Language?

Language teaching professionals have asked throughout the ages how a person becomes a proficient user of a language. What processes underlie second language acquisition? While we may never have an answer to that question, there are many theories about how languages are learned that have been informed by research and observations in second language classrooms. We will start with the view of language acquisition that is no longer held by most ESL professionals. It is a theory that held its ground for many years, however, and it shaped much of language instruction throughout the 50s, 60s and continues to shape instruction in many venues around the world today. That theory is **behaviorism.**

1.2.4 Behaviorism

Behaviorism (Skinner 1957) is the theory that human beings learn new behaviors through a stimulus and response cycle. In language learning it holds that language is learned through mimicry and memorization of forms, which leads to habit formation. It suggests that the goal of instruction is to replace bad habits (errors in production) with good ones (grammatical utterances). This theory resulted in the creation and extensive use of the Audiolingual Method (ALM) for teaching foreign languages. This method of teaching relied heavily on the use of memorization of set dialogues and extensive repetition and drilling. It was developed in the 50s as a method for teaching foreign languages to military personnel very quickly. Its focus on drills and repetition was probably welcomed by that particular student body. However, when used in the public schools and universities throughout the world, it fell short of producing competent users of foreign languages. Why is that? As we set forth in this book, language production is not based on predictable, set dialogues. Language use can be unpredictable and it will vary depending on the contexts in which is produced.

Behaviorism is a psychological theory that is held by many areas of learning. There is no doubt that human beings have behavioral responses to certain types of input, for example, we automatically slow down when we see brake lights on the car ahead of us. There may be certain areas of language that are learned through mimicry and memorization, for example, formulaic greetings (*How do you do? Fine, thank you. Nice to meet you.*), or pronunciation of unfamiliar sounds. This theory does not go very far in explaining the complex processes that go into learning a language, however.

1.2.5 A Shift Away from Behaviorism

Noam Chomsky (1959), a noted linguist, was the first to refute behaviorism as an explanation for the process of language acquisition. If humans learn through the imitation of forms they have heard, why is it that they create novel utterances and new combinations containing language they have never heard before? Chomsky suggests that as human beings, we are all endowed with the ability to create innumerable forms based on a limited amount of input. We are somehow "hard-wired" to learn language and we use this innate ability to analyze and make guesses about the language. The guesses that we make as language learners often result in ungrammatical production. How many of you have heard children say things like this:

- **a** We goed to the zoo today.
- **b** We bringed it.
- **c** We boughted it last week.

If we say *looked*, why not *goed*? The last example was spoken by my seven-year-old son, Jonas, just this week. He is not imitating anyone; he is making logical guesses about how to form the past tense. He applies the rule of adding the *-ed* ending, even after learning the irregular past of buy (bought). You've probably heard your adult ESL learners make similar overgeneralizations about rules of the language. These errors provide us with evidence that language learning involves far more than imitation. Many others have supported Chomsky's view that language learning is an innate process rather than a behaviorial one, and a number of the theories that followed have helped to shape the current communicative, learner-centered approaches most prevalent in language teaching today.

1.2.6 Krashen's Model of Language Acquisition

Stephen Krashen (1982) proposes an influential model of second language acquisition that includes a number of hypotheses. We'll look at each in turn and discuss how they relate to classroom instruction.

1 **Order of Acquisition Hypothesis** Krashen has suggested that learners acquire forms of language in a predictable sequence independent of their first language and of what is taught in the classroom. Many researchers have argued that there is not a hard and fast sequence all learners follow. However, studies have shown a degree of consistency in the stages of forming questions (Pienemann, Johnston, and Brindley 1988) as well as other forms. What does this mean for you as a teacher? It is important to understand that not all

learners are at the same developmental stage and, as a result, they may not all be ready to acquire certain areas of language at the same time or rate. Some may even be at what Krashen calls a preproduction stage or **silent period,** when they are able to take language in, but not produce it.

2 **Input Hypothesis** In this hypothesis, Krashen (1985) proposes that in order for individuals to acquire a second language, they need to have adequate **comprehensible input.** Comprehensible is the key; it's not a question of simply being immersed in the target language. Language input needs to be at a level just beyond the learner's current level, what Krashen calls **i + 1** (*i* is input at the learner's current proficiency level, and + *1* means a step beyond that level). The language can be made comprehensible in the following ways:

TABLE 1.5 Strategies for Making Language Comprehensible to Learners

Use visuals, realia (real objects such as fruit, tools, etc.), and gestures.	Provide a visually rich classroom environment for your learners; include multiple means of instruction that appeal to a variety of learners.
Provide input that is meaningful to learners.	Thida's teacher would need to draw on background knowledge and experiences that are very different than those for Yurie.
Build redundancy into your teaching.	Say things in more than one way; have students see the language, hear the language, "do things" with the language (sorting pictures, ranking, etc.).
Create achievable tasks for your learners.	Learners with limited literacy can demonstrate understanding by pointing to pictures and sorting pictures as they complete a listening activity.

3 **Acquisition vs. Learning** Krashen suggests that there are two very different processes going on for any learner: **acquisition vs. learning.** Acquisition refers to natural, unconscious processes that children go through as they acquire their first language. Rules are not analyzed or learned through formal instruction or analysis. Rather, like Chomksy, Krashen believes that we have an innate ability to acquire languages through sufficient input and exposure. Learning, on the other hand, refers to consciously learning the rules and patterns of the language. Many of us who have studied foreign languages have "learned" the language, but oftentimes feel inadequate as fluent users of the language. Krashen suggests that learned language may be less permanent, or less automatic, than language that has been fully acquired. How does this theory play out in a second language classroom? See Table 1.6 for some ways a teacher can promote acquisition of language.

TABLE 1.6 Promoting Acquisition as Well as Learning

Focus is on meaning and use, not on analysis of rules.	Learners engage in real-life interactions in the classroom. Remember Teacher B from earlier in the chapter? She takes this view in her lesson, going beyond grammar and pronunciation.

Input is natural and authentic.	The teacher uses authentic materials (books, articles, broadcasts, songs, etc.) and authentic contexts for practicing language.
Language rules are presented inductively.	The teacher uses discovery-based learning with little or no emphasis of grammar rules.

4 **Monitor Hypothesis** The **monitor hypothesis** relates to the learning side of the learning/acquisition coin. Learned language acts as a monitor that edits and corrects language. Krashen argues that overuse of the monitor can inhibit fluent language production and ultimate acquisition of the second language. This is especially true in oral production where use of the monitor can result in halted, heavily interrupted speech. Many teachers can think of learners who exhibit this kind of language production, particularly learners whose language learning experiences consisted of rule-based, grammar-translation approaches to teaching. There can be great benefit to using the monitor when learners are working on their writing, when they have time to edit and revise their language production. In the classroom, teachers may choose to include practice that is more focused on "getting it right," but ultimately will want to provide learners with ample opportunities for communicative, spontaneous practice that is not interrupted by heavy use of the monitor, for example, role-plays, information-gap activities (tasks that include a genuine exchange of information), discussions, and skits, all of which are described in Chapter 3.

5 **Affective Filter Hypothesis** Finally, Krashen's **affective filter hypothesis** states that anxieties associated with learning can act as a filter, which inhibits acquisition. Those anxieties may include stress, fatigue, and embarrassment about performing in a second language, among others. The role of the teacher is to lower the affective filter by providing a supportive classroom, free of constraints, that can act as a filter. Here are some ways a teacher can do that:

- Provide encouragement that is meaningful.
- Allow for mistakes.
- Don't spotlight learners.
- Allow for different learning styles and needs.
- Show respect for all learners.

Table 1.7 summarizes Krashen's principles.

TABLE 1.7 Summary of Krashen's Five Hypotheses of Second Language Acquisition

1 Order of Acquisition	A natural order of acquisition of particular features of the language exists (e.g., questions, negation, verb endings).
2 Input Hypothesis	Abundant comprehensible input is needed in order for language acquisition to occur.

3 Acquisition vs. Learning	Acquisition refers to language picked up by learners without conscious focus on rules or forms. Learning refers to conscious analysis of language. Krashen suggests that acquired language is more permanent.
4 Monitor Hypothesis	The learned language acts as a 'monitor', checking and correcting language output. Overuse of the monitor can result in stilted, unnatural speech.
5 Affective Filter Hypothesis	The affective filter represents barriers to learning such as stress, anxiety, and embarrassment. Our goal is to lower the affective filter.

1.2.7 Interactionism

One of Krashen's propositions that have been put into question is the input hypothesis. Can acquisition occur simply through exposure to abundant comprehensible input? Michael Long (1983) suggests that while receiving comprehensible input is a desired characteristic of second language acquisition, it is not enough. In addition to input, there needs to be *interaction*. It's the interaction itself that helps to make input comprehensible. This theory is called **interactionism.**

Long proposes that it is through interactions with competent users of the second language that we move forward in our use of that language. He likens it to the progress children make in their interactions with parents and other sympathetic listeners who modify their language. The modified language has certain features, and it's through these modified interactions that language acquisition occurs:

- The listener uses comprehension checks.
- The listener asks for clarification.
- The listener repeats or paraphrases what he or she has understood.
- The listener simplifies his or her speech.

The listener does not need to be a native speaker or the ESL teacher in the classroom. The listener can be another student, but this means that the classroom practices need to allow for ample and meaningful interactions. The teacher needs to make these interaction strategies somewhat explicit to students, i.e., teach them how to ask for clarification or check understanding.

1.2.8 Taking Learners beyond Basic Interpersonal Communication Skills

One other theory to look at connects very closely to item 7 of the cultural adjustment checklist at the beginning of this chapter: **Education and level of literacy in first language/Previous exposure to English and other languages.** Think about these questions for few minutes:

How long does it take a person to achieve oral skills sufficient to interact and survive in a new culture (such as language needed to shop, interact with co-workers, and access health care)?

How long does it take to acquire oral and literacy skills sufficient to function fully in the new culture (read newspapers, manufacturing instructions, textbooks; take notes, write memos; follow complex directions; state opinions, etc.)?

Jim Cummins (1979), an expert in bilingual education, has researched the differences between oral proficiency and level of literacy with learners in academic settings. He suggests that there are two types of language proficiency. The first is **Basic Interpersonal Communication Skills (BICS)** which require approximately two years to acquire, provided the learner is immersed in the second language and has opportunities to use the second language. The second is what he calls **Cognitive Academic Language Proficiency** skills **(CALP)** which can take anywhere from seven to fifteen years to acquire, depending on a learner's experience with formal education and level of literacy in the first language. What are some factors that determine one's ability to acquire CALP?

- Prior schooling and experience using complex language.
- Level of literacy in the first language.
- Amount of exposure and practice in the second language.

Cummins's work looks specifically at K–12 learners in school settings. Central to its purpose is developing the understanding that an immigrant child's ability to make small talk, follow simple directions, etc., is not an indicator of his or her ability to complete cognitively demanding academic work in the second language. Those skills need to be developed if they haven't already been developed in the first language.

So what are the implications of this for those of us working with *adult* ESL learners? Often there is a mismatch between an individual's mastery of basic communication skills and advanced literacy skills. This results in inaccurate assessments and misperceptions about a second language learner's abilities in the classroom and in the world at large. Read a supervisor's comments about his employees:

> Sometimes a worker won't mark down that a defective part was thrown out. We have a form to use, but sometimes they won't even know where to mark it down. They don't seem to understand why this is a problem.

He shared with me that the team is very fluent in English, but as he described other incidents like the one above, it became apparent to me that many of his employees had mastered Basic Interpersonal Communications Skills, but lacked the literacy skills needed to perform tasks that involved completing complex forms or reading technical manuals. Because the employees had highly developed BICS, the employers expected the same level of understanding in completing literacy-related tasks.

> Whenever I ask this one worker to do something, he doesn't seem to understand. It surprises me since I know he was an engineer in Russia and has studied English.

In the second example, the supervisor is making the assumption that an advanced education equals advanced oral proficiency in a second language. Varying ability in different areas of language is an enormous issue in almost every ESL classroom. Cummins's model helps to give us some understanding of the cause of the discrepancies between basic communication skills and literacy skills.

1.2.9 Age and the Acquisition of a Second Language

A final area to consider here is the effect that age has on one's ability to acquire a second language. If you go back to Yurie's and Thida's stories, you may recall that Thida's children acquired the language very quickly. I can attest to the fact that Yurie's son, Gregor, has mastered some areas of language (pronunciation, in particular) much more fully than either of his parents. Is this due to age, or do other factors come into play?

It has been suggested that there is a **critical period** for learning a second language which begins at birth to around puberty. Some suggest the period ends as early as five or six years old. Changes that occur in the brain at or around puberty make it more difficult, if not impossible, to become a native-like speaker of the language. We have all seen that young children pick up a native-like accent with little or no effort, and most of us would agree that far fewer adults attain the same degree of proficiency, at least in terms of accent.

But is accent really an important measure of proficiency? Many times adolescents and adults can actually acquire other areas of language (literacy, grammar, vocabulary) more quickly than children can. Older learners can bring the experience of learning other things through formal or informal education to the task of learning a second language. Developed literacy or learning strategies from their first language can be transferred to the second language. Many adults are able to attain very intelligible pronunciation provided that they have adequate input and opportunities to interact in the new language. In fact, factors such as motivation, identity, and access to adequate input may play a more important role than the age at which one begins learning a language.

An adult learner may be in a job that does not require extensive use of language and, as a result, is not strongly motivated to learn English beyond a certain level. Often adult immigrants and refugees can get by with limited English in their communities and they are more concerned about their children acquiring the skills needed to thrive in school and in the community. A refugee may have hopes of returning to his or her country of origin and not feel particularly driven to acquire anything beyond very basic skills. Often adults have a desire to maintain their identity as a member of their own cultural community. Adults often have far less input in the second language than children have. Children enter regular mainstream classrooms where there are numerous opportunities to hear and use English every day, whereas some adults may have limited input depending on their work status, mobility within the community, and exposure to and interactions with English speakers. All of these factors can have an impact on the adult learner's progress toward learning a language, and they are not related to aptitude or a critical period for learning.

Based on the considerations discussed in Part II of this chapter, it is important to keep the following in mind in your role as a teacher of adult learners:

- Adults **are capable** of acquiring a second language.
- Adult learners need **ample and accessible language input;** provide extensive practice with listening to authentic language in your classroom. Support that language input with visual aids and other tools for making language comprehensible.
- Adult learners need **meaningful and authentic opportunities to use language** in order to acquire language; help your learners to learn beyond the classroom and to become active members of their communities.

CONCLUSION

In this chapter, you have been given a glimpse of some of the challenges faced by adult learners of English as a second language. Their journeys to a new country as well as the contexts in which they are living and working make for a vast array of needs and expectations in any adult ESL classroom. It is crucial that adult ESL teachers tap into the experiences and knowledge that learners bring into the classroom. It is also important to understand the complex nature of second language acquisition. Teachers need to provide a classroom environment that is supportive and engages learners in activities that are purposeful and meaningful. Throughout this book, we will explore teaching principles and strategies that help ESL teachers achieve these goals.

KEY TERMS

CHECKLIST OF KEY TERMS	On your own, or with a partner, provide an example or brief definition for each concept.
acculturation	
minority culture	
dominant culture	
assimilation	
intergenerational tension	
learner-centered	
communicative competence	
behaviorism	
silent period	
comprehensible input	
acquisition vs. learning	
monitor hypothesis	
affective filter hypothesis	
interactionism	
BICS	
CALP	
critical period	

Applying What You Learned

1 Cultural Adjustment and Adult Learners

If you're already teaching. . . identify a learner in your class who seems to be having particular difficulty with learning English and adjusting to the new culture. What do you need to know about this student? How can you know more? Based on information you have about the student, write a description similar to the ones of Thida and Yurie. Try to include as much information as possible about the learner (reason for coming, current situation, family, etc.). Use the following checklist to examine your student's journey as I did with Yurie and Thida, and reflect on the questions that follow.

Student's Name	
1 Country of origin	
2 Reasons for coming to the U.S.	
3 Age at which the person emigrated	
4 Financial resources	
5 Difficulties in the journey/Extent of life disruption and trauma during war	
6 Immigration status	
7 Education and level of literacy in the first language/ Previous exposure to English and other languages	
8 Extent of family separation	
9 Experience living in another country	
10 Status of cultural group/Amount of discrimination they face	

It may not be possible to gather all of the information you'd like. Even though you cannot have a complete picture of your learners' life circumstances, this exercise gets you to think about the questions you need to ask yourself about your students' lives.

If you're not teaching. . . use the following story of a migrant worker from Mexico and complete the checklist.

> Josefina is a migrant worker from Mexico who has joined her husband in southern California. He came two years before Josefina and managed to get a work permit and find a job in a factory. Josefina is here with her three children illegally, but she is in the process of applying for legal

residency. She tries to take ESL classes in a community program, but is having difficulty finding the time to attend classes. Her husband often works double shifts at the factory and Josefina has no one to care for her children. Josefina does have a tenth grade education and can read and write in her first language.

What did this process reveal to you about some of the obstacles your learner might be facing? What are some concrete steps you might take to help this learner in light of what you've learned?

2 The Learner-centered Classroom

If you are already teaching, give examples of the ways you have incorporated the following principles into your teaching. If you aren't teaching, observe a lesson and see whether the teacher seems mindful of any of these principles in the choices she or he makes in the lesson.

Lesson Observed	
The learners' knowledge and experiences are validated.	
The learners have active roles in the classroom.	
The learners make choices about content and classroom activities.	
The learners control the direction of activities.	
The content of instruction is relevant to the students' needs and interests and draws on their experiences and knowledge.	
Classroom interactions and tasks are authentic.	
Teachers use authentic language in their interactions with learners.	
Learners acquire strategies that help them learn inside and outside of the classroom without the help of a teacher.	
Teachers listen actively for themes that emerge from learners.	
Teachers constantly assess teaching and learning in relation to learners' needs.	

3 Teaching Learners to Become Communicatively Competent Users of English

If you're already teaching. . . look at a lesson you've taught over the past two weeks. What areas of language were included in your lesson?

Language Forms	
Social Interactions	
Language Skills	
Learning Strategies	

Are you satisfied with your coverage of different areas of language? What would you add or change to make sure you've taken the broadest view possible of the language you're teaching? Do learners practice language purposefully and meaningfully?

If you're not teaching. . . choose a chapter in a textbook used for adult ESL and evaluate the degree to which it teaches to the four areas above. What would you add or change in the chapter?

4 Promoting Second Language Acquisition

If you are already teaching. . . reflect on and write about these questions:

1 What are you doing to make input comprehensible to your learners?

2 What are three things you could do to make input comprehensible to your learners that you haven't thought of before?

3 What are you already doing that serves to lower the affective filter in your classroom? What are some other ways that you could create a classroom environment that is conducive to learning?

If you are not teaching. . . respond to these questions:

1 What are three ways a teacher can make input comprehensible to learners with very limited English?

2 What are some ways a teacher can lower the affective filter in the classroom? Think of a number of things you would do to create a classroom environment that is conducive to learning.

Recommended Reading

Auerbach, E. 1992. *Making meaning, making change: A participatory curriculum development for adult ESL literacy.* Washington DC and McHenry, IL: Center for Applied Linguistics and Delta Systems.

The author shares the experiences of the University of Massachusetts Family Literacy Project in planning and implementing a participatory curriculum for adult literacy. The book provides the reader with ideas for collaborating with learners to develop relevant curricula that respond to learners' needs as parents, workers, and community members.

Fadiman, A. 1997. *The spirit catches you and you fall down.* New York: Farrar, Straus and Giroux.

A powerful account of a Hmong family's experience with U.S. doctors and the health care system.

Lightbown, P. and **N. Spada.** 1999. *How languages are learned.* Oxford: Oxford University Press.

An introduction to the main theories of first and second language acquisition.

Nunan, D. 1988. *The learner-centred curriculum.* Cambridge: Cambridge University Press.

This guide combines research and practice to give teachers insights into planning, implementing, and evaluating learner-centered language courses.

Useful Websites

Focus on Basics

http://www.gse.harvard.edu/~ncsall/fob/index.htm

Focus on Basics is a publication of the National Center for the Study of Adult Learning and Literacy (NCSALL). It contains highly practical and accessible articles on best practices, current research on adult learning and literacy, and the ways research is used by adult basic education teachers, administrators, and policy makers.

National Immigration Forum

http://www.immigrationforum.org/index.htm

Information about immigration policies and trends from immigrant rights groups. Particularly useful for teachers new to working with immigrants are the "Immigration Facts."

Cultural Orientation Resource Center

http://www.cal.org/CORC

This Website offers up-to-date information about refugees and their concerns. It also includes Fact Sheets with pertinent country and cultural background about such groups as the Sudanese, Iraqi Kurds, Somalis, Haitians, and Cubans.

2 Approaches and Program Options in Adult ESL

Part I ◆ Approaches in Adult ESL

2.1.1 Introduction

Teachers of adult ESL learners find themselves in a variety of settings with a variety of roles. Public school systems, community colleges, community-based programs, correctional facilities, libraries, or volunteer organizations provide ESL instruction for adult immigrants and refugees. ESL teachers may work with learners one-on-one, with families in their homes, at drop-in centers, or in classrooms with groups of learners. Each situation will have its unique challenges both in terms of curriculum and teaching approach. What will work best in a given situation? No one approach will meet the needs of all learners in all situations. As with any teaching, a blending of approaches and methods is necessary. Part I of this chapter provides a brief overview of the most common approaches to teaching adult ESL from which a teacher can draw ideas and inspiration. In Part II, the most common program options offered in adult ESL are described. Let's begin by taking a look into Rosie's Adult Basic Education ESL class.

Checklist

After reading this chapter and completing the activities, you should be able to

- explain the rationale for taking a multifaceted approach to teaching ESL.
- identify and describe current approaches to teaching ESL to adult learners.
- explain the factors that affect the types of programs offered in communities.
- describe program options and their purposes.

Getting Started

Task 2.1

Read this class description and talk to your partner or write in your journal about the following questions:

1 What challenges does Rosie face in working with such a diverse group of learners?

2 What do different learners in this class need to work on in their English?

3 Could Rosie use one approach with all of these learners?

Rosie's beginning-level ESL class is comprised of 24 students ages 17–75 from 14 different countries including Thailand, Laos, Cambodia, Vietnam, Russia, Ukraine, Kirghistan,

Somalia, Peru, Mexico, and Colombia. Some of the students have professional degrees from their country, while others have no formal education at all. The level of first and second language literacy varies greatly as well. None of the students have had experience in interactive classes (pair or group work) and many of the students rely heavily on writing everything down and checking words in their dictionaries. Rosie has found that a number of her students balk at activities that seem like 'fun and games,' while others are eager to take part in role-plays, language games (bingo, word searches, etc.). Some of the learners are in class to improve their chances of finding employment, some hope to enter higher education, and others want to acquire basic survival skills. One goal they have all expressed is a desire to improve their ability to speak English.

2.1.2 Taking a Multifaceted Approach to Teaching

There are no easy answers to the questions in Task 2.1. Just as there are varying views on the processes that underlie second language acquisition, there are numerous methods and approaches to teaching ESL from which classroom teachers can draw. Rarely does a teacher or program adhere to *one* method or approach to teaching. The choices we make hinge on a number of factors:

- Who are the learners and how do they learn best?
- Why are they learning English?
- What experience have they had with formal and informal education?
- What are their views of teaching and learning?
- What is your own view of teaching and learning?
- What are the overall goals of the program? Who decides or mandates these goals?

When you think about Rosie's class in relation to these questions you can see that there are many complex issues involved in teaching adult ESL. There is tremendous variation in her students' backgrounds, education, and needs. How can a teacher find an approach that responds to such varying backgrounds, wants, needs, and learning-style preferences? Looking at our own experiences as learners can shed light on just how complex these choices can be.

Task 2.2

Think of a recent experience you've had learning a language, a new skill (cooking, gardening), or how to use a new a computer program or an apparatus at work or home. Reflect on the experience by answering these questions in your journal or with a partner:

1 What helped you learn best? Listening to someone describe things to you? Using the language, skills, machine, etc.? Using your hands? Moving around?

2 How did you figure things out? Did the teacher give you examples and have you deduce rules, patterns, and procedures, or did the teacher just tell you these things?

3 What feedback did the teacher give you? Corrections? Praise? What helped you the most?

4 What did you discover to be the most effective elements of this experience?

Follow-up Now share your answers with several other people in your group, or with friends or family if you are on your own. From my experience working with teachers over the past 15 years, there is always tremendous variation in the responses to the questions above. Far too often, teachers find themselves teaching as they were taught. All of us learn differently, and what may have worked well for you may not work well for the students you find yourselves teaching.

The ways in which a particular learner learns best has a tremendous impact on the success he or she will have in a given classroom situation. Howard Gardner suggests that there are at least seven *intelligences* that learners draw on to process and understand the world. Different learners may have some *intelligences* that are stronger than others, and approaches that are responsive to **multiple intelligences** are more likely to appeal to a broader audience of learners. These seven intelligences (Gardner 1993) are as follows:

- Verbal/Linguistic
- Musical
- Logical/Mathematical
- Spatial/Visual
- Bodily/Kinesthetic
- Intrapersonal
- Natural/Environmental

A kinesthetic learner who benefits from physical action may not be very successful sitting in a desk for hours at a time. A learner who has strong logical/mathematical intelligence may prefer analyzing grammar over an indirect, inductive approach to teaching and learning. All learners benefit from developing multiple means of processing information, as Gardner and others have shown, so a multifaceted approach to teaching is going to provide a richer learning environment for all students, one that is responsive to the multifaceted ways in which individuals acquire language.

Just as there are different intelligences, there are different learning-style preferences. Educators have proposed a variety of models for describing these preferences, for example, one can be *analytical* (prefer to analyze smaller pieces of information) vs. *global* (prefer to look at the whole). Some people are said to be random (they do not process information in a linear fashion) vs. *sequential* (prefer when information is presented in a logical order). Labeling learners as "random" or "global" can have negative effects, as it limits the expectations you have of students. What is key to this discussion is that we all learn differently, and there are many differences among students, even those from the same culture. No one approach to teaching is going to be responsive to all learners, so drawing on multiple approaches to teaching has become the norm in adult ESL instruction.

What do all ESL classes have in common? They are comprised of adult learners who need to take on a variety of roles within society, who have different ways of learning, and who have diverse backgrounds and needs. The goal of instruction, regardless of the approach we take as ESL teachers, is to help these diverse groups of learners acquire the tools they need to thrive in society as parents/family members, citizens/community members, and workers (Stein 2000). In choosing teaching approaches, we need to ask ourselves the following questions:

- What roles do learners and the teacher take on in this approach?
- What are the purposes for learning?
- What types of activities does the learner take part in within this approach/method? Are a variety of intelligences and learning styles considered?
- What skills are developed in this approach?

2.1.3 APPROACHES IN ADULT ESL

The following overview of current approaches to teaching ESL provides you with a range of options from which you can shape instruction. Some of them have a heavier focus on developing oral/aural skills (e.g., the Natural Approach), while others integrate both the **receptive skills** of listening and reading and **productive skills** of speaking and writing from the start (Communicative Language Teaching, Whole Language, competency-based education, content-based instruction, participatory approach). Project-based learning is a type of extensive activity that can be used within a variety of approaches. It is included in this chapter because of its focus on learner participation and community involvement. The Language Experience Approach (LEA) is also commonly used for literacy development with learners who have very limited literacy skills in any language. That approach is described in detail with illustrations of classroom application in Chapter 5.

Many of these approaches, particularly the Natural Approach and Communicative Language Teaching, emerged as alternatives to the Audiolingual Method (ALM), which grew out of behaviorism in the 1960s. The Audiolingual Method relies heavily on memorization of dialogues, drill, and repetition; there is little room for meaningful use of language in this method. While there are certainly elements of ALM that are integrated into instruction (more limited use of drills and dialogues), it is generally not used as a stand-alone method among adult ESL practitioners today.

Task 2.3

As you read about these approaches, use the chart below to identify the core principles as well as classroom practices from each. While all of these approaches have merits, see if some are more responsive to the needs of adult ESL learners than others.

Approach	Core Principles	Sample Classroom Practices
Natural Approach		
Competency-based Education		
Communicative Language Teaching		
Whole Language		
Content-based Instruction		
Participatory Approach		
Project-based Learning		

2.1.4 NATURAL APPROACH

CORE PRINCIPLES

The **Natural Approach** is an approach used with learners who have minimal language skills. It shares many of the same principles found in Communicative Language Teaching (2.1.6), its primary difference being a focus on comprehension first and production later. Stephen Krashen and Tracy Terrell developed the Natural Approach (1983) based on Krashen's input hypothesis, which holds that language acquisition occurs in a classroom with abundant comprehensible input. Based on the belief that all learners will experience a **silent period**, learners engage in activities that allow them to demonstrate understanding of a particular language point before they are expected to produce it. The goal of the Natural Approach is to replicate the conditions under which children acquire their first language.

CLASSROOM PRACTICES

The teacher uses frequent comprehension checks, visuals, and gestures to convey meaning to learners. The following example illustrates a typical teacher-student exchange in a class using the Natural Approach:

Lesson Theme: Body parts and ailments

Level: 1
1 Teacher displays visual of a person with body parts labeled. She begins by pointing to words and saying body parts (students repeat words only if comfortable with language).
2 Teacher removes labels, distributes them, and has each learner affix label to correct body part.

3 Teacher removes cards again. Students in class have a set of yes/no cards (yes one color, no another color). Teacher points to and says a body part, sometimes correctly and sometimes incorrectly. Learners hold up yes/no card according to whether the teacher said the right or wrong word.

One of the primary goals of the Natural Approach is to allow learners to demonstrate their understanding of language forms and vocabulary before they are able to produce the language. The practices above provide learners the opportunity to do that. In later lessons, the learners would take on the teacher's role, directing activities, asking one another questions, and engaging in simple paired activities. These 'silent' techniques are not unique to the Natural Approach, and are used at any point when the teacher wants to check for learner understanding.

2.1.5 Competency-based Education

Core Principles

Competency-based education (CBE) emerged from a study conducted in the 1970s (Adult Performance Level Project at the University of Texas, as cited in Savage 1993, p. 17), which identified five areas of knowledge needed for adults to function in society: occupational, consumer, health, government and law, and community resources. The skills of listening, speaking, reading, writing, interpersonal relations, problem solving, and computation were considered requisite to function fully in each of the areas above. Outcomes within each area and skills were identified in terms of performance objectives (learners will be able to...), which became the basis for curricula. While CBE was originally developed for all Adult Basic Education programs (GED, Diploma for native-English speakers), it quickly became the basis for ESL programs that were welcoming waves of refugees throughout the 70s and 80s.

Classroom Practice

Competency-based education has more to do with *what* is taught rather than *how* it is taught. Rather than defining goals of instruction only in terms of grammar, functions, and vocabulary, it is defined in terms of competencies (or daily tasks) that learners need to perform. Learners need to acquire the vocabulary and grammar needed to perform competencies as well, so the outcomes of a competency-based lesson could look like these:

- Learners will be able to read clothing labels to determine size and washing instructions.
- Learners will be able to select clothing they need from a newspaper circular.

A teacher using a competency-based approach may draw on techniques from a number of methods or approaches that are compatible with the level, needs, and learning styles of the students. The sample that follows illustrates the kind of activity learners could engage in within a competency-based lesson on returning an item to the store.

Competency: Returning an item to the store

Learners will be able to • Explain reasons for returning an item. • Demonstrate understanding of return policies: a refund, an exchange, or store credit.
Sample activity Half of the class is assigned the role of store clerk. Each clerk is given store policies: • Must have a receipt for a refund. • Purchase made less than 30 days ago. • Must have packaging for a refund. Each of the other students in class is given an item to return; some are given a receipt; some have item in the box; some have item with no packaging.
Role-play Students return items to the appropriate store. Redistribute items and assign new clerks.
Follow-up Did you get a refund, a new item, or a store credit? Why? Did you get what you wanted? What were the store policies and how did they affect you?

2.1.6 Communicative Language Teaching

Core Principles

Communicative Language Teaching (CLT) has its origins in a movement in Europe in the 1970s to make foreign language teaching responsive to the communicative, functional demands of people working across cultures, in workplaces, and in international organizations. Likewise, in the United States, linguists embraced the idea of communicative competence as the goal of instruction. Course curricula included language functions (greetings, making invitations, making requests, etc.) and notions (time, money), which was a departure from the grammar-based curricula of the previous decades. Communicative Language Teaching was also a departure from the rote learning found in Audiolingual teaching, giving primacy to communication. CLT is viewed as an approach or philosophy to teaching, not a set method; it sees fluency and the ability to communicate in a variety of settings and in a variety of ways (verbal and nonverbal, written) at the core of teaching and learning. Although teachers throughout the world would describe their approach to teaching as CLT, you could walk into classes that look very different in terms of activities, materials, and interactions. All of the teachers could still embrace the core principles of CLT, which are outlined in Table 2.1.

Table 2.1 Key Principles of Communicative Language Teaching

• The goal of instruction is learning to communicate effectively and appropriately.
• Instruction is contextualized and meaning-based.
• Authentic materials are incorporated from the start.
• Repetition and drilling are used minimally.

TABLE 2.1 Key Principles of Communicative Language Teaching

• Learner interaction is maximized; the teacher acts as a facilitator of learning.
• Fluency is emphasized over accuracy.
• Errors are viewed as evidence of learning.

(Adapted from Richards and Rodgers 1986, p. 67)

CLASSROOM PRACTICE Communicative Language Teaching (CLT) can be thought of as an umbrella under which an array of methods and techniques can be used. Learners take on very active roles as they engage in role-plays, discussions, or debates. They work with samples of authentic language, for example, news reports, articles, or taped interviews. Practice activities should represent real-world uses of language that correspond to the strengths, wants, and needs of the students in class. Students develop listening, speaking, reading, and writing skills concurrently through this integrated approach to teaching ESL. The sample lessons presented in Chapters 3, 4, and 5 provide extensive illustrations of how Communicative Language Teaching can be applied in adult ESL classes.

2.1.7 WHOLE LANGUAGE

CORE PRINCIPLES **Whole Language** is an overall philosophy to learning, which views language as something that should be taught in its entirety, not broken up into small pieces to be decoded. As with other holistic approaches, whole language classrooms integrate all language skills, make use of authentic texts (literature, poetry, etc.) rather than simplified or graded readers, and view the learner as the center of learning.

CLASSROOM PRACTICE As a philosophy to teaching and learning, Whole Language is not seen as a method of teaching. In fact, many teaching ideas throughout this book might be found in a whole language classroom, which adheres to the principles outlined in Table 2.2.

TABLE 2.2 Whole Language Practices

• Project-based learning (see 2.1.10)
• Reading, writing, listening, speaking skills development
• Language Experiences (see 5.1.4A)
• Writing using inventive spelling from the beginning of instruction
• Little attention paid to errors
• Use of 'whole' texts

Whole Language has its critics because of mixed results in classes using the approach. Any lack of success probably has more to do with a mismatch between the whole language philosophy and the standardized tests that are used to measure learner outcomes. Many practitioners have embraced a **balanced literacy** approach, which combines the principles of Whole Language with other types of instruction (the balanced literacy approach is described in Chapter 5) including phonics (see 5.1.4) as well as other techniques that focus on the development of grammar, vocabulary, and oral production.

2.1.8 Content-based Instruction

Core Principles Considerable research has been conducted on the benefits of teaching language through content that is meaningful and relevant to students (Brinton, Snow, and Wesche 1989, MacDonald 1997, Sticht 1997). **Content-based instruction** is an approach to teaching that makes subject matter such as history, environmental studies, math, or citizenship, the basis of the curriculum. CBI is used extensively in academic settings because it prepares students for the work they need to do when they enter degree programs with native-English speakers and faculty who are not language teachers. Some teachers are hesitant to adopt this approach, which requires knowledge of a particular content area; many ESL teachers are not as comfortable with the content area as they are with teaching language skills.

Classroom Practice Citizenship is an example of content-based instruction within adult education. Learning about American history and systems of government becomes the basis for instruction, along with the language needed to read about and answer questions about that content. In a content-based class, learners take part in language activities that are typical of any communicative classroom: prereading, prelistening, role-plays, or discussions. Teachers work on structures and vocabulary as needed to understand and talk or write about the content. The sample activities below illustrate a variety of ways students in a content-based citizenship class might practice for a citizenship test, which requires knowledge of history and government as well as an ability to understand different types of questions.

Sample activities to practice the content of the citizenship test as well as question forms.

1 Jeopardy

Sample categories: Leaders in History, Government System, Important Events

Sample clues: I was the first president of the United States.

Fifty of us represent your state and we work in Washington, D.C.

2 Twenty Questions (Can use yes-no or information questions—who, what, etc.)

Each learner is given a card with an event, person, policy, or process from the test.

Sample cards

The House of Representatives

The Civil War

Use the names of students' current state and local representatives.

3 Find the Question

Give half the class the sample test questions and half the class the answers. Students mingle to find the person with their question. Mix up cards and repeat several times.

Students in vocational English classes often need to prepare for job-specific certification tests. The activities above could be used in that context as well.

Content-based instruction is common to pre-academic ESL programs. In this setting, instruction would include development of listening, speaking, reading, and writing skills. Much of the focus of instruction would be on developing Cognitive Academic Language Proficiency (CALP), including note taking, predicting, analyzing and synthesizing information, or organizing information, all of which is needed to succeed in a higher education.

2.1.9 PARTICIPATORY APPROACH

CORE PRINCIPLES

The **participatory,** or **Freirean approach** to teaching ESL grew out of Paulo Freire's work in literacy development. Freire, a Brazilian scholar and educator, developed an approach to teaching first language literacy that has been implemented in developing countries all over the world. His approach has the goal of empowering learners to have a voice in their communities. He views education as a means for people "to liberate themselves from the social conditions that oppress them" (Spener 1993:77). ESL practitioners have embraced the core principles of Freire's approach, namely that learning must derive from learners' lives and personal issues within their social context so that they can take action to improve their lives. In the words of Elsa Auerbach: ". . . the central tenet of a participatory approach is that curricula must emerge from and be responsive to the particular context of each group of participants. . ." (Auerbach 1992:1). As such, a participatory approach does not rely on textbooks, set outcomes or curricula. Rather, the curricula and outcomes emerge and evolve through learner input and teacher guidance.

CLASSROOM PRACTICE

In adult ESL, participatory education can take many forms, but it will share these features:

- Content evolves from learners' real-life issues and concerns, what Auerbach calls an **emergent curriculum** (1992).
- **Problem posing** (identifying problems) is central to the approach, followed by **problem solving** (gaining tools to deal with these issues); looking at causes of problems and possible remedies (Auerbach 1992).
- The approach emphasizes dialogue and collaboration among learners and between teacher and students.

"Problem-posing is more than a technique that teaches critical thinking; it is a philosophy, a way of thinking about students and their ability to think critically and to reflect analytically on their lives" (Nixon-Ponder 1994). Auerbach (1992) proposes a series of steps in the process of problem-posing, which are illustrated below through a classroom experience from Sarah Nixon-Ponder (1994). Sarah noticed that the issue of child care was of great concern to the women in her class.

Steps in the Problem-posing Process	Problem-posing in Action
Describe the content.	The teacher shares pictures, a short story, and a newspaper article about the topic of child care. She shares the story of her divorced sister and her two children.
Define the problem.	Learners discuss reasons for the lack of good affordable child care, which ranged from money issues, to unreliable (or no) transportation, to physical isolation from others, to cultural beliefs about who is qualified to care for someone else's children.
Personalize the problem.	Learners bring in relevant reading materials and share their own stories on the problem of child care. They write their feelings about the discussions in dialogue journals and share these with others.
Discuss the problem.	They research different laws on child care facilities and they learn about cooperatives and discuss reasonable alternatives to this problem.
Discuss alternatives to the problem.	Their solution is to organize a system for child care on their own by sharing their resources. They plan schedules for taking care of each other's children, and those with reliable transportation arrange for carpools. They plan meals for their children and caregivers and organize a system for funding their project.

This process allowed the learners in Sarah's class to identify the problems underlying their concerns, and to arrive at a number of solutions unique to their own lives and situations. While few approaches are so fully anchored in learners' lives, many of the approaches discussed in this chapter and in Chapter 5 are participatory in nature, particularly project-based learning and the Language Experience Approach.

2.1.10 Project-based Learning

Core Principles

In her article "Teaching Less Learning More," Susan Gaer recounts how she was dissatisfied with the traditional, grammar-based approaches she found herself using:

> I was a traditional teacher using a grammar-based curriculum along with dialogues and drills to teach English for speakers of other languages (ESOL) to immigrant populations when I arrived at the Visalia Adult School in central California in 1989. There I found a population of Southeast Asian Lao, Hmong, Mien, and Lahu refugees who had been in beginning-level ESOL classes since their arrival in the United States in the early 1980s. Most of the instructors were using the type of instruction I did; it was not working with the group at all. The students seemed resistant and had little confidence in their ability to learn English (Gaer 1998).

In her exploration of alternative ways of learning, Susan encountered Elsa Auerbach's book *Making Meaning, Making Change.* Auerbach promotes a participatory approach to language development where learners work on meaningful projects (Auerbach 1992). Susan describes the successes she had with her learners as they created a book of folktales, a cookbook and, in a later teaching situation at a community college, a school newspaper.

Project-based learning (PBL) is an approach that allows for maximum learner involvement and choice in the learning process. Heide Wrigley, another expert in adult ESL teaching and learning, describes it in this way: "In its simplest form, project-based learning involves a group of learners taking on an issue close to their hearts, developing a response, and presenting the results to a wider audience" (Wrigley 1998:1). It is based on the premise that the best learning is that which draws from the learners' own lives and contexts.

CLASSROOM PRACTICE

There are number of steps a teacher needs to consider in planning and facilitating projects. As Wrigley suggests, there is no set procedure to follow when students are engaged in developing a project, but she has observed that the following steps are common (Wrigley 1998):

TABLE 2.4 Project-based learning: Steps to consider

Identification of a problem	What do your students want to learn more about? In the case of Susan Gaer's Southeast Asian students, they wanted to be able to record and pass on their folktales, which were traditionally passed on orally, to their children.
Preliminary investigation	Where can we learn more about the topic? What resources are available? What do we already know and what do we want to learn?
Planning and assigning tasks	Who is responsible for each piece of the project? This is determined by the students.
Researching the topic	Different learners take on different responsibilities depending on their interests and language abilities. This could include guest speakers, visits to the library, and Internet research.
Implementing the project	What is the best way to present what has been learned? This may result in a booklet, poster, or presentation. Susan Gaer's learners created visual storyboards to accompany the telling of their folktales.
Drafting and developing a final product	What language support is needed to finalize the project? Peer editing and feedback are necessary. Language development activities with the teacher or volunteer may be needed.
Disseminating the product	Who is the audience for the project? One school in Minneapolis sold their class cookbook as a fundraiser for the school. Susan Gaer's students presented their folktales to a class of eighth graders.
Evaluating the project	How is the success of the project evaluated? Audience participation is a measure of success. Self-evaluations on personal and group participation can be conducted. Completing the process is in itself a sign of great accomplishment.

The following chart describes a project developed by EL civics students to improve communication with the staff and teachers at their children's schools. Their ultimate goal was to develop a booklet about accessing schools to share with others in their community.

Civics education: Accessing schools

Materials and resources needed	School directory, PTO chair or other parent, school maps and literature about the school (translated or simplified), list of after-school course offerings, film and/or disposable cameras
Sample unit activities	**1** In-class practice of telephoning; request to meet teacher; role-plays **2** Guest speaker from PTO; prepare for visit with prelistening activities; provide listening tasks at time of visit **3** School visit: prepare questions to ask guide; role-play questions; practice following direction; map reading activities **4** Language Experience activity: Group text about the visit; multiple activities using text **5** Take photos of children and parents at the school to include in final booklet **6** Create a list of appropriate free/low-cost after-school activities for children

Project-based learning need not be used as the sole means of instruction, in fact, projects many be implemented within any teaching approach. An on-going project might be a once-a-week activity. One teacher reported using classroom project stations, which learners would go to when finished with other class work. PBL is ideal for a multilevel class like Rosie's, described at the beginning of this section, in which learners' strengths vary. Learners comfortable with computers may gather information on the Internet; more verbal students may audiotape stories as part of the project. Taking part in a project develops collaborative skills, which benefits learners seeking employment, and a project is likely to appeal to a variety of learning styles and multiple intelligences.

CONCLUSION A multifaceted approach to teaching means combining elements from different approaches in ways that are most responsive to a particular group of learners. In completing your chart, you may have discovered that some approaches promote more active participation by the learners than others; some may promote development of a wider range of skills. Now we turn to the program options that exist within adult ESL. As you read about these options, start thinking about the ways these varied approaches might best serve students in these different settings, for example, how can project-based learning be used in English language civics?

Part II ◆ Program Options

2.2.1 INTRODUCTION

Adult ESL programming and curricula can take on many forms, including integrated-skills general English, family literacy, native language literacy, citizenship, English language civics, vocational English, workplace/work readiness, and pre-academic programs. It is not uncommon to incorporate work-readiness outcomes in general English or family literacy programs; civics education can become a component of any type of adult ESL class. What determines the classification of a program largely depends on the funding source and current needs in a community (e.g., increase in citizenship programs after a government amnesty). In this section, you will learn about the goals of different program options as well as the factors that determine what is offered and which learners find themselves in your classes.

Getting Started

TASK 2.4

With a partner, read the descriptions of three adult ESL classes and discuss which type of program you think each exemplifies: integrated-skills general English, family literacy, citizenship, English language civics, vocational English/workplace/work readiness, or pre-academic?

Group A

This class consists of 15 members of the housekeeping staff of a large hotel in Minneapolis. Most of them are recent immigrants from Latin America with little formal education. The purpose of the class is to help them function effectively on the job. There will be 20 hours of on-site instruction over a period of two months.

Group B

This class prepares immigrants to enter a nursing assistants' program at a community college in St. Paul. Students work on test-taking strategies, reading skills, as well as job-specific skills such as completing patient in-take interviews, and taking patient food orders, all of which the students need to know for the practicum they complete in their training.

Group C

This group of mothers and preschool children from Central America meets three mornings a week at a local elementary school. The mothers are working on developing literacy as well as basic skills in English. The children spend time playing games, working on art projects, and learning letters, rhymes, and songs. Each week, the mothers share with their children the stories they have created in class.

Follow-up Compare your answers with another pair in class. What seems to be the dominant emphasis of each program? Are there any that seem to respond to multiple purposes (e.g., vocational and pre-academic)? What teaching approach might be most responsive to each setting?

2.2.2 Moving beyond Survival English

While there's no question adult immigrants need to attain the language, knowledge, and skills in areas that have traditionally been called survival skills—things such as shopping, registering children at school, opening bank accounts—there is far more one needs to know in order to *thrive* in the new culture. Auerbach and Burgess (1985) suggest that active participation in all aspects of the community is what ESL instruction ought to be about. They argue that courses that adhere to a survival English approach hinder an immigrant's or refugee's ability to become an active participant in society. The following section outlines the range of options that go beyond survival English available in many communities.

In Task 2.2, the three cases illustrated different types of program options: A. workplace, B. a combination of pre-academic/vocational, and C. family literacy. How does a community or adult education site decide what types of programs to offer? There are a number of factors that determine the types of services provided in any community.

Funding Most programs rely on state and federal funding, much of which is earmarked for specific program types. Funding for EL civics, for example, rose to over $70 million in 2001, which meant a sharp rise in the number of sites developing civics curricula. With the rise in welfare-to-work programs in many states, there has been an increase in funding specifically for work readiness or workplace programs. Grantors require that programs adhere to specific guidelines and outcomes (see Chapter 10 for a discussion of meeting grantor expectations). So it's often the case that the program offerings and outcomes are determined by funding trends and resources.

Community size Large urban areas with multiple adult education centers can offer an array of services. Small communities often have one ESL site that must provide everything from workplace ESL to family literacy. Multilevel classes are the norm at these sites.

Community resources Are there teachers with expertise in adult ESL in the community? If not, does the state provide training for teachers? Many small, rural communities have experienced sudden and rapid increases of immigrant populations and are ill prepared to respond to their needs. Are there volunteers available?

Ideally, learners would enter the type of program that best corresponds to their personal and professional needs: a learner with vocational goals chooses a work readiness program; a parent of school-age children attends to a family literacy program. Regrettably, this is not always the case. There are a number of factors that determine the type of program learners choose to enter:

Location of the program/Transportation Programs need to be accessible to learners using public transportation.

Personal schedule Employed students have time constraints, especially those living in smaller communities with limited class offerings.

Availability of services Waiting lists may prevent a learner from attending in his or her neighborhood.

Legal status State sponsored programs accept only legal immigrants. Some community-based programs do not check learners' legal status.

Work/welfare status Some states require attendance in a work readiness program in order to receive public assistance. If a student is a recipient of certain types of funding, for example, Temporary Aid for Needy Families (TANF), he or she may be required to attend a work readiness program.

Level of literacy Ideally, adults with limited or no literacy should attend programs offering literacy-level courses.

Child care Some programs, particularly family literacy programs, have free on-site child care. Parents of small children are often limited to this option, even if that is not the best program fit for them.

One or more of these factors come into play as learners or sponsors select program options. The fact of the matter is that many learners do not have the luxury of researching numerous options and choosing the one that best fits their professional and personal goals. It may be that factors related to location and personal schedule will determine their choice. What does that mean for you as an ESL teacher? Regardless of the type of program within which you teach, more often than not, you need to teach to a wide range of purposes and outcomes. What are those program types and what are the central purposes of each one?

Task 2.5

To help you make connections between teaching approaches and program options, use the following grid to identify the purposes for learning in each context, as well as approaches from Part I that you think might be particularly suitable within that context.

Program Option	Purposes for learning	Suitable approaches to teaching in this setting
Integrated-skills General English		
Citizenship		
EL Civics		
Family/ Intergenerational Literacy		
VESL/Work readiness/ Workplace		
Pre-academic		

We start with what is probably the most common type of program in adult ESL: Integrated-skills general English.

2.2.3 INTEGRATED-SKILLS GENERAL ENGLISH

Many newcomer programs within Adult Basic Education (ABE) can be described as **integrated-skills general English** programs. The language focus may include literacy development, listening, speaking, functions, and grammar, all in keeping with the needs of the particular group of students. Unlike content-based programs, for example, Citizenship, where learners have a shared goal for learning English, students in these programs may have divergent wants, needs, and goals for learning English. Therefore, the themes for instruction are drawn from what are considered to be general needs. At the lower levels, learners need to acquire **basic skills,** or language needed to fulfill basic needs in the community (often called survival English). At the intermediate to advanced levels, practice in reading, writing, listening, and speaking, as well as high-level grammar, functions, and vocabulary, are integrated. Instructional themes often revolve around culture or current events. Integrated-skills general English classes often draw on core textbooks (see 8.1.2), which include practice in all skills areas.

2.2.4 CITIZENSHIP

Courses preparing immigrants to pass the citizenship exam have been in existence since the beginning of adult ESL, going back to the turn of the century. Clearly, the approach to teaching those courses has not always been the same, but the government has had a long-standing commitment to assisting immigrants in their quest to become citizens. To become a citizen, an immigrant must demonstrate English literacy and knowledge of civics through an application and interview process. Applicants are expected to have knowledge of U.S. history and government systems. Becker and Lindt (1996) suggest that the following components be included in citizenship classes:

- The benefits of citizenship.
- The naturalization process.
- Preparation for the oral and written exams including teaching language skills, culture, and content.
- Test-taking strategies.
- Confidence building.
- Referrals for legal advice.

2.2.5 ENGLISH LANGUAGE CIVICS

In more recent years, funding has been given for expanding services to include civics education, which entails a broader notion of citizenship. **English language civics** (EL civics) promotes active citizenship and participation in all aspects of the community including voting and civic involvement, involvement in neighborhood programs, active participation in children's schooling, and taking full advantage of community services such as libraries, shelters, or community centers. These topics and themes are not unique to EL civics; family literacy programs share many of the same goals, and many integrated-skills general English programs draw on the same themes. What is special about civics education is that civic involvement becomes the central goal; while the vocabulary and language that learners need to navigate within their communities is taught, civics lessons go beyond simply being language lessons. Table 2.5 illustrates some ways in which civics classes can meet the goal of civic participation.

TABLE 2.5 Comparing and contrasting general English and civics education

General English/Basic Skills	Civics
Getting around the neighborhood	**Accessing neighborhood facilities**
Map reading activities.	Scavenger hunt: Collect information as a class or individually about neighborhood stores, organizations, etc.; bring findings back to class to share with others.
Matching vocabulary to pictures of a bank, stores, school, etc.	Invite Neighborhood Watch leader to class.
Class-generated dialogues for shopping, banking, and asking for directions.	Visit local library and apply for library card (as a field trip, or as out-of-class assignment).
Role-plays to practice dialogues.	

As you compare the two settings, you can imagine that students in both classes would learn similar vocabulary, language functions, and structures. What is unique about civics? Learners step out of the classroom and into the community. They take part in activities that actually require them to participate as active citizens, and in many instances, to take action. In *Civic Participation and Community Action Sourcebook*, edited by Andy Nash, teachers describe programs involving AIDS awareness, domestic violence, and dealing with prejudice. Civics education provides an opportunity for teachers to go beyond basic survival issues, and to delve into the multitude of social issues and dilemmas many ESL students encounter every day.

2.2.6 FAMILY AND INTERGENERATIONAL LITERACY

The correlation between parental involvement and school success for children has been well established and adult immigrants are as eager as U.S.-born parents to see their children reach their highest potential. However, there are numerous factors that can impede parental involvement for language minority parents, including lack of language proficiency and familiarity with North American school norms (Mulhern, Rodriguez-Brown, and Shanahan 1994).

The overarching goal of family literacy programs is to promote connections between homes and schools by promoting literacy among adults and their children in order that children reach their highest academic potential. Equally important in this equation is that schools acknowledge and draw on the multiple perspectives and experiences of immigrant families.

Family literacy programs work concurrently with at least two generations within a family: parents or grandparents and children. Family literacy programs also have the goal of promoting self-sufficiency among parents, which means that a portion of the curriculum may focus on basic survival and work readiness skills. First-language literacy development is another component found in some programs working with adults who are not literate in their first language.

In *Family Literacy for Language Minority Families: Issues for Program Implementation*, Mulhern, Rodriguez-Brown, and Shanahan have drawn from the research of Auerbach and others on family literacy practices and identified the features in Table 2.6 as necessary for successful programs.

TABLE 2.6 Successful family literacy programs are those which . . .

• Address parents' personal goals.
• Value families home languages, traditions, and values.
• View families as a resource.
• Provide families with access to information and resources that encourage success for children.
• Draw on previous experiences with education.
• Recognize the skills and knowledge families already have; take a *strengths* rather than *deficit* view of adult learners.
• Promote shared literacy experiences in the home (creating stories together, reading together).

(Adapted from Mulhern, Rodriguez-Brown, and Shanahan 1994, p. 2)

Initially, family literacy programs focused on families with preschool children (e.g., Even Start), but there are many learners arriving in the U.S. at a later age, which means that family literacy programs need to look at educational issues from preschool through high school. In some instances, adult literacy programs are offered at the elementary and secondary schools attended by participants' children, a model which allows parents to visit classes, take part in school activities, and become acquainted with the school and teachers (Holt and Holt 1995). This also provides an opportunity for the schools to learn from immigrant parents and families. Holt and Holt report an increase in parent participation in school activities for adults enrolled in these school-based programs.

What is crucial in all of this is that educators not take a **deficit** view of adult learners and their families; programs should not be designed solely to transmit school culture and language to immigrant parents (Auerbach 1995).

Learners' homes are not linguistically impoverished—parents and children interact and collaborate, they use many forms of literacy, they educate one another. The interactions and literacy practices used in homes may be different, but no less valid, from those used in institutions. "Program design should recognize the existence of multiple literacies and literacy behaviors in the home and community and attempt to integrate home and school literacies" (Kerka 1991). In other words, literacy experiences and practices can move from homes to schools as well as from schools to homes.

2.2.7 Work Readiness/Workplace/VESL

Work readiness programs are those offered before employment, and often focus on the skills needed to attain employment, such as reading job ads, resume writing, and interviewing. One goal that many work-related programs share is to help learners develop **SCANS,** a set of skills proposed by the Secretary's Commission on Achieving Necessary Skills (Whetzel 1992). In 1990, the secretary of labor appointed a commission to determine the necessary skills for success in the workforce today. These skills are commonly integrated into workplace ESL texts (Price-Machado 1998), and workplace ESL programs. Grognet (1997) has identified ways in which these workplace competencies can be integrated into work readiness or workplace ESL instruction. The following themes can become part of any work-related curriculum, varying the content of instruction based on the industries in which learners are employed or hope to be employed:

Workplace Competencies

- Resources: allocating time, money, materials, space, staff
- Interpersonal skills: working with others
- Information: locating, evaluating, organizing, and processing information
- Systems: understanding, managing, and improving systems
- Technology: interacting successfully in all aspects of technology use

In addition to workplace competences, SCANS identifies the following foundation skills:

Foundation Skills

- Basic skills: reading, writing, mathematics, speaking, and listening
- Thinking skills: thinking creatively, making decisions, solving problems, and reasoning
- Personal qualities: responsibility, self-esteem, sociability, self-management, and integrity

Grognet (1997) highlights the importance of going beyond a vocabulary-based, generic curriculum in workplace ESL, given the complex demands learners encounter in workplaces of today. She suggests that learners need more than just language needed to *get* a job. Learners also need to *survive* and *thrive*, or have mobility.

Workplace ESL programs are those offered at work sites or with a group of learners from the same work site, focusing on the very specific needs of the learners' job. In many states, Adult Basic Education funding is earmarked for on-site ESL instruction, meaning that ESL teachers who have thought of themselves as general ESL teachers may find themselves working in highly technical, job-specific settings. These programs fall under the umbrella of **vocational English as a second language,** or **VESL.** VESL programs may also be offered pre-employment, for example, a specialized English class for nurses, carpenters, or bank tellers. In any setting, VESL has unique challenges and rewards for both students and teachers. Because the needs are so specific, for example, "follow instructions for filling drive-shaft molds," instruction becomes highly focused and goals are often more attainable than general goals, such as "speak more fluently." The challenge is that the terminology can be highly technical and the work processes can be unfamiliar to the teacher and students. The key to success is to conduct a thorough needs assessment and learn about the company and industry within which you work. In addition to job-specific language and processes, the workplace ESL instructor needs to integrate the SCANS competencies, as well as the skills Grognet suggests are needed to thrive and survive in the workplace (Table 2.7).

TABLE 2.7 Work readiness programs should address the language and skills needed to. . .

• Get a Job: give personal information; express ability; express likes and dislikes; and answer and ask questions.
• Survive on a Job: follow oral and written directions; understand and use safety language; ask for clarification; make small talk; request reasons; find facts or specifications in text materials; and determine the meaning of technical vocabulary.
• Thrive on a Job: participate in group discussions; give as well as follow directions; teach others; hypothesize; predict outcomes; state a position; express an opinion; negotiate; interrupt; and take turns.

(Grognet 1997 p. 3–4)

2.2.8 PRE-ACADEMIC ESL

The primary goal of **pre-academic** ESL programs is to prepare students to enter higher education institutions: community or junior colleges, technical schools, or universities. Some of the adult learners in these programs are pursuing their first degree, while others are retraining in the same or similar profession they held in their country of origin. The focus of instruction in these programs is most often on academic skills and strategies development:

- Reading extended texts.
- Writing for academic purposes: research papers, reports, essays.
- Finding resources: using libraries, journals, Internet sources.
- Listening to lectures and note taking.

- Test-taking strategies; depending on the legal status of learners, some may need to prepare for the TOEFL.
- Study skills.

In some cases, the pre-academic program is taught in conjunction with a training program, allowing the ESL teacher to integrate the field-specific content (the nursing assistants' program described in Task 2.4 is an example of this). Many community and technical colleges and universities offer pre-academic programs, but they may require students to pay tuition that is beyond their means. State-sponsored Adult Basic Education programs have traditionally focused on helping learners at lower proficiency levels. Even those that offer advanced courses do not necessarily prepare learners for the demands of higher education. There is often a mismatch between the content and goals of Adult Basic Education programs and the goals of academically bound adult learners (Rance-Roney 1995). Adult Basic Education **transition programs,** which instruct students in skills and strategies needed in higher education settings, are a solution and are becoming more common within Adult Basic Education programs. In fact, through an initiative of the New England Literacy Resource Center, 20 new ABE transition programs were launched in 2002 in the New England area (New England Literacy Resource Center 2002).

2.2.9 Distance Learning

Distance learning is a recent trend in adult ESL, particularly for those learners who lack transportation, have work commitments, or live in areas where there is limited adult education support. It provides learners added flexibility in choosing the time and place of instruction. Distance learning is characterized as "separation of place and/or time between the learner and the instructor, among learners, and/or between learners and learning resources. Interaction between the learner and the instructor, among learners, and/or between learners and resources is conducted through one or more media" (NIFL 2000). A National Institute for Literacy (2000) report cites the following delivery modes for distance learning:

- *computer technology*, such as the Internet, e-mail, CD-ROMs.
- *video technology*, such as videoconferencing, cable, satellite linkage, and videotapes.
- *audiographic technology*, such as radio and audiotapes.
- *telephone technology*, such as teleconferencing.

Any of the program types described in this chapter can be delivered through distance learning, and the outcomes and standards are the same as those for face-to-face instruction. Many of the resources developed for distance learning can also be used by students in on-site classrooms, enhancing their educational experience. Web-based lessons, video, or audio programs provide self-study opportunities for any learner.

CONCLUSION In this chapter, we have looked very broadly at some of the most common approaches to teaching adult ESL as well as the program options available. It is essential that teachers new to adult ESL understand that there are many connections between and among all of these approaches and options. There is no recipe for good teaching. What works successfully in one setting may not in another. Through thorough needs assessment, on-going observation, and abundant opportunities for learners to express their needs and concerns in the classroom, teachers shape their curricula accordingly, drawing from a variety of approaches, techniques, and materials.

In the chapters that follow, teaching techniques and strategies that help learners develop both language and social/cultural knowledge are examined and illustrated through sample lesson plans, activities, and guidelines. The tools and techniques you will learn about can be used within many of the approaches and program options discussed in this chapter.

KEY TERMS

CHECKLIST OF KEY TERMS	On your own, or with a partner, provide an example or brief definition for each concept.
multiple intelligences	
receptive skills	
productive skills	
silent period	
emergent curriculum	
problem posing	
problem solving	
basic skills	

Applying What You Learned

1 Reflecting on Your Own Learning Experience

In reflecting on approaches to teaching, it can be useful to think about our own experiences as learners. At the beginning of the chapter, you briefly discussed a learning experience you've had. This activity allows you to examine in greater depth the ways your own learning may shape or inform your teaching.

If you have studied a second language, reflect on your own experiences as a language learner as you answer these questions. For those of you who haven't learned a second language, think of a different classroom experience you've had, either for academic or vocational purposes (computer classes, professional training) or for personal growth (piano, gardening, etc.). Write your answers in your journal or discuss them with others in your class:

a What is your overall recollection of the experience? Was it positive or negative and what made it so? Did you feel you learned something or not?

b How many students were in your class? How was the classroom arranged? What roles did the students and teacher take in the classroom? Would you describe the class as learner-centered or teacher-centered? Why?

c What areas of language did you practice, or, for nonlanguage classes, what content or skills did you learn?

reading, writing, listening, speaking, grammar, language functions, vocabulary

d Did the teacher speak the target language or your native language during class? What about the students?

e What happened when students made errors? What find of feedback worked best for you?

f What topics and themes were covered? To what extent did you have a say in course content?

g How do you think your own experiences as a learner can shape and inform the choices you make about approaches to teaching adult ESL?

h What did you discover to be the most effective elements of your own language (or other) classes? What helped you learn best?

i Do you recognize any of the elements from the approaches in Part I in the approaches used by your own teachers?

2 Approaches to Teaching Adult ESL

If you are already teaching. . . choose one of your classes and answer the questions from Part I of this chapter:

- Who are the learners?
- Why are they learning English?
- What experience have they had with formal and informal education?
- What are their views of teaching and learning?
- What is your own view of teaching and learning?
- What are the overall goals of the program?

How would you describe the approach you are currently using with this group of learners? What other approaches would you like to try with this group of learners?

If you are not teaching. . . contact an ESL teacher in your community and ask if you can observe his or her class.

Before class: Interview the teacher using the questions above?

After you observe, answer these questions: How would you describe this teacher's approach to teaching? Is there an approach described in Part I you think might work well with the group you observed?

3 Program Options in Your Community

What program options are offered in your community? Call your adult education department of your state department of education and ask for the following information:

a Where are adult ESL services provided through your state? Community colleges, public schools, community-based programs, other?

b What program options are available? General English, family literacy, etc.?

c What are the requirements for teachers of adult ESL in your state?

Recommended Reading

Nash, A., A. Cason, R. Gomez-Sandford, L. McGrail, and **M. Rhum.** 1992. *Talking shop: A curriculum sourcebook for participatory adult ESL.* Washington, DC and McHenry, IL: Center for Applied Linguistics and Delta Systems.

This book includes teachers' first-hand accounts of how they applied a participatory approach in their classrooms. The writers address learner roles, first language literacy as well as ways to involve learners in shaping the curriculum.

Weinstein-Shr, G. and **E. Quintero,** (eds.) 1995. *Immigrant learners and their families.* Washington, DC and McHenry, IL: Center for Applied Linguistics and Delta Systems.

This book provides models of innovative family and intergenerational literacy programs from across the country.

Wrigley, H. and **G. Guth.** 1992. *Bringing literacy to life: Issues and options in adult ESL literacy.* San Mateo, CA: Aguirre International.

A comprehensive overview of the connections between theory and practice in adult literacy development. The authors provide information on methods and approaches, assessment, technology, teacher development as well as promising practices from literacy programs across the country.

Useful Websites

National Center for ESL Literacy Education (NCLE)

Center for Applied Linguistics

www.cal.org/ncle

NCLE provides information on adult ESL language and literacy education to teachers and tutors, program directors, researchers, and policy makers interested in the education of refugees, immigrants, and other U.S. residents whose native language is other than English. This Website provides links to a plethora of articles on a broad range of issues including teaching practices, working with learners with special needs, assessment, and workplace instruction, just to name a few. Many of these articles are cited in this book. For an extensive list of links to resources on a broad range of topics, be sure to visit the NCLE "Worth a Visit" page at http://www.cal.org/ncle/links.htm#plans, which also includes a section of Websites for learners.

System for Adult Basic Education Support SABES

Massachusetts Department of Education

http://www.sabes.org/index.htm

SABES is a training and support initiative for adult education teachers. The Website provides links to many valuable online resources, newsletters, and reports, including *Bright Ideas* (1991–1999), now redesigned as *Field Notes,* and *Adventures in Assessment,* which include timely and practical articles from experts in the field of adult ESL education.

Literacy Online (National Center on Adult Literacy)

http://litserver.literacy.upenn.edu/

Publications including newletters and research reports from NCAL and the International Literacy Institute (ILI) as well as links to national and international sites.

English Literacy and Civics Education (EL/Civics)

Colorado Department of Education

http://www.cde.state.co.us/cdeadult/ELCivics.htm

This site provides numerous links to civics education materials and resources.

3

Contextualized Language Teaching

Part I ◆ Developing Integrated and Contextualized Language Lessons

3.1.1 Introduction

We have looked at a number of approaches to teaching ESL as well as program options offered in most communities. Each program type has a particular focus, but they share the goal of helping learners communicate within their communities more effectively. Whether the need to communicate is for work, school, family, or community involvement, students come to classes to improve their ability to use English. In this chapter, we explore an integrated approach to developing ESL lessons that is both learner-centered and contextualized. We examine the different areas of language learners need to acquire as well as the contexts in which the language is used outside of the classroom. We explore activities that promote natural use of language so that learners gain confidence in using English in the safe environment of the classroom. As with any type of lesson, teaching begins with understanding your learners' strengths, wants, and needs.

CHECKLIST

After reading this chapter and completing the activities, you should be able to

- define language competencies and language functions.
- describe the rationale for taking an integrated and contextualized approach to presenting and practicing new language.
- create an integrated and contextualized language lesson.
- choose activities that promote meaningful practice of language competencies, functions, and forms.
- explain considerations for deciding when and how to correct learner errors.

Getting Started

Task 3.1

Jessica teaches adult ESL to a diverse group of learners in Portland, Oregon. They have been placed in the low-intermediate level class. The main focus of her program is on survival skills and general English for new immigrants, although many of her students have been in the United States for over five years. She surveyed her students' needs and interests at the beginning of the session. Here are some of the responses from her students:

Use the telephone	Find jobs in the newspaper
I want grammar	Understand my child's schoolwork
I need vocabulary	Talk to my landlord about problems
Go to the bank	Interview for jobs
Talk to doctors and nurses	I can't talk to the teachers at school
I can't understand people	Go shopping
Learn English for college	Talk to people at my job

Jessica is struck by the variety of needs and expectations from her students and is not sure where to start. Her own experience as a language learner in high school and college was to practice grammar and vocabulary, but she can see that her students need something more than that. She knows that some students want nothing but grammar, while others want to learn how to communicate in English with their children's teachers. How can she bring all of this together?

Work with a partner to identify at least three key themes that could guide Jessica's choices for her class:

Themes for Jessica's class
1
2
3
Others

3.1.2 An Integrated Approach to Language Learning and Teaching

Key themes that arose from Jessica's class are highlighted below, along with topics from the needs assessment, and others that might be addressed within each theme. How does this compare to your list above?

Theme 1: Getting around the community

Going shopping

Going to the bank

Using the telephone

Accessing medical care

Talking to doctors and nurses

Making doctor appointments

Finding housing

Talking to landlords

Theme 2: Interacting with school staff and teachers

Talking to teachers at parent-teacher conferences

Understanding class assignments

Reporting an illness

Reading school correspondences

Theme 3: Finding jobs and interacting at work

Reading advertisements

Interviewing

Talking about skills

Calling in sick

Talking to co-workers

These themes can be translated into a variety of language needs:

LANGUAGE COMPETENCIES

These are real-life skills that enable us to complete the tasks we need to accomplish in our daily lives or at our jobs.

Examples: Making appointments

Calling in sick to work

Asking a co-worker for help

LANGUAGE FUNCTIONS

Functions represent the ways we use language forms and phrases in social interactions.

Examples: Greetings and introductions

Making invitations

Making polite requests

Complaints and apologies

LINGUISTIC COMPETENCE: GRAMMAR, VOCABULARY, SPELLING, PRONUNCIATION

Learners need to develop their linguistic competence, but it should be done within broad, real-life contexts.

CULTURAL COMPETENCE

Learners need to acquire skills to navigate in the new culture; they need to be able to advocate for themselves, and understand how and where to access services.

LANGUAGE SKILLS

Lessons also need to take into account the modes of communication that we use: speaking, listening, reading, and writing. We call those modes of communication the four **language skills.**

Effective language lessons depend on identifying the purposes for which learners need to use English, then identifying the competencies, functions, grammar, vocabulary, and skills needed to gain confidence and proficiency for those purposes. All of this comes together in an **integrated approach** to teaching. To illustrate what this means, let's take an example that derives from Jessica's list of learner needs at the beginning of the chapter: *Making a complaint to a landlord.* Table 3.1 illustrates the variety of components that go into making complaints and approaching resolution with a landlord.

TABLE 3.1 Components of an integrated lesson

Language Competency	Making a complaint to a landlord
Language Functions	Introducing a complaint: I've had a problem with . . . My _____ is broken . . . The _____ doesn't work. Requesting action: Could you please replace . . .? Would you mind sending someone to fix the _____ ? Coming to a resolution to the problem
Skills	Speaking to the landlord over the phone or in person. Listening to the landlord. Reading tenant policies. Writing letters of complaint.
Cultural Competencies	Knowing how to access consumer advocate offices. Knowing whom to contact at the housing agency or complex if the problem isn't resolved.
Grammar	Modal verbs (*can, may, could*) Question forms
Vocabulary	Household appliances and items. Repair, fix, replace. Rooms of the house.

Making a complaint to a landlord entails everything from knowing how to make requests appropriately to knowing the vocabulary for household items. It also involves learning how to access community organizations such as consumer advocates or housing agencies. One aspect of language does not stand alone without the others. In this chapter, you will learn how to bring all of this together by taking an *integrated and contextualized approach* to teaching.

Contextualized Language Lessons

Lessons in which the teacher focuses on a particular language competency, function, grammar point, or set of vocabulary used in real-world contexts. While each lesson you teach may have a particular language focus (e.g., calling in sick to work, making polite requests, talking about the weather, or using the simple past tense), many skills and areas of language are integrated into each lesson.

3.1.3 Contextualized Language Lessons

Teachers and researchers have through the years proposed a variety of models and procedures for language teaching. After the fall in popularity (in most corners) of the Audiolingual, drill-response approach to teaching, more meaning-based approaches emerged. One such approach to teaching language lessons, called the PPP model, is seen in Table 3.2.

TABLE 3.2 Presentation/Practice/Production

Presentation	Show how language is used and formed through a story or dialogue, for example; highlight the target forms; check for learner understanding through accurate reproduction activities.
Practice	Highly controlled activities, drills, dialogue repetition. (While more meaning-based than the strict mechanical drills, these activities are carry-overs of the Audiolingual Method.)
Production	Freer activities that allow learners to try the new language more spontaneously: information-gap activities and role-plays, for example.

This approach to teaching ESL has come under increasing criticism for a variety of reasons. It implies that, as Jeremy Harmer has pointed out, "students learn in 'straight lines'—that is, starting from no knowledge, through highly restricted sentence-based utterances and on to immediate production" (Harmer 2000:82). We know that such a linear approach does not represent the complex processes that go into learning a second language. A lesson that focuses too narrowly on a particular language point, and presents and practices it with a set procedure, has the following shortcomings:

- It may not account for the fact that language forms are used in combination with a variety of skills and other language forms. Lessons need to integrate and combine these various skills and forms.
- Language forms are used differently in different settings. A narrowly focused lesson may result in learners completing a lesson not fully understanding the range of uses a language point might have or how to use them in different settings, e.g., informal vs. formal settings, personal vs. vocational.
- Language learners bring different knowledge and skills to a lesson. Teaching needs to validate and draw on that knowledge, allowing learners to shape the direction of the lesson. Lessons that follow a prescribed set of steps may overlook the role learners can play in shaping the lesson.
- Language use is unpredictable, so highly controlled practice activities won't necessarily replicate real-world use when your students leave your classroom.

A number of ESL educators have suggested alternatives to the strict PPP progression. Jim Scrivener proposes a model he calls **ARC: Authentic use, Restricted use,** and **Clarification and focus.** He suggests that most classroom activities can be described in one of those ways. Role-plays, listening to news reports, or interview tasks are examples of Authentic use. Restricted use refers to activities that focus on accuracy such as drills and repetition activities. Clarification and focus represents those instances in a lesson when the teacher and learners describe or discover rules and patterns of the language, or when corrective feedback is given. Scrivener suggests that all of these elements can exist in a lesson, but that they don't need to happen in a particular order. The ARC Model provides a description of effective language teaching rather than a prescription of what it should look like. The examples provided in this chapter are intended to do the same, i.e., guide your language teaching in ways that promote learner involvement.

So, what are the benefits to teaching **contextualized language lessons** that *do* focus on a particular competency or area of language? Presenting and practicing language competencies, functions, and grammar points, *can* have the following benefits for beginning to intermediate-level learners:

- This type of lesson allows the teacher to respond specifically to a language need of a group of learners.
- Working through small chunks of language with a logical progression can be very reassuring to beginning-level students; there's a sense of accomplishment in getting it right.
- Many adult learners have had formal instruction in languages and benefit from the opportunity to notice and focus on particular language forms.

As you will discover, the key to effective contextualized language lessons is that they include a variety of practice activities that use language in real-life, meaningful ways. In addition to that, they need to include a variety of learner options so that, for example, learners with fewer literacy skills can have the same learning opportunities as more literate learners. Perhaps the most important factor is that lessons have learners using language in ways that are as authentic as possible. Whenever possible, learners should take on roles in class that replicate the roles that they need to take on outside of the classroom. We have to be careful when using the term *authenticity* in language teaching. After all, the learners are in classroom and, as David Nunan (1991) stresses, nothing we do in a classroom can be truly authentic. That said, we do want to strive to replicate real-world language use as much as we possibly can.

Finally, lessons need to take into account the social contexts in which language is used. The language we choose to use is defined by the personal relationships and social situations of interactions with others (Kramsch 1996). Lessons need to account for socially accepted norms of formality and politeness, which means that we need to include practice of both formal and informal usage:

- Greeting a government official at a citizenship interview as well as greeting friends and neighbors.
- Understanding social and cultural norms of communicating on a first-name basis with co-workers, teachers, and even supervisors. Also understanding that using first names is not a sign of disrespect.

In the pages that follow, I am sharing sample contextualized language lessons practicing ESL teachers and I have developed for our students. They are not intended to be prescriptions of how to teach a language lesson, but rather examples of how experienced teachers each constructed a lesson for a particular group of learners. Each lesson has a different language focus:

Sample 1: A competency lesson: making phone calls for a variety of purposes

Sample 2: A grammar lesson: sharing life stories using simple past tense

Sample 3: A vocabulary lesson: colors and clothing

Not every lesson has the same types of objectives or outcomes; those vary depending on the focus of the lesson. Sample 1 focuses more on the functional language and speaking and listening skills needed to make telephone calls. Sample 2 focuses on using the simple past tense with accuracy and fluency. Sample 3 focuses on vocabulary that could later be used in a variety of competency-based lessons, for example, shopping, comparing prices of clothing, or reading labels.

This contextualized approach does not require that you create everything in a lesson from scratch. While none of these sample lessons came out of a textbook, they represent what is commonly found in many current ESL textbooks, which provide similar contexts, stages, and activities (see Chapter 8 for a detailed discussion of using textbooks). In fact, in most cases, teachers have a textbook from which they can develop lessons like these. All three examples contain three general stages, which are outlined in Table 3.3. As Scrivener suggests, a teacher needs to move freely between these stages in response to learner participation and understanding in a lesson.

TABLE 3.3 The Contextualized Language Lesson

1 Language Used in a Real-world Context	Show how and when the language is used. Get learners to notice patterns and phrases they can use (Clarification and focus). Check for learner understanding through activities and questions that check comprehension.
2 Practice in Meaningful Contexts	Practice that begins with simple repetition, semiscripted role-plays, information-gap activities (Restricted use), and moves to spontaneous language practice—a dry run for the real world (Authentic use). The teacher may move back and forth between less controlled and more controlled activities depending on learner ability. These activities will be defined further in Part III of this chapter.
3 Application/Extension	Application/Extension is taking learning out of the classroom and into the real world—making phone calls, collecting information from the community, attending an activity at a child's school.

Task 3.2

As you read the following lesson plan, look for answers to the questions below. Write your answers in your journal or discuss them with a partner.

1 How does the teacher connect learning to students' lives?

2 What makes language practice authentic for the learners?

3 When do the teacher and learners focus on learning patterns?

4 Which activities help learners attain accuracy with the language of telephoning?

5 When and how are the four skills (reading, writing, listening, speaking) practiced?

SAMPLE LESSON 1 Calling for Information over the Telephone

I taught this lesson to a group of adult immigrants in St. Paul, Minnesota, but it would also respond to Jessica's students' desire to improve their ability to talk on the telephone if she were to construct dialogues that are situated in her learners' community.

CLASS DESCRIPTION 26 adult low-to-intermediate level ESL students

SETTING Community-based Life Skills ESL Class

TIME 90 minutes

Objectives	
Competencies	Students will be able to make telephone calls for a variety of everyday purposes: calling for hours and information, leaving a message. Students will alphabetize names. Students will listen for and record phone numbers.
Functional	Students will be able to greet and introduce themselves. Make requests over the phone.
Listening	Students will listen for the gist of a topic/conversation. Students will listen for specific information.
Grammatical	Students use correct modals (*may, can, could*) + simple form of verb (*speak, take, leave*) in making requests.
Vocabulary	Telephoning words and phrases.

Assumptions: Adults use the telephone for many purposes and often need to communicate with English speakers on the phone. They are therefore likely to be motivated to learn words and phrases to help them express themselves more clearly.

Anticipated Problems: Difficulty with authentic listening tasks; need to assure learners to listen for only the information needed; need to replay calls numerous times to complete each task.

Materials: Handouts, tape and tape recorder; cue cards; telephone; phone books

A. Language Used in a Real-world Context

Purpose	To establish a context for using the target language (telephoning); to motivate students by showing real-world use of language

T	Do you have a telephone? How often do you use it? When do you use the telephone? What language(s) do you usually speak on the phone? When do you need to use English? Who makes the most calls in your house?
Elicit responses	(Possible responses: call friends and family, to make appointments, call school, call for store hours)

The following listening activities are based on telephone calls Ana made, which were transcribed and recorded for use in the classroom. Alternatively, the teacher and students can co-construct dialogues similar to the ones below. The teacher elicits from students what is said at each stage of a conversation, and writes their suggestions on the board (reformulating their language as needed) to create a class-generated dialogue. The teacher can then proceed with similar activities.

T We are going to hear Ana make two calls (see transcript of what learners hear below).

Task 1	Identify the call (learners listen to get the gist of the calls). On board or handout: ______ calling a department store for store hours ______ calling the doctor ______ calling a friend about work ______ calling school
Task 2	Listen for details Complete details
Call 1	Target is open from ______ to ______ on Saturday and______ to ______ on Sunday.
Call 2	Ana is calling ______. Ana's number is __ __ __ - __ __ __ - __ __ __ __. She will be up until ______.
Task 3	Dialogues cut in strips. Listen and put dialogue strips in the correct order.

Transcripts of taped dialogues

Call 1	Good evening, Target Roseville.	How late are you open tonight?
	9:30.	And what about your hours over the weekend?
	Um. . . –Saturday ten to nine.	Uh uh.
	No, I'm sorry nine to nine.	Uh uh.
	And Sunday ten to six.	OK, thank you very much.
Call 2	Hello.	Hi. Is Martin there?
	No, he isn't.	Could I leave a message, please?
	Oh, OK.	Could you ask him to call Ana?
	Oh yeah, sure.	It's about work.
	And what's your number?	It's 651-644-8763.
	OK. Are you going to be home?	Um...I'll be home and I'll be up until about ten.
	OK. I'll tell him to give you a call.	Thanks a lot.
	Sure.	Bye.
	Bye-bye.	

Focusing on the language

Purpose	To highlight and focus attention on the language used to ask for information on the phone and take/leave messages. You can modify the number of language options you give depending on the level of your learners.

T

How does Ana ask for Martin?

How does she ask for store hours?

What does she say to leave a message?

Elicit learner responses

Learners choose sentence strips and teacher writes phrases on board. Elicit other ways learners know to ask for someone, ask for information, or leave a message. Their responses are written on flash cards to be used for a checking activity that follows.

Checking learning

Purpose	To check understanding of what the language means and when and how to use the language
Cue cards	Learners will match the language functions with the phrases that can be used for each (can be done at a table, or cards could be taped to the board)

Ask for someone on the phone	Ask for information	Leave a message
Is Martin there? May I speak to Martin? Can I speak to Martin?	How late are you open? What are your hours? When do you close?	Could I leave a message? Could you ask him to call Ana? Please tell him Ana called.

B. Practice in Meaningful Contexts

Purpose	Provide opportunities for practice, moving from more to less controlled as appropriate for your learners.

1 Discourse Chains (students are given the two sides of a dialogue and each takes one part):

Directory Assistance.

Calling the bank for hours.

Leaving a message.

Pairs fill in missing words in discourse chains.

Check as a group.

Practice each one with a partner.

Repeat for each scenario.

Meaningful Practice: Sample Discourse Chains

Create these dialogues using genuine information based on community shops, services, and the learners in the class. Learners take turns with one side of the dialogue.

Calling for Bank Hours

Caller	Bank
	Hello, First Bank.
How ___ are you ___?	
	We're open until 4:30.
What ___ Saturday?	
	We're ___ until 12:00.
Thank you.	
	Thanks for calling. Good-bye.
Bye.	

Leaving a Message

	Hello.
Hello, is ___ ___?	
	No, ___ ___ home now.
	Can I ___ a message?
Sure. This is ___.	
	What's your ___?
My number's ___.	
	That was ___?
Yes. Thank you.	
	No problem. I'll tell ___ to ___ you. Good-bye.
Good-bye.	

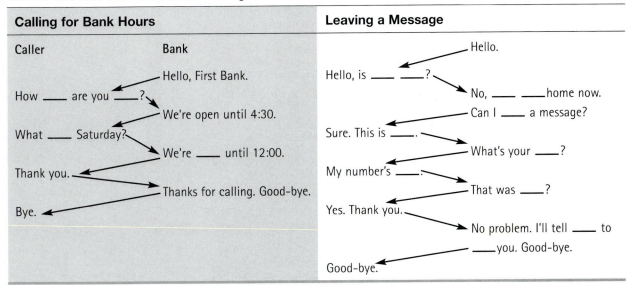

2 Role-play Pairs are given cue cards with information needed to make a phone call.

Sitting back to back, they make calls.

T circulates to listen.

Rotate cue cards to change scenarios and roles.

Give feedback on outcomes and language.

Sample cue cards for role-plays (use genuine information from the community and class).

1A	Call a parent from your child's school. You have a question about a class assignment. The parent's name is Xavier Martin.
1B	Answer the phone. Xavier isn't home. Take a message.
2A	Call JC Penney. Ask for their hours.
2B	You work at JC Penney. The hours are: Monday—Saturday: 10:00 A.M.—9:30 P.M.
3A	Call the Metropolitan Transit Commission (bus company). When does the #4 bus leave Francis and 5th Street going south? (Use names from your community.)
3B	MTC. Bus #4 leaves every 15 minutes (12:15, 12:30, 12:45, etc.)
4A	Call the post office. Ask for their hours.
4B	Post office is open Monday—Friday: 9:00—5:00 Saturday: 9:00—12:00 Sunday: closed

3 Phone Books Students may want to contact one another outside of class. Students mingle to collect numbers. This activity could be done only with groups who are comfortable providing personal information to others. An alternative could be to give each learner a name and number of a local service that would be useful for students to have and the group mingles to fill in phone books.

ABC Name: Chen, Ah-li Phone Number: 906 425-9988	**GHI** Name: Phone Number:
Name: Phone Number:	Name: Phone Number:
DEF Name: Phone Number:	**JKL** Name: Phone Number:
Name: Phone Number:	Name: Phone Number:

C. Application/Extension

Purpose	To provide learners with opportunities to apply what they learn in class outside of the classroom.
Community calls	Learners gather useful information to report to the class in the following lesson. As a class, brainstorm a list of places learners have called or need to call (provide an example: Call motor vehicle department for times and cost of driver's education courses). Assign each student one place to call, or have students assign tasks to one another.

In the lesson above, learners needed to have some degree of literacy in English in order to complete many of the tasks (filling in answers to the listening tasks, reading and filling in the discourse chains, reading the role cards). In this competency-based lesson, learners practice a variety of functions as well as vocabulary associated with telephoning. How can this approach work with beginning-level learners, particularly those with limited or no literacy? In the next section, we turn to sample lessons for beginning-level learners, including those with limited literacy skills in their first language and in English.

3.1.4 Working with Learners New to English

Beginning-level learners need to acquire basic language skills before they can move on to to more extensive use of the language. That is not to say that they should be learning small pieces of language one at a time. What they do need is sufficient input and modeling in order to produce extended spoken or written language. The input also needs to be supported with visuals and gestures in order to make it comprehensible to students. Production may be very limited at this stage, but students can point to pictures, order pictures, or respond with yes/no cards, all of which demonstrate their accomplishments in language development.

The following contextualized language lessons on *Telling our Stories* and *Clothing and Colors* were designed for beginning to high-beginning level learners in two different settings. The students came from a variety of cultural backgrounds, some with limited formal education, others with degrees from their country. What they shared was a desire to acquire literacy and basic skills in English. In Sample Lesson 2, the teacher uses the context of sharing life stories to present and practice the simple past tense. While the focus in this lesson is on grammar, you will see that many other areas of language are integrated as well. Sample Lesson 3 focuses on clothing vocabulary and colors, a lesson which prepares learners for subsequent practice with prices and shopping.

Task 3.3

Use the same questions as above to reflect on these lessons. Two questions are added that help you think about techniques and strategies for working with lower-level students:

1 How does the teacher connect learning to students' lives?

2 What makes language practice authentic for the learners?

3 When do the teacher and learners focus on learning the grammar point?

4 Which activities help learners to attain accuracy using the simple past tense?

5 When and how are the four skills (reading, writing, listening, speaking) practiced?

6 Identify the techniques used that are particularly suitable for beginning-level students.

7 How is the lesson different from the one above from learners at the low-intermediate level?

SAMPLE LESSON 2	Sharing Life Stories/Simple Past Tense
CLASS DESCRIPTION	16 adult beginning-level ESL students
SETTING	Family Literacy Program
TIME	90 minutes

Objectives	
Functional	Students will be able to tell others where they're from and share key milestones in their lives.
Grammatical	Students will practice the simple past tense of regular verbs and irregular verbs *to get* and *to have*; students will form questions in the simple past tense.
Writing	Students will work together to write short biographical paragraphs.
Reading	Students will read or retell their stories.
Vocabulary	Students will practice words about education and family.

Anticipated Problems: Some members of the class may not be comfortable talking about their life journeys (remember from Chapter 1 that difficulties in the journey and extent of life disruption and trauma during war need to be considered when working with immigrant and refugee students).

A. Language Used in a Real-world Context

Purpose	To establish a context for using the target language; to motivate students by showing real-world use of language

Students and teacher around table with photographs (T shares pictures of highlights of her life)

First day of school	High school graduation	First group of ESL students
Wedding	First apartment	First home
First child	Second child	

On table, flashcards with these dates:

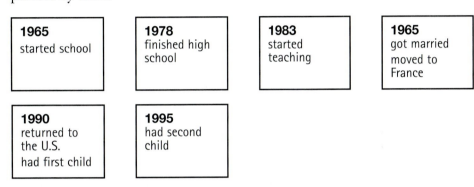

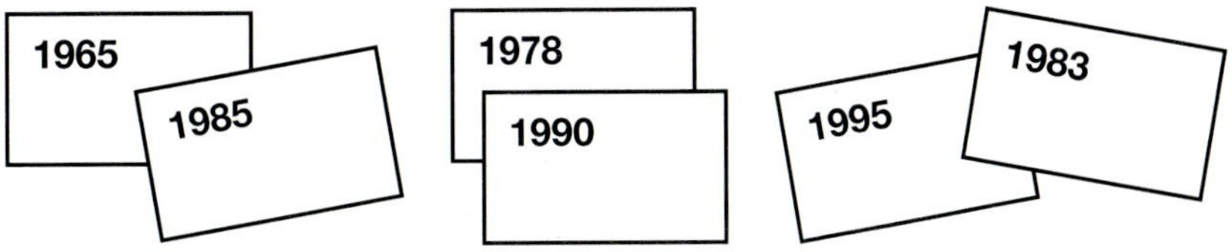

Ask students to put pictures in order. Provide nonverbal support with fingers for first, second, and so on; model by choosing two pictures and ask: *Which comes first?*

T tapes pictures on board; writes dates under pictures.

Pairs guess what each picture represents. T confirms guesses and writes phrases by dates:

1965 started school	**1978** finished high school	**1983** started teaching	**1965** got married moved to France
1990 returned to the U.S. had first child	**1995** had second child		

Focusing on the language

Purpose	To highlight language needed to talk about milestones in our lives

T asks appropriate questions of learners based on his or her knowledge of students, for example:

When did you get married?

When did you finish high school?

When did you move to the U.S.?

T tries to elicit question form by showing a flashcard of a question mark: *?*

T writes student answers on the board to use as models for the class members and highlights the past tense forms:

When did you start school?

I started school in 1970.

Checking learning

Purpose	To check understanding of what the language means and when and how to use the language

Group stands in a circle; each learner chooses a question to ask a classmate. T helps students by reformulating the questions and answers as needed. I sometimes have students take turns by throwing a beanbag or a soft ball to the student they want to ask:

When did you start school?

When did you move to the U.S.?

When did you get married?

B. Practice in Meaningful Contexts

Purpose	Provide opportunities for practice, moving from more to less controlled as appropriate for your learners.

Pairs work together to create a timeline for their partner. Each given a blank line with some dates:

1960	1970	1980	1990	2000

Task 1 Students ask questions to complete timeline with milestones. Nonliterate learners draw pictures.

Task 2 Students help each other write a simple autobiography (one paragraph). Use models from teacher's story on board. Volunteers or the T can help transcribe the stories.

C. Application/Extension

Purpose	To provide learners with opportunities to apply what they learn in class outside of the classroom.

T takes pictures of each student and the group members collate pictures and autobiographies to create a class book. Students take books home and read (or tell) stories to other family members.

SAMPLE LESSON 3 Talking about Clothing and Colors

CLASS DESCRIPTION 22 adult beginning-level ESL students

SETTING Basic Skills Community-based ESL Program

TIME 90 minutes

Objectives	
Vocabulary	Students will review names of stores in the neighborhood. Students will learn and practice names of clothing. Students will review and practice names of colors.
Grammar	Students will use prepositions of place to describe location of clothing items in a room.

Anticipated Problems: Some of the students have very limited literacy skills; all of the words are represented visually and with labels. Some learners may need extra time to process written representation of words.

A. Language Used in Real-world Context

Purpose	To establish a context for using the target language; to motivate students by showing real-world use of language

WARM-UP/REVIEW TYPES OF STORES

Students mingle in class to gather information from classmates about where they shop for clothes and food.

What is your name?	Where do you buy clothes?	Where do you buy food?

T Where does Aye Lee buy clothes? What do you buy there, Aye Lee?

T elicits from class all of the clothing items they can think of, establishing what they already do and do not know.

T shows picture of clothing item and adds those not already on the list. Affixes picture to board and writes name under picture.

ITEMS INCLUDED

dress, blouse, skirt, shirt, tie, belt, pants, jeans, shoes, suit, hat

REVIEW OF COLORS

What color is the dress? What color are the pants? T writes color name next to each picture.

Whole class Repeats names of clothing and colors after T.

REPETITION USING CHAIN DRILL

T Reina, what color is the dress?

Reina Blue. Angel, what color are the pants?

Continue until all students have asked and answered a question.

Checking learning

Purpose	To check understanding of what the language means and when and how to use the language

Removes pictures and gives one to each student; T points to and says word on board; student with that card puts picture next to that word.

MATCHING Put words and pictures on small cue cards in envelopes; students match picture to word.

B. Practice in Meaningful Contexts

Purpose	Provide opportunities for practice, moving from more to less controlled as appropriate for your learners.

Color spelling practice Complete missing letters and color in box with colored pencils (this is done for all colors reviewed):

____ell____w ☐

____ree____ ☐

____ra____ge ☐

BINGO Students are given blank grid and asked to draw or write the name of clothing item in each box:

dress	**pants**	**tie**
skirt	**shirt**	**belt**
shoes	**suit**	**hat**

T distributes pennies or tokens; T calls out clothing items and first learner to have three in a row calls Bingo. Pairs practice using same Bingo grid.

GUESSING GAME Pairs prepare a description of someone in the room: ____ is wearing . . .

Read descriptions; class guesses which student is being described.

FIND THE CLOTHING IN THE ROOM Present class with picture of room with items all over. Students look at picture and answer questions with a partner (sample questions):

1 The belt is on the chair.	Yes	No
2 The dress is on the chair.	Yes	No
3 The shirt is on the chair.	Yes	No
4 The hat is under the chair.	Yes	No

(For groups that are accustomed to using **information-gap activities** (see Table 3.4), you can move onto this freer task.) Find the difference: Using the same picture plus one that has four things that are different.

Student A: One picture with clothing around room.

Student B: Same picture with four differences.

Without looking at each other's picture, describe where clothing is in room and try to identify the four differences (in one picture the hat is on the chair and in the other it is under the chair).

C. Application/Extension

Purpose	To provide learners with opportunities to apply what they learn in class outside of the classroom.

FINDING CLOTHING ITEMS IN NEWSPAPER CIRCULARS

Distribute one circular for local department or discount store to each learner. Put students in A/B pairs. Give each learner a list of items and the question: Can you find ____?

Student A's list	Student B's list
pants	skirt
tie	shirt
hat	belt
shoes	jeans

Taking turns, learners look for item and circle it in the ad.

For extension and preview of next lesson on pricing, use same circular and work in pairs to find answers to questions like these:

1 How much is a girl's shirt? ________

2 How much are boy's jeans? ________

3 How much are women's pants? ________

(Thanks to Patsy Vinogradov for inviting me to observe parts of this lesson. Some activities have been added and modified based on activities the author has used in similar lessons.)

CONCLUSION

In this section, we have examined one approach to preparing lessons that focuses on the development of language competencies, functions, grammar, and vocabulary. Learning is made meaningful by:

- Presenting and practicing language that is real (authentic phone calls, teacher and learners sharing their own stories, finding vocabulary in a circular).
- Student interaction is maximized (discourse chains, role-plays, pair work with timelines, bingo, find the difference).
- Learning is extended outside of the classroom (calling services, sharing class stories with family).

The approach is based on the belief that ESL teachers need to view learners as active participants who contribute to the direction and content of activities. ESL teachers still have a prominent role in promoting language acquisition. In fact, many would argue that learner-centered teaching takes more planning and creativity than traditional teacher-centered approaches. Our presence is just as important as ever, but that presence is more evident in the planning stage than in the classroom.

In all of these lessons, the teachers used a variety of practice activities, some which were fairly controlled (chain drills), and others that promoted more spontaneous use of the target language (making community phone calls). In Part II, we turn to the process of selecting or designing practice activities that generate use of a particular language point in order to build learner confidence with language that is new for them.

Part II ◆ Meaningful and Communicative Practice Activities

3.2.1 Introduction

In planning contextualized lessons, teachers need to make choices about practice activities that are most suitable for the ability level and needs of students. These activities may be in an assigned textbook, they may be part of a curriculum that has already been developed by the school, or teachers may need to create their own. In a contextualized language lesson, there needs to be a balance between fairly controlled activities that help learners attain confidence in using new language, as well as authentic, communicative tasks, which allow them to use language spontaneously.

Task 3.4

Before you read on, think about your own experience as a language learner, or as a learner of any new skill. Talk to a partner for a few minutes about the characteristics of good practice activities (or write your ideas down if you're working alone). What helps you remember things? What engages you as a learner?

3.2.2 Language Practice Activities

There are several factors to consider in choosing and developing practice activities, as outlined in Table 3.4.

Table 3.4 An appropriate practice activity is one that...

involves genuine communication (e.g., an information gap).	Information-gap activities are those where one student has certain information that a partner or other class members do not have. In order to complete the task, students need to find the missing information. This type of activity provides learners with a genuine reason to communicate.
is meaningful, not mechanical.	Mechanical activities involve the pure manipulation of forms with no attention to meaning. Beginning-level learners benefit from repetition and controlled practice, but the activities designed for this purpose need to be meaningful, i.e., allow production of relevant and truthful statements about the students' lives, the classroom environment, or the world at large. Repeating set dialogues can become meaningful by including names of local stores, companies, or attractions. Personal information about students can be used in place of fictitious information.

is based on a real-life task and authentic use of language.	Activities should, as much as possible, replicate what we actually say and do in the real world. Students should practice calling local services, for example, rather than a family member, with whom they normally use their first language.
maximizes student-student interaction.	Activities should be designed in such a way that learners have multiple opportunities to speak, i.e., not just one response and the activity is finished.
integrates a variety of skills.	When possible, choose and design activities that use a variety of skills. In multilevel classes, there can be multiple options for the same activity. Literate learners can write responses, while preliterate learners record information with pictures, for example.

Practice activities can fulfill different purposes in language development. The continuum below illustrates the key differences between controlled (or Restricted use) activities and free (or authentic, communicative) activities. Activities that fall on the controlled end of the continuum can be thought of as language-oriented, i.e., working on mastery of particular language point. There is a place for both types of activities in your lessons, and you will move back and forth between the two depending on learner level, needs, and outcomes, as outlined in Table 3.5.

TABLE 3.5 Practice Activities Continuum

Controlled ————————	———————— Free
Focused on use of target language.	Spontaneous, unpredictable language.
Focused more on accuracy.	Focused on fluency.
Feedback and correction is often given.	Errors noted and handled after task or in later lessons.
Build confidence in using target language.	Integrate new language with old.
Teacher as conductor.	Teacher as facilitator, monitor.
Check how much has been understood.	Check ability to extend language use.

Task 3.5

The sample lesson plans in Part I (*Telephoning*, *Telling our Stories*, and *Clothing and Colors*) included a number of practice activities. Working with a partner or on your own, review each activity and answer the following questions:

- What competencies, function(s), grammar point(s), and skill(s) are being practiced?
- Does it have the qualities of an appropriate practice activity, as listed in Table 3.4?
- Where does it fall on the continuum of controlled to free?

(The above checklist and exercise were developed in collaboration with Julia Reimer, TEFL Certificate Program, Hamline University).

In this section, a sampling of activity types is presented, starting with highly controlled, language-oriented activities, followed by communicative activities.

A. Highly controlled, language-oriented activities

LISTEN AND REPEAT

At the very beginning of language production, learners need opportunities to say new words and phrases numerous times through listen and repeat activities. While it may seem tedious to us, it won't to your students. Repetition can be an excellent confidence builder as the learners tackle new sounds in the language. That is not to say that repetition activities should be mindless, mechanical drills. Use colorful, interesting photographs as prompts; draw on your learners' community for content.

TOTAL PHYSICAL RESPONSE (TPR) ACTIVITIES

The **Total Physical Response (TPR)** method has inspired activities that are ideal for initial presentation and practice of language forms and vocabulary before students have sufficient oral proficiency to create extended sentences. TPR is based on the belief that second language acquisition can occur much in the same way that first language acquisition occurs, namely through responding physically to input the way a child responds to parents at a very young age. In a TPR activity, the teacher directs learning through a series of commands, which learners perform. The learners, in turn, take the lead and give commands. TPR is often used to teach grammatical structures, e.g., imperatives, prepositions of place or direction, and vocabulary. The following classroom exchange illustrates TPR in action:

Sample of TPR in action
T to whole class: Walk to the front of the room (T performs action as giving command).
Learners respond by walking to the front of the room.
T asks individual learners to perform action.
T adds actions: Walk to the window. Put your hand on the window.

In this exchange the learners are getting exposure to imperatives *(walk, put)*, prepositions *(to, on)*, and vocabulary *(window, hand)*. After abundant practice with following the directives of the teacher, the learners begin to practice the language by taking on the teacher's role, trying new combinations of language: *Walk to the table next to the window. Put your hand on the table.* The physical response appeals to kinesthetic learners and, as with any classroom aid, may enhance memory. Relying on the classroom environment, realia, and visual aids makes learning familiar and comprehensible to learners who have had limited exposure to English.

CHAIN DRILLS

T or student begins the chain by asking a set question (high focus on accuracy). In a lesson on the simple present tense and question forms to talk about job routines, prompts from which students choose their answers can be written on the board.

corrects homework *helps sick people* *repairs cars*

T Raphael. What does a doctor do?

Raphael A doctor helps sick people. Min, what does a teacher do?

Min A teacher corrects papers. Yoon. What does a mechanic do?

BINGO

Bingo is an excellent vehicle for reviewing and solidifying understanding of new vocabulary. It provides opportunities to repeat the words numerous times, but for a communicative purpose, i.e., playing the game. Bingo can be played with the whole class, with the teacher or a student as the caller, or in pairs. Students can prepare their own grids by copying words from the board, which is very useful for learners with basic literacy skills.

B. Communicative Activities

(These activities can fall anywhere on the continuum from controlled to free depending upon the amount of language the teacher provides for the students).

FIND SOMEONE WHO. . .

"Find someone who. . . " activities are common in many classroom contexts. In the language classroom, they can provide learners practice in using the target language in a controlled, yet purposeful and communicative, fashion. Completing the activity is highly repetitive, but production is always meaningful provided that the teacher draws on personal information about the students to design the task. Look at the following example used in a lesson on talking about past activities using "used to":

Find someone who. . .

__________________ used to live in Vietnam.

__________________ used to ride a bicycle to school every day.

__________________ used to work as a teacher.

And others.

IN-CLASS SCAVENGER HUNTS

Many of the themes in ESL curricula involve learning the vocabulary for everyday objects found at home, work, or school. The following in-class scavenger hunt serves to check understanding of new words (kitchen items), compound nouns (stress on the first word), and the *...is used for/is made of...* structure.

Place common kitchen utensils around the classroom. Form four teams, and give each a list of items to find (see sample prompts that follow).

Team A

Find something that is used for peeling carrots.
It's called a ________________ ________________.

Find something that is used for pressing garlic.
It's called a ________________ ________________.

Find something that is used for serving soup.
It's called a ________________ ________________.

Find something that is used for opening cans.
It's called a ________________ ________________.

Fill in the Grid

Fill-in-the-grid activities are used extensively in ESL classes for both controlled and communicative practice. In this example, the class has been working on expressing likes and dislikes with the theme of food. The food items are set at stations around the room, and students work in small groups at stations to fill in the grid with information about their classmates. The activity is controlled because sample questions and verbs are provided, yet it allows learners to express their true feelings and interact with one another in a meaningful way.

Ask your classmates questions like this:

Do you like the smell of garlic?
Do you like the smell of onions?

Use these words to describe how you feel:

love	*adore*	*really like*	*like a lot*	*like*
like a little	*don't like*	*don't like at all*	*hate*	*can't stand*

Student Name	cinnamon	nutmeg	coffee	onion	garlic
Betsy	loves	really likes	adores	doesn't like	likes

Once a grid is completed, other activities can evolve from the information on the grid. In this lesson, the teacher moves on to practicing the forms: *so do I/does he/she* and *neither do I/does he/she:*

I love the smell of cinnamon, and so does Cristina.
Jin doesn't like the smell of nutmeg, and neither does Gao.

Grid activities can be used from the very beginning of instruction and are common in adult ESL textbooks, such as the one below for beginning-level learners from *Contemporary English* (Simons and Weddel 1999). This task allows learners to practice basic yes/no questions while at the same time being meaningful as the learners find out about each other's jobs:

WRAP-UP

Work in a group of 3. Ask the yes/no questions below. Give short answers. Write yes or no on the chart. Share your chart with other students.

QUESTIONS	ANSWERS		
	Student Name	**Student Name**	**Student Name**
1. Are you a restaurant worker?			
2. Are you a factory worker?			
3. Are you a hotel worker?			
4. Are you a store clerk?			
5. Are you a worker?			

(Simons and Weddel, Contemporary English, Book 1, *Contemporary Books, 1999)*

Other types of activities that fall on the free end of the continuum are role-plays, surveys and questionnaires, and community tasks. We will look at these kinds of communicative tasks in more detail in Chapter 4 when we turn to teaching the skills of listening and speaking.

COMMUNICATIVE WRITING PRACTICE Practice activities should not be restricted to oral production of the language. In creating writing activities to practice a particular language point, the same principles of activity choice should apply. Most importantly, writing activities should represent real-life purposes for using written language. The following practice activity is from a lesson on describing personal qualities and traits.

Students are instructed to write a short ad to place on a bulletin board either asking for help or offering a service. Provide a variety of scenarios from which learners can choose. Pairs work together to plan and write the ad.

Help Wanted: Baby Sitter

Looking for someone who is ______________________________

____

____

____

Need Your Car Repaired? Car Mechanic Available

I am an experienced mechanic. I am ______________________________

____

____

____

Post ads around the classroom and have the students read the ads and choose one that is of genuine interest to them. Have them respond by role-playing a phone call to the writer of the ad.

The examples of activities in this section can be used to promote practice of particular competencies or language points. This is only the beginning of the discussion of practice activities in this book. In Chapter 4, you will learn about listening and speaking activities that can be used within any curriculum for learners at the beginning, preproduction, level, including those with little or no literacy in their first or second language, all the way up to advanced-level students. In Chapter 5, you will learn more about principles and practices for teaching reading and writing skills, but before turning to teaching those skill areas, the place of error correction in contextualized lessons is considered.

Part III ◆ Correcting Learner Language

3.3.1 INTRODUCTION

This chapter has focused on means of presenting and practicing language competencies, functions, grammar and vocabulary to learners. Many of the activities in Part II are form focused, i.e., they promote accuracy in using the new language. What is the place of correction in these activities? How and when does the teacher intervene? How can the teacher promote self-correction? These questions are the focus of this final section.

Getting Started

Last week I entered my yoga class and found that I didn't have my usual teacher. As I was struggling to move my body into a new pose, this new teacher was calling out my name telling me how to move my thigh muscles and shoulder blades. I couldn't seem to get it right in her class. Had my other teacher been too easy on me? I didn't think so. She had moved around the room working with individuals, coaxing their arms into the right positions. I missed her gentle encouragement. These two teachers had very different styles, and there are undoubtedly many who would appreciate the direct approach of my second teacher.

Task 3.6

What approach to feedback works best for you? Think of a time you were learning something new (a language, a craft, a sport). What kind of feedback did you receive? What feedback was most beneficial to you and motivated you to learn? What discouraged you? Take a few minutes to talk to a partner or write your answer. Now talk to others in class, or to friends or family, and identify any similar themes that arise.

Helpful forms of feedback	Not-so-helpful forms of feedback

Follow-up In discussing your answers, did you find a range of preferences? Did some people like being corrected immediately when they were doing something wrong? Was encouragement as important as correction? How did people feel about being spotlighted in class?

Errors are a natural part of language learning. They show us where learners are in their understanding of language structures; they provide evidence of learning as students over-generalize a rule or pattern, as in the following example:

> José cans come at 5:00.
> (adding third-person singular *-s* to the modal verb *can*)

Learners go through developmental stages of language acquisition, and correct forms tend to emerge over time with increased frequency. The fact that learners worked on the past tense and were corrected for weeks does not necessarily mean they will produce the past tense consistently. That does not mean learning has not occurred, however. Over time and with attention to that feature of language, accuracy will most likely increase.

3.3.2 Considerations in Handling Learner Errors

One of the most important considerations in error correction is learner affect. Constant attention to errors and over-correction only serves to raise what Krashen (1982) refers to as the affective filter, or emotional barriers to learning. Imagine the beginning-level learner who can barely construct a complete sentence. Clearly you would be very careful not to overcorrect. What about an advanced-level student practicing a presentation that she will be giving at work the next day, or learners who have expressed a desire to be corrected, perhaps as a result of the language learning experiences common to their culture? In these cases, correction may be more prevalent. In all cases, it is imperative not to interrupt instruction to correct learner errors all the time. Table 3.6 provides an overview of the many considerations teachers should make in deciding how to handle learner errors.

Table 3.6 Considerations in deciding when to correct learner errors

Who is the learner?	• Consider the learner's level. A beginner will make mistakes all of the time. Correcting every utterance that passes through a student's lips only serves to raise the affective filter. Always remember to focus on what those learners get right. • Consider the learner's confidence level. A more confident learner may be ready for more corrections. A hesitant speaker may become more so if corrected too frequently. • Consider learners' readiness, or stage, in their acquisition of English. All learners make attempts to create utterances using language that is new or difficult for them. Make corrections that correspond to what you believe that student understands about the language. • Consider cultural issues. Learners from some cultures may lose face if singled out in class. Find ways to provide feedback individually to those students who you notice seem embarrassed. Older learners may not appreciate being overtly corrected in front of younger learners, particularly those from the same culture.
Might the error cause the student embarrassment?	Most of us who have learned a second language have experienced this type of error, and would agree that a speedy correction can be greatly appreciated. It could be that a mis-pronunciation results in a word that is inappropriate, or a word in one language means something very different in another (the English-speaker who says *embarazada* in Spanish, which means pregnant, when they mean embarrassed).
Is the learner making a mistake or an error?	A learner who says something incorrectly that she or he has used correctly many times before is just making a mistake, the kind of slip of the tongue we all make. When some thing is said or written incorrectly numerous times, it's more likely an error that could benefit from correction or further practice.
Does the error cause a breakdown in communication?	Errors that result in a breakdown in communication are worth addressing. This breakdown can be signaled by misinterpretation by a peer during a paired activity or by the response of the listener. Help learners to recognize signals that what they've said isn't clear.
What is the stage of the lesson and purpose of the activity?	At the beginning of a lesson, you are assessing what learners do and don't know. Heavy correction is premature at this point. During activities that focus on accuracy (repetition, drills, etc.), correction is helpful. During fluency activities such as role-plays, mingle activities, discussions, errors can be noted and responded to after the activity.

What is the focus of instruction?	If you are teaching a grammar lesson, focus corrections on the structures in question. If you are working on speaking fluency, listen for and record errors that cause a breakdown in communication or are recurrent.

3.3.3 Providing Correction

Now the question is: *How do I correct my students in ways that are sensitive and helpful?* One answer to that question is: *Don't do the corrections for them.* Far too often teachers supply corrections immediately after students make a mistake or error, which ends up being a very passive activity for the students. Many times students do not even notice that they are being corrected, especially in classes where the teacher tends to echo learner responses.

Task 3.7

Before reading about strategies for responding to learner errors, look at the exchange between a teacher and her students and identify what the teacher does for each of the following correction strategies:

Strategies used to respond to Mira's language

Help a learner notice the error
Try for the correct form
Let the student know they have it right (or let it go)
Let the learner repeat the language

This high-beginning class is working on the difference between the simple past and present perfect when talking about the students' new lives in North America. The exchange below is between the teacher and Mira. The class has generated a story about one of the other students, so there are models of the language on the board:

T Mira, how long have you been in Cleveland?

Mira I be here for six month.

T Um, Mira, *I've been* (T emphasizes a bit) here for eight years. You. . . ?

Mira I been here for six month.

T Listen: I've been here for six months. (Points to example on the board.)

Mira I've been here for six month.

T Good. Say that again.

Mira I've been here for six month.

T OK, so Mira has been here for six months. Masha, how long have you been here?

Follow-up In looking back at the considerations in Table 3.6, it seems that the purpose of this activity is to develop accuracy, so that is one of the considerations that is guiding the teacher's decision to help Mira construct an accurate sentence using the present perfect tense. This is what I identified as the strategies used with Mira. How does this compare to your answers?

TABLE 3.7 Strategies used to respond to Mira's language

Help a learner notice the error	**T**	"Um, Mira, *I've been* (T emphasizes a bit) here for eight years. You. . . ?" The teacher speaks about her own personal history and emphasizes the correct form with the hope that Mira notices the difference between her own language and the teacher's.
Try for the correct form	**T** **Mira**	"You . . . ?" "I been here for six month." The teacher invites Mira to try again, which results in some progress with the form (she uses the past participle *been*). "Listen: I've been here for six months." (Points to example on the board). Now the teacher uses a more overt correction, pointing to the model already on the board. This results in Mira getting the present perfect correct: "I have been here for six month."
Let the student know they have it right (or let it go)	**T**	"Good."
Let the learner repeat the language	**T** **Mira**	"Say that again." "I've been here for six month."

Notice in the exchange above that the teacher focused on the correct form of the present perfect (*I have been*) and did not spend time at that moment on the other error (or perhaps mistake), *6 month*. Generally, it is most useful to focus on one language area at a time if accuracy is our goal.

The activity and analysis above represents error correction in accuracy-based activities. During spontaneous conversation with learners, during fluency-based activities, or when learners are presenting information to the class, less obvious means of error correction may be used. Even a raised eyebrow may result in a learner self-correcting. The error correction strategies below move from more subtle to more overt.

Help a learner notice the error. As a teacher makes the decision to respond to a learner error, the first thing she or he generally does is help a learner notice that an error has been made. Often the learner will immediately self-correct if the language form is the focus of instruction that day, or if the learner is ready for the correction.

- The least overt and most naturalistic approach is to use **reformulation,** or restating a learner's utterance correctly in as naturalistic a way as possible.

Reformulation

S Yes, on Saturday I go to St. Paul on trip.

T You're going to St. Paul. That'll be nice.

S Yes, I'm going to St. Paul, and we see Winter Carnival.

T Have you seen the Winter Carnival before?

S No, this is first time.

T Really, the first time. So, Sonia's going to the St. Paul Winter Carnival. And what's everyone else doing?

This approach involves responding to the content of what learners say by reformulating errors they've produced in a way that is as natural as possible. Not every learner will notice the correction, but the technique is ideal for those times when a teacher wants to encourage fluency. It also provides the affirmation more proficient learners may desire when they notice their peers' inaccuracies in the language.

- Nonverbal means can be used to help learners notice errors; use a questioning facial expression; use a gesture, for example, a motion behind you to indicate that a verb needs to be past tense, or a lengthening movement of the hands to indicate present continuous instead of simple present. For word stress errors, clap or tap the correct pattern.

- For recurrent errors, for example, the omission of the *–s* ending on third person singular verbs or with plural nouns or possessives, have a large *S* sign on the wall and point to it to indicate that kind of error has been made. For verb tenses, have simple timelines on the wall like the one below for the simple past tense. Point to the timeline to indicate an error with that verb tense has been made.

The choice of signs can be negotiated with or created by the learners, assuring that the representations being used for correction are understood by all.

- Repeat up to the point where the learner made an error:

Student She is taller George.

Teacher She is taller. . .

At which point the student often 'fills in the blank' as she or he notices the error.

- Say the sentence leaving a blank where the error was made (I often hum through the blank):

Student She is taller George.

Teacher She is taller (hum) George.

Or write the same thing on the board leaving a blank.

- If there are samples of the language being practiced on the board or on a chart in the room, point to the correct form, as the teacher above did with Mira.

These are only some of the many strategies you can use to help a learner notice an error. Doing so engages the student in the process of thinking about the language and trying to self-correct, which will have a more lasting impact than if the teacher provides the correct form immediately.

Try for the correct form. In cases where a learner does not notice the error right away and self-correct, let the student try more than once. In the exchange above between Mira and her teacher, the teacher tried different strategies to help Mira self-correct. If a learner continues to struggle, invite another student to help by asking, for example: *Who can help Mira?* If all else fails, repeat the correct utterance and move on in the lesson.

Let the student know they have it right (or let it go). Once the student gets it right, affirm the response. Also, focus on and affirm one language form at a time. There are times when a beginning-level learner will not be able to make a correction, which signals that they are probably not ready for it. Let it go at this point and make note of the fact that this is an area that needs more work for the student.

Let the learner repeat the language. Depending on the circumstances of the class (number of learners, type of activity, time), let the student say the word, phrase, or sentence again. This can help to solidify the language as well as build learner confidence with the language.

Some common pitfalls Learning how to respond appropriately to learner errors takes time and practice for new teachers. Comparing different approaches can help new teachers avoid some of the pitfalls. What are the advantages and disadvantages of each of these approaches to providing on-the-spot verbal correction?

Echoing

S I am born in Mexico City.

T I am born in Mexico City?

S Yes, I am born in Mexico.

T I was born in Mexico.

Teachers echo learners all the time. Often they say they echo because learners cannot hear one another. To that I'd suggest that the teacher invite a learner to repeat what they said louder. When echoing is used for error correction, the learner has no way of knowing if the teacher is confirming what they said, asking for clarification, or making a correction. Also, when a teacher echoes an entire sentence, there is no indication as to what is wrong with it. Generally speaking, echoing is a class routine teachers need to use sparingly, if at all.

Think of the times you would echo another native English speaker in natural conversation.

Speaker 1 Jan's moving to Brazil.

Speaker 2 Jan's moving to Brazil?

In this example, Speaker 2 is expressing disbelief or maybe excitement about the prospect of Jan's move. Think about the ways you hear teachers echo learners or the way you echo students in your class. Are you echoing language in ways that represent authentic use of language, or is the echoing a teacher routine that does not add anything to learners' understanding of language?

Overt correction (Use of grammar terms)

S I can to go with you.

T You shouldn't use the infinitive with *to* after modal verbs. Use the simple form of the verb.

Unless your student is well versed in grammar terminology, this technique can be lost on many students. While many students know terms such as infinitive, gerund, or modal verb, you do not want them thinking about those terms as they work on fluency. This approach gives the learner the impression that they should always be thinking about grammar terms and structures as they speak, which, as Krashen points out, often leads to hesitant, stilted speech (see the discussion of the monitor in 1.2.6.). If a teacher senses that a learner appreciates overt corrections, it is preferable to respond this way:

S I can to go with you.

T Try *go* after can: I can go.

This highlights the importance of observing and identifying the types of correction your learners benefit from most. Do they know the grammar terms and, if not, do they need to know them? Discuss this with your students; find out what their expectations are regarding correction when possible.

CONCLUSION

Teaching language in context using an integrated, learner-centered approach takes careful planning on the part of the teacher. It also requires careful observation of students in order to be genuinely responsive to their needs. This is a lot to think about for a new teacher. Whether you are working from a set curriculum, a textbook, or teacher-generated lessons, consistently ask yourself the questions that follow about each lesson you teach. If you answer affirmatively to even some these questions, you have already come a long way from being the center of attention in your classroom to putting your students center stage.

Do my learners have active roles in the classroom?

Do they make choices about content and classroom activities?

Do they control the direction of activities?

Is the content of instruction relevant to the students' needs and interests? Does it draw on their experiences and knowledge?

Are classroom interactions and tasks authentic?

You will continue to explore more ways to achieve these goals throughout the book.

KEY TERMS

CHECKLIST OF KEY TERMS	On your own, or with a partner, provide an example or brief definition for each concept.
competencies	
functions of language	
the four language skills	
Authentic use	
Restricted use	
Clarification and focus	
information-gap activity	
contextualized language lessons	

APPLYING WHAT YOU LEARNED

1 Understanding the Components of Integrated Language Lessons

Look at following competencies and identify the functions, grammar, and vocabulary needed to successfully use the competency:

Competency	Functions needed	Grammar	Vocabulary
Ex: Returning an item to a clothing store	Asking for help/ Offering help Stating the problem "I'd like to return this because. . ."	Modal verbs (*could, would, may, can*) Question forms	Clothing items Words that describe problems: too small, too big, tear, rip
Calling school about a child's illness			
Reporting an accident at work			

2 The Contextualized Language Lesson

If you are already teaching. . . think about a lesson you taught last week that did not engage your students as much as you might have liked. Evaluate your lesson using these questions:

a Did I present and have learners practice language that is real (e.g., authentic phone calls, teacher and learners sharing their own stories)? What could I have done differently?

b What did I do to promote maximum student interaction (e.g., discourse chains, role-plays, pair work with timelines)?

c How was learning extended outside of the classroom (calling services, sharing class stories with family)?

Based on what you discover, rewrite your plan using the three stages of the contextualized language lesson:

Class Description (time, level)
Objectives (competencies, functions, grammar, vocabulary, skills):

1 Language used in authentic context

2 Practice in meaningful contexts

3 Application/extension

If you aren't teaching yet. . . choose a language competency, language function, or grammar point and develop a contextualized language lesson for a group of your choice.

3 Assessing Practice Activities

If you are already teaching. . . Using the checklist of practice activities from Part III, assess three activities you used last week in class. Based on your evaluation, is there anything you would do to make the task more authentic, meaningful, or interactive?

Characteristics of Practice Activities	Activity 1	Activity 2	Activity 3
Involves communication (ex: information or opinion gap)			
Is meaningful, not mechanical			
Is based on a real-life task			
Maximizes s-s interaction			
Integrates a variety of skills			

If you aren't teaching. . . choose three activities from an ESL textbook and do the same analysis. Based on your evaluation, how would you implement each activity to make sure it is authentic, meaningful, or interactive?

4 Error Correction

If you are already teaching. . . tape record a segment of your class and complete the task below as you listen to your lesson.

If you are not teaching. . . either observe a class or ask someone in class if you can use their taped segment.

Collect samples of student errors and record how the teacher responds to that language. Review the principles in Table 3.6 and the recommended steps for error correction. Which error correction strategies helped the students self-correct? At which points in the lesson did the teacher do more error correction? In what other ways did the teacher give feedback to the students about their performance? Your samples might look like this.

Student's language	Teacher's response (correction or praise)	Student's response to correction or praise
Example: "I no have time."	"I no have time?" "I ______ have time.	Student looks puzzled. "I don't have time."

(Adapted from Reimer 1998)

Recommended Reading

Auerbach, E. 1992. *Making meaning, making change: Participatory curriculum development for adult ESL literacy.* Washington, DC and McHenry, IL: Center for Applied Linguistics and Delta Systems.

The author shares the experiences of the University of Massachusetts Family Literacy Project in planning and implementing a participatory curriculum for adult literacy. The book provides the reader with ideas for collaborating with learners to develop relevant curricula that respond to learners' needs as parents, workers, and community members.

Lewis, M. 1997. *New ways in teaching adults.*

This collection of highly integrated and communicative tasks is organized by sources of input, from teacher-directed instruction to out-of-class activities based in the community.

Maley, A. 1992. *Learner-based teaching.* Oxford: Oxford University Press.

A collection of easily adaptable activities that draw on learners' experience and knowledge.

McKay, H. and **A. Tom.** 1999. *Teaching adult second language learners.* New York: Cambridge University Press.

A teacher resource with a multitude of classroom activities appropriate for the adult ESL classroom.

Nunan, D. 1991. *Designing tasks for the communicative classroom.* Cambridge: Cambridge University Press.

This book provides principles for developing communicative tasks for use at all levels with learners in diverse settings.

Pennington, M. (ed.) 1995. *New ways in teaching grammar.* Alexandria, VA: TESOL.

This book contains activities drawn from practicing teachers; these communicative activities promote practice of grammar points in motivating and realistic contexts.

Ur, P. and **A. Wright.** 1992. *5-Minute activities: A resource book of short activities.* Cambridge: Cambridge University Press.

The short activities in this book can be used for practicing particular language points, as ice breakers or warm-ups, or for supplementing a course book.

Ur, P. 1988. *Grammar practice activities.* Cambridge: Cambridge University Press.

This book includes principles of grammar teaching, suggestions for designing activities as well as a collection of nearly 200 interactive activities for practicing a wide range of grammar points.

Useful Websites

ESL Special Collection

National Institute for Literacy/Western/Pacific Lincs

http://www.literacynet.org/esl/home.html

An extensive collection of materials, lesson ideas, Web links, and resources for adult ESL teachers and tutors.

Dave's ESL Café

www.eslcafe.com

Dave's ESL Café offers links to innumerable Websites with ideas for activities and lesson plans. It also offers a forum for teachers to pose questions about teaching.

Spring Institute ELT Website

http://www.springinstitute.com/elt

This site has full-text online publications with ideas for integrating pre-employment training and ESL (including SCANS), program planning and evaluation, teaching tips and lesson ideas, and back issues of their newsletter, *Compass Points.*

Tower of Games

http://www.towerofenglish.com/games.html

This site includes ideas for interactive games, word games, and puzzles, as well as links to other ESL teaching resources and ideas.

4 Developing Listening and Speaking Skills

Part I ◆ Listening Skills Development

4.1.1 Introduction

In the previous chapter, we examined an integrated approach to teaching language lessons that was both contextualized and learner centered. While the integration of all four skills (listening, speaking, reading, and writing) was part of the approach, the focus of the lessons was on the acquisition and understanding of specific language competencies, functions, grammar points, and vocabulary. In this chapter, we take a closer look at the development of listening and speaking skills. While none of the skills are taught and practiced in isolation, there are many principles to teaching each one that will shape and guide your practice. What is involved in teaching listening and speaking skills? The answer to that begins with understanding the nature of oral communication, particularly informal communication that your learners encounter every day.

Checklist

After reading this chapter and completing the activities, you should be able to

- define schema theory and describe its implications in creating listening lessons.
- define top-down and bottom-up processing and the role each plays in understanding language.
- create a listening lesson with prelistening, listening, and follow-up activities.
- identify the features of a good fluency activity.
- explain intelligibility and the factors that can affect intelligibility for adult learners.
- discuss the rationale for incorporating pronunciation in Adult ESL curricula.

4.1.2 The Nature of Informal Communication

Look at this list of characteristics of language your students need to decipher each day. How does this compare to language found in many textbooks?

- Extensive use of slang and colloquial expressions (*off the top of my head*).
- Ungrammatical utterances: *There's people in the room.*
- Reduced speech: *wanna, gonna.*
- Hesitations, false starts, and fillers such as *well, you see, um...*

Were we to rely solely on commercially produced ESL texts or scripted taped dialogues, we would not provide students with the rich input they need to move forward in their acquisition of English (see discussion of Krashen's i +1 theory in Chapter 1). We also need to consider the amount of time learners actually spend listening in a second language. Nunan (1999) suggests that learners spend more than 50% of their time listening in a second language, so it's imperative that part of our curricula be dedicated to developing effective listening skills. In Part I of this chapter, we look at what goes into teaching listening comprehension skills. We identify what learners need to listen to and understand in their new English-speaking environment, as well as the skills and strategies they need in order to access the meaning of what they hear.

Conducting lessons that focus only on a particular language point will not prepare learners for the communicative demands of spontaneous interactions outside of the classroom. In Part II we will turn to the topic of teaching speaking, specifically, considering how to help ESL learners become fluent users of the language. Finally, in Part III we consider the place of pronunciation in ESL curricula; most importantly, how we can help learners become *intelligible* speakers of English. Let's start with a look into David's plans for a listening lesson on the theme of celebrations.

Getting Started

Task 4.1

Working with a partner or on your own, read the following description of David's plans for his lesson and answer the questions that follow:

David is doing a unit on celebrations in the United States and around the world with a diverse group of immigrants. He wants to include a listening lesson in this unit and has recorded an interview he conducted with Farid, an immigrant of French and Iranian decent. David asks Farid about his favorite holidays from the two cultures. The conversation is not scripted. David asks Farid about the various customs, foods, and special clothing for the holidays (see transcript on p. 120).

What do you think David could do with this interview in his lesson?

What could students do before they listen to the interview?

What could they do while they're listening?

4.1.3 Getting Students Ready to Listen

One of the greatest challenges to teaching a diverse group of learners is that everyone comes to class with different experiences and expectations. When a teacher prepares students to listen to a passage, she or he needs to do so in ways that will reach all the students. In David's lesson, he needs to prepare students for the theme of holidays, but where should he start?

SCHEMA THEORY Prior knowledge and expectations that we bring to any situation are based on our cultural background, education, and life experiences. We have 'scripts' in our mind about how events in the world unfold, and these scripts are called "schemata." **Schema theory** suggests that prior knowledge shapes our expectations and understanding of what we hear. The closer our schema is to the content of what we hear, the easier it will be for us to understand. In David's lesson on holidays, each learner brings different expectations and perceptions about celebrations. Some may have some prior knowledge about Iran and France, while others may have none at all. What they all share is experiences with celebrations, albeit different types. The first thing a language teacher needs to do is to tap into learners' prior knowledge about the theme of the lesson through **prelistening** activities. Before examining what David could do to activate his learners' prior knowledge, however, we'll examine the relationship between Schema Theory and ESL instruction in more detail.

Much of what learners encounter in a new culture is unfamiliar to them, from shopping and banking to making doctor appointments. The theme of health and wellness serves as a good example for exploring how prior knowledge affects learning. What goes through your mind when you hear the phrase "going to the doctor"? What images and events do you visualize? Write your response in the box below:

Task 4.2

Images of Going to the Doctor

Now compare those images with a partner, or with a friend or family member. Do you have the same images? There's a good chance that if you were raised in the same part of the world and live in the same area now, your images are quite similar.

When I lived in France, going to the doctor was a very different experience from what I expected it to be. I walked up to a turn-of-the-century stone apartment building. When I opened the door of the doctor's office, I found myself in a room lavishly decorated with rugs and antiques. The doctor wore a skirt and blouse and sat behind a massive mahogany desk. The examination table was a converted antique dining table. This unfamiliar setting was unsettling for me as a newcomer to France, even though I was sufficiently proficient in French to understand the doctor's questions. Where was the sterile, white table? Why wasn't the doctor wearing a white coat? Why wasn't I given a gown to wear? My script, or schema, for going to the doctor was very different from what I was experiencing in this visit to the doctor.

Now imagine how different the experience of going to the doctor is for many immigrants and refugees. Here are some of their stories:

In Russia, we go to the clinic and wait. Sometimes we wait for hours to see the doctor.

We sent for the Shaman in Laos, who would rid the house of spirits causing our illness.

The interactions, settings, and routines that we encounter in our daily lives vary greatly from culture to culture. Identifying these differences and familiarizing students with these new routines will help their comprehension tremendously. If you know what to expect in a given situation, you will understand a great deal more of what you hear. So when you tell students to listen to a conversation between a patient and receptionist making a doctor appointment, it's quite possible that they will not share the same perceptions and images of what that conversation will entail. The first thing you need to do in a listening lesson is activate your learners' prior knowledge and provide them with crucial background information that will aid them in comprehending what they are going to hear. In a lesson on making doctor appointments, for example, the teacher would start with questions like these:

What do you do when you're sick? Do you see a doctor?

When do you see a doctor? (for a simple cold or only serious illness)

Do you need to make an appointment in your culture? Do you call the doctor before you go? Have you gone to the doctor in the U.S.? What was different here compared to in your country?

Now thinking back to David's lesson on celebrations, look at the following prelistening activity. How does this compare to the ideas you generated at the beginning of the chapter?

CELEBRATIONS AROUND THE WORLD

Prelistening I interviewed Farid about two holidays his family celebrates. He was raised in two different cultures: French and Iranian. Look at the activities and customs he talks about in the box below and answer these questions with your partner:

1 What kind of celebrations do you think he will talk about in the interview? Which of the customs, activities, or food do you think are French and which are Iranian?

2 Which of these activities or customs are practiced in your culture?

start of spring	fresh fruit	white fish	rice
herbs	visiting family	going on picnics	jumping over fires
new clothes	French Revolution	1789	marches
dances	airplanes	eating outside	wear red, white, and blue

The purpose of this task is to preview the key concepts the learners will encounter in the interview. It allows students to make some educated guesses about the content of what they are about to hear as well as to connect that content to their own lives and experiences. Every time you use a listening passage with your students, you need to begin with a prelistening task. Now that students are ready to listen, what will they do *while* they are listening to the interview?

4.1.4 How Do We Listen?

Before we think more about David's listening lesson, take a few minutes to reflect on how you listen to language differently depending on your purpose for listening. Talk to a partner or write down your ideas:

Task 4.3

How do you listen to each of the following:

Messages on your answering machine	
A weather report	
The news	
Advertisements	
An announcement at a store	
An announcement at an airport	
Directions from a supervisor	
A lecture	

What did you notice about the way you listen to different types of passages? Do you listen attentively to announcements at a store? What about at the airport? Missing a boarding call would have more dire consequences than missing out on a promotional offer at a department store. When do you listen for the general ideas and when do you listen for more detail? All of this depends on our *purposes* for listening. There are innumerable purposes for listening, but here are some that exemplify my everyday purposes for listening:

- **To seek specific information:** In listening to a weather report, I'll listen for low and high temperatures, the chance of rain or snow, so that I can dress my children for school appropriately.
- **To gain a general idea of the topic:** In listening to news reports on TV, I pay attention to those headlines in the news that interest me or have an impact on my life. I may ignore detailed information.
- **To gain knowledge:** In a class or training session, I may listen more attentively for detail because I need to learn a new skill.

As we listen for different purposes, we employ a variety of listening skills:

- **Anticipating content:** We approach a listening situation with certain expectations (the weather report will give high and low temperatures and the extended forecast; if the sky is blue, we expect to hear that there's little chance of rain).
- **Listening to confirm predictions:** As we listen, we check to see if our predictions are right or wrong.
- **Listening for gist:** In listening to the news headlines, we may filter out many of the details and just hone in on key concepts of importance or interest to us.
- **Listening for specific information:** In listening to our voicemail messages, we may listen only for the names and phone numbers and write those down. Don't you sometimes skip ahead after you have this crucial, specific information?
- **Listening for details:** If you have detailed directions on a message telling you how to get to a job interview, you probably listen for details and may even replay the message a few times. Listening for detail involves what we call **intensive listening**, or trying to understand the listening passage in its entirety. We may listen intensively to lectures, dialogue in a film, or directions from a supervisor, for example.
- **Making inferences:** As we listen, we interpret and make inferences about what we hear. After hearing a politician's views on a particular issue, we make guesses about the way she or he might vote on an upcoming bill. We also make a decision as to whether or not we'll vote for that politician in the next election.

4.1.5 Applying Listening Skills Practice in the Classroom

Almost everyone uses the listening skills above in their first language. If you are already teaching ESL, however, you may have noticed that your ESL students don't necessarily transfer those skills as they listen to passages in English. They may have a tendency to try to understand every word they hear and, when they are unable to understand, they may become frustrated and overwhelmed. As you'll discover, trying to understand every word in a listening passage is not the most productive approach, especially for beginning-level language learners.

BOTTOM-UP VS. TOP-DOWN PROCESSING

In listening to passages (or in reading, as we'll see in Chapter 5), we can use either bottom-up processing or top-down processing. **Bottom-up processing** involves attempts to decode and understand a listening passage word-for-word, whereas **top-down processing** involves listening more globally and trying to understand the overall meaning of what we hear. Top-down processing also involves making educated guesses about content based on prior knowledge and visual clues (facial expressions, context, etc.). Efficient listeners and readers do not rely solely on bottom-up processing in their own language, so why should they in a second language? Most ESL learners will not understand a good number of the words in a given text; as a result, they can become overwhelmed by the barrage of new words coming their way as they listen to an authentic dialogue, newscast, or even their ESL teacher's instructions. A listener who manages to connect key words to prior knowledge and make guesses based on extralinguistic cues (visuals, body language, context), on the other hand, is likely to understand the main ideas or pick out specific information.

Our job as ESL teachers is to help learners practice top-down processing so that they can begin to access the wealth of language they are exposed to day to day, much of which is highly colloquial, full of reduced speech, and delivered at a rapid pace. In order to do this, we need to develop listening tasks that allow learners to draw on prior knowledge, make guesses, and listen selectively, i.e., focusing on the information they need. In other words, the goal of listening instruction is to help learners develop effective listening skills that they can use inside and outside of the classroom. Now let's return to David's lesson on celebrations.

The interview with Farid had many of the features highlighted at the beginning of the chapter: false starts, ungrammatical utterances, and hesitations. David has developed activities that promote selective listening, as well as opportunities to connect the ideas generated in the prelistening portion of the lesson to what they understand from the interview.

Task 4.4

Look at the activities and identify the listening skills learners practice in each one:

Celebrations From Around the World

Task A: Students listen and check predictions from prelistening: Where is Farid from? Which of the customs relate to Iran and which to France?

Task B: In this listening activity, notice that students are assigned to two groups and are responsible for listening for only half of the information in the charts.

Complete the tables with the missing information

Group A	Nowrouz in Iran	Bastille Day in France
History/origin of holiday		Freeing of Bastille Prison French Revolution 1789

Group A	Nowrouz in Iran	Bastille Day in France
Special Food	Fresh fruit White fish	
Activities		Marches Military marches Dances and music
Clothes	New clothes	

Group B	Nowrouz in Iran	Bastille Day in France
History/origin of holiday	Celebrates start of spring	
Special food		Eating outside
Activities	Visiting family Going on picnics Jumping over fire	
Clothes		Anything red, white and blue

Task C: A's get together and B's get together to check their answers. Then, students work in A-B pairs and share the information from their grids (not reading from one another's grid, but sharing orally what they understood). Notice that this activity is designed so that peers can provide feedback and correction.

In completing the activities in David's lesson, learners listened to check predictions and they listened for specific information. Remember that we generally listen for a particular purpose, which often entails acting on what we listened to in some way: discussing what we've listened to with a friend; acting on the request of a supervisor; making a decision or choice based on what we learned. What would be a logical response to the interview for David's learners? To complete the listening segment in the celebrations unit, David includes a follow-up or postlistening activity. The purpose of this stage in the lesson is to extend learners' understanding of the content of what they heard, respond to it in an authentic manner, and apply it to their own lives.

Follow-up/Postlistening Now think of one of your favorite holidays and write or draw the origin, foods, activities, and clothes for that holiday (students from the same country could work together on this stage):

Country and Holiday: ______________________________

Origin	Foods	Activities	Clothes

Now talk to three other people in the class and find some customs that are the same and some that are different for your countries:

Things that are the same	Things that are different

4.1.6 Summary of Listening Skills and Activities

There were three stages in David's listening lesson: prelistening, listening, and follow-up. Each listening lesson can include a number of different activities, each one practicing a different skill (confirming predictions, listening for gist, listening for specific information). The number of listening skills practiced would depend on the nature of the listening passage, the level of the learners, and the purposes for listening. Table 4.1 provides a summary of the stages that can be included in a listening lesson, along with suggested activity types for each stage. Not every lesson will include all the steps, however, every lesson should begin with prelistening activities and end with a follow-up activity. Students new to English may do nothing more than listen and point to a picture of what they have understood, whereas intermediate to advanced-level learners need to practice listening for detail, opinion and attitude, and making inferences about the meaning of the listening passage. As with everything we have talked about in the book, always remember the interrelatedness of language skills, particularly listening and speaking. The listening activities in Table 4.1 are often combined with speaking, reading, and writing practice, or they are used within contextualized language lessons.

Table 4.1 Stages of Listening Lessons and Suggested Activities

1 Prelistening	Objective: to generate the learners' schemata. Prelistening tasks serve to get the learners thinking about and talking about the content of what they are about to hear. This will enable them to anticipate content and facilitate comprehension of the listening passage. Possible tasks: Questionnaires True/false predictive questions Discussions Look at words from the passage and guess what it will be about. Pictures that set the scene Preteach vocabulary
2 Listening to confirm predictions	Objective: to enable learners to confirm predictions made during prelistening Possible tasks: Match predictions with what's heard. Check answers to prelistening activities.

3 Listening for gist (main idea)	Objective: to give learners practice in understanding only the main ideas of a passage. It is not always necessary for us to understand the details of what we listen to. We need to give learners practice in the skill of discriminating the main ideas of a passage. Possible tasks: Listen and answer true/false, yes-no, or open-ended questions about the main ideas of the passage. Provide a list of statements and check off those that reflect the main ideas. Choose a picture that corresponds to the main idea of the text.
4 Listening for specific information	Objective: to give learners practice in picking out specific information in a text without expecting them to understand every word. Possible tasks: Jigsaw tasks: different groups listen for different information; exchange info in new groups Fill in missing words/numbers in a text. Provide a list of specific information and check off those ideas that are heard. Listen and point to pictures/words as they appear in the passage. Order information as it appears in the text using pictures or words. Choose the correct word, number, etc. (multiple choice) Correct misinformation in a text. Fill in a grid/table with words or draw pictures.
5 Listening for detail	Objective: to practice listening intensively for details of the text. Learners move from identifying short, factual information to interpreting the meaning more deeply. The types of activities you use will be similar to the ones listed in Parts 3 and 4. above. What will be different is the *content* of the questions you ask. Listening for specific information with news headlines might entail simply identifying the countries mentioned and the event that occurred in each one. A more detailed listening could require learners to identify the players, the time, or the exact location of the events. This means that you can use the same news headlines with a variety of levels, but simply change the nature of the task you assign.
6 Making inferences	Objective: to give learners practice in analyzing, interpreting, and evaluating the meaning of a text. While beginning-level learners will be challenged enough by determining the gist and specific information from a listening passage, intermediate to advanced-level students need practice with making inferences and going beyond the factual information presented to them. Possible tasks: Discuss underlying messages e.g., view advertisements and determine the target audience for the ad. Problem-solving or decision-making activities. Choose statements that could be inferred from the listening passage. This could be with true/false statements or multiple choice.
7 Follow-up	Objective: to give learners further practice using the content of the text; to further check understanding of the text through another medium Possible tasks: Discussion questions Role-plays Writing tasks: reports, summaries, journal entries Interviews and surveys conducted in or out of class Community research and reports back to class

4.1.7 Sources of Listening Passages

For the sample listening lesson in this chapter, David conducted and recorded an interview. There are many other types of listening passages that you can use. Work with a partner or on your own and brainstorm sources for listening passages:

Task 4.5

Sources for Listening Passages

Sources for listening passages will generally fall into one of these categories: Authentic texts (radio broadcasts, songs, anything that was produced for public use that is unmodified); Teacher-generated (the interview with Farid falls into this category); ESL textbooks (commercially produced ESL texts are full of listening passages and activities from which you can draw). Now look at your list above and decide which you would consider teacher-generated, and which you would consider truly authentic:

Task 4.6

Authentic Texts	Teacher-generated

Follow-up Look at this list of sources and see how it compares to yours:

Authentic Texts:

- Short radio reports (or audio on the Internet)
- TV reports
- News headlines
- Songs
- Interviews on TV or radio
- Advertisements
- Instructional videos or tapes

Teacher-generated:

- Taped interviews
- Taped conversations/dialogues, preferably unscripted: Scripted dialogues are useful when presenting particular language points (as with the telephoning dialogues in Chapter 3). When teaching listening skills, however, we want to expose learners to language as actually spoken with false starts and hesitations.
- Story telling: using a set of prompts, teachers can use themselves as an invaluable source for listening practice. This has the benefit of allowing students to pick up on visual clues such as gestures and facial expressions. Students can also ask for clarification as they would in real-life interactions.
- Videotaped real-life scenarios: teachers can tape everyday interactions at stores, banks, restaurants, schools, or home, and use them as the basis for listening practice. These have the added benefit of visual support.

Integrating various technologies into your lessons, and choosing and developing classroom materials will be covered in more detail in Chapter 8. For now, we have taken a brief look at the array of sources from which you can draw. We have also examined the importance of connecting your learners' prior knowledge to the content of the listening passages we choose. As noted throughout this book, no language point or skill is taught or learned in isolation. Learners in David's class interacted with one another throughout, using speaking as well as minimal reading and writing skills. Now let's turn to what you need to consider in order to engage learners in speaking and fluency development.

Part II ◆ Developing Speaking Skills

4.2.1 FLUENCY AS THE GOAL OF INSTRUCTION

INTRODUCTION In a learner-centered, communicative classroom, just about anything you do, provided the learners are communicating with one another, serves to develop their speaking skills. There is much more to teaching speaking than simply getting students to talk, however. As with listening, we normally have specific purposes for communicating with others, such as asking the time of the next bus, asking for help at a store, or describing a problem to a supervisor. These are examples of **transactional dialogue**, the purpose for which is to transmit factual information. We also take part in **interpersonal dialogue**, for example, making small talk with a co-worker or talking to a friend about a concern at home (Nunan 1991). The language we encounter can be more or less predicable depending on our shared knowledge and experience with our interlocutors (Brown 2001). We need to be fluent users of language in order to handle the communicative demands of day-to-day interactions outside of the classroom. What does it mean to become a fluent user of the language?

Table 4.2

Characteristics of Language Fluency
• The ability to handle unpredictable language.
• The ability to anticipate the direction a conversation will take.
• The ability to make oneself understood and negotiate meaning (e.g., ask for clarification, paraphrase what one understands); use compensation strategies (point to something when you don't know the word for it, describe an object for which you don't know the name).
• The ability to convey meaning and "get things done" with the language, even with limited words or accuracy.
• The ability to pick up on and use visual cues from the environment and other speakers/listeners.

As we looked at language lessons that focused on a particular competency, function, or language point in Chapter 3, practice activities fell on a continuum from controlled (with more emphasis on accuracy) to free (with a focus on fluency). All of the activities were designed to generate use of particular language points. For example, in a lesson on "Calling in Sick to Work," the teacher would develop activities that include greetings, stating the problem, asking permission for time off, and closures. Of course the goal of such a lesson would be the ability to communicate effectively, and success with the language would be measured by the ability to complete the task of calling in sick (even though the learner may make some errors in production). In a grammar lesson, the teacher would be looking for some degree of accuracy with the language as well as the ability to integrate grammar use in meaningful, real-world contexts, e.g., using the past tense to talk about work experience in a job interview. In order for learners to become fluent users of the language, they need time to develop the traits highlighted in Table 4.2. Lessons need to include activities during which learners communicate ideas and negotiate meaning as they need to do outside of the classroom. How can we facilitate that in our classes?

4.2.2 Developing Interactive Speaking Activities

Look at these two speaking activities and discuss the following question with a partner: Which activity will generate more language production and why?

Task 4.7

Activity 1
Talk about your hobbies and interests in small groups. You have 15 minutes.

Activity 2

How do you like to spend your time after work or on the weekend? Circle three things you like to do. Cross out three that you never do. Write three other things you like to do in your free time.

swim visit family listen to music go to the library
garden cook for friends and family visit friends
sew watch television take walks exercise read

Three other things you like to do: ______________________________

Now talk to the other students in class and find the person who has the most things in common with you. Ask that person the following questions:

How often do you do that activity?

What do you like about that activity?

What are some things you did in your country that you can't do in the U.S.?

Simply telling students to talk to a partner about a particular topic for 15 minutes will not necessarily generate much production. With Activity 1, more verbal students are likely to monopolize the discussion since there are no clear roles assigned to participants. There is no specific direction or outcome to the task. While Activity 2 might appear quite controlled, the structure of the task allows all students an equal opportunity to participate. It also has a concrete outcome, which gives the task a clear purpose or goal. It allows for multiple interactions as the students mingle around the classroom and talk to everyone, rather than just the two or three people in the small group.

There are many challenges to dedicating substantial amounts of class time to fluency development. Many of your learners will come to class with the expectation that the teacher should be teaching grammar lessons and leading the class through repetition activities. While providing learners with extensive opportunities to speak in your classes should be your goal, it is important to make the outcomes and purpose for doing communicative speaking activities clear to your adult learners:

- Explicitly state how the fluency activity will help them outside of the classroom, for example, that the activity will give them practice in making small talk with co-workers.
- Use content that is generated from students or that you know is connected to their life circumstances and needs.
- Balance fluency practice with lessons that are more language oriented and focused on accuracy.
- Include mini grammar lessons or short drills in preparation for a fluency activity. For example, in preparation for an interview task, work on question formation as a class.

For fluency to develop, learners need genuine reasons to communicate with one another. The activities that follow demonstrate a variety of ways you can promote this kind of purposeful communication among students. Learners at all levels need practice developing their speaking fluency, but this can be challenging with learners at the preproduction level. A number of the activity types that follow can be used with even Level 1 learners.

A. Picture stories

Picture stories can be used with all students, particularly those with limited literacy skills. Learners can interpret a story based on a picture sequence, as with the example below from *Picture Stories* (Ligon and Tannenbaum 1990). Alternatively, each student is given a picture of a story sequence. Students work collaboratively to put the story in the correct order. Once they have done so, they stand in a circle and tell the story.

UNIT 1 ½ Cup

A. Talk about the pictures. Then listen to the story.

½ Cup 1

(Ligon and Tannenbaum, Picture Stories, *Longman, 1990)*

B. Information-gap activities

As noted in Chapter 3 (3.2.2), information-gap activities require that students exchange information in order to complete a task. There are many activities that fall into this category (and many texts with ideas for activities in the resource section at the end of Chapters 3 and 4). Information-gap activities are often used to practice specific language points, and they are also ideal for general fluency practice. While not all the sample activities that follow are appropriate for all learners, they serve to illustrate what constitutes an information-gap activity.

Find the Other Half

Each student is given half of a picture:

Mingle and ask questions:

Is your person wearing a red shirt?
Is it a man?
Is it a woman?

Even very beginning-level students could use one-word utterances to complete the task.

Find the Difference

Students are given two similar drawings or pictures with several small differences. They must ask one another questions to find the differences:

Is there a ball under the table?
Is there a picture on the wall?

Calendars/Schedules/Grids

In a general-English class, give each student a schedule for the week to fill in with all appointments, classes, etc. they have for that week. Tell the students they need to talk to other students in class to find a time they would all be free to form a study group before or after class.

In a work-readiness program, you can create scenarios like this one:

Student A: You are calling in sick to work today, but you need to know your schedule for next week. Ask your supervisor over the phone and fill in the schedule below:

Schedule	
Week of ____________	
Monday	
Tuesday etc.	

Student B: ______ is calling in sick and needs his or her schedule for next week.

(Student B is given the completed schedule.)

Prepare two schedules so that students can repeat the task taking on new roles.

C. Groupings

Finding connections among objects, concepts, and ideas is a good way to enhance understanding and remember new words or concepts in a second language. This activity can be done around any theme and with any set of words students have been working with. It's ideal for review or for previewing a theme and can be done with any level. We'll use the theme of jobs to illustrate how this works. Give each student a picture depicting a particular job: carpenter, doctor, nurse, server, mechanic, beautician, etc. Ask students to create job groups based on different criteria for the picture they are holding, for example:

Indoor vs. outdoor jobs
Jobs traditionally held by men/women
Jobs that require specific training (group by type of training needed)

Have students group based on criteria of their choosing.

In creating groups, learners need to negotiate, justify their choices, and describe the job depicted in the picture they are holding. The task generates language production of varying degrees depending on the learners' oral proficiency, making it ideal for multilevel classes. If you are working with parents of school-aged children, making groups based on school supplies is an ideal way to learn about the names and uses of the items

D. Mingle activities

A mingle activity involves learners milling around and gathering information from other students in the class on a given topic. Mingle activities have the benefit of maximizing student participation for learners at all levels. The most proficient students may talk to everyone in class within the assigned time frame, while the students who are less proficient can be equally engaged through talking to just a few students. This sample activity could be used in a lesson on health and wellness.

Home remedies

Many of us choose NOT to go to the doctor when we have a minor illness. What are some home remedies in your culture for common illnesses? Talk to the other students in class and find out what they do in their cultures?

Student/Country	Illness	Remedy
Mira/ElSalvador	Cold/fever	Hot tea

Mingle activities can be continued outside of class by having students interview family, neighbors, or friends as homework. They can report their findings during the next class period.

E. Discussion activities

Any learner can take part in a discussion to some degree, but we normally use discussion activities with low-intermediate to advanced students who have sufficient language to engage in sustained conversation in English. Successful discussion activities have the following features:

- An identified purpose and outcome.
- Clear roles for all participants: facilitator, scribe, timekeeper, for example.
- A clear time frame.
- A genuine reason to communicate. The group needs to make a decision, create groups, reach consensus, or generate a list, for example.

Discussions can be about current events, cultural issues, education, work, or anything that is relevant to your learners' lives.

F. Problem-posing activities/Problem solving

Problem-posing activities have all of the characteristics given for discussion activities. They revolve around particular problems learners have encountered in their lives, for example, a conflict between an immigrant and her U.S.-born in-laws regarding childrearing. Learners pose the problem, identify the issues, and discuss the possible solutions. Problem posing is an integral part of a learner-centered adult ESL curriculum; in fact, it provides the foundation for participatory approaches to teaching. Similar to problem-posing and discussion activities, problem-solving tasks revolve around more practical, day-to-day issues, for example:

- You're locked out of your house.
- You can't come to the last day of class when the final test is given.
- You had your wallet stolen.
- You forgot an appointment.

Learners work together to come up with a solution to the problem. Further practice can involve comparing and ranking class solutions. Problem posing and problem solving can be used at any level of instruction.

G. Role-play

Role-plays are used with any level of learner for a variety of purposes. They can be used to practice particular language points, as we saw with the telephoning role-plays in Chapter 3, or for general fluency practice. Because learners are taking on a different persona to a degree, they sometimes are less inhibited than they might be with other fluency activities. On the other hand, role-playing is new for many learners and may appear frivolous. Therefore, careful planning and implementation are crucial. Here are some tips that will help make role-plays successful:

- Model the role-play with a student.
- Provide language support to successfully complete the role-play (put samples of language needed on the board, use familiar language in role descriptions).
- Include an incentive to communicate (shopkeeper is out of a particular item so the shopper has to make another choice).
- Assign roles that are achievable for students of varying ability levels.
- Use realistic scenarios.
- Incorporate realia and visual aids (menus for a restaurant, food items for a grocery store).

CONCLUSION This section has included a variety of examples of speaking activities that you can use with students at different levels with the goal of promoting fluency in English. Keep in mind that the activities presented in this chapter can also be used in the following ways:

- Prelistening, prereading, or prewriting activities (the last two are covered in Chapter 5).
- Warm-up or review activities.
- Follow-up activities.
- "Authentic use" practice activities in contextualized language lessons.

It is important to keep the following in mind as you choose and develop tasks for your students:

- Assure students that there is a true communicative purpose to the activity.
- Provide clear guidelines and outcomes for the activity.
- Assign roles according to learners' strengths and abilities. As learners become more familiar with one another and comfortable with fluency activities, they can self-assign roles.
- Use visuals and realia to provide context and add authenticity (e.g., real menus in a restaurant role-play; real maps for an information-gap activity).

An aspect of speaking that is often of utmost importance to your students is pronunciation. We complete this chapter with a discussion of the place of pronunciation instruction in ESL classes as well as techniques for promoting awareness of and intelligibility in pronunciation with students.

Part III ◆ The Place of Pronunciation in ESL Instruction

4.3.1 MAKING A CASE FOR PRONUNCIATION IN YOUR CURRICULUM

There has been extensive debate over the past decade about the role pronunciation should play in adult ESL curricula (Morley 1991). Some would argue that within a communicative approach to teaching, attention to discrete phonemic features of the language is counter to current meaning-based approaches to teaching. What are your own views about pronunciation and adult ESL instruction?

Task 4.8

Take a few minutes to complete this questionnaire and, if you're working in a group, discuss your answers with a partner:

Rate yourself from 5 (strongly agree) to 1 (strongly disagree).

1 Most adults have extreme difficulty acquiring a native-like accent.

2 A pronunciation component should be included in most any ESL curriculum.

3 Native-English speakers make negative judgments about people with a non-native accent.

4 Pronunciation drills are the best way to help learners acquire intelligible pronunciation.

Explicit pronunciation instruction has taken a backseat to other areas of language with the advent of communicative teaching approaches. One reason for this is that early approaches to pronunciation instruction focused heavily on mechanical drills and practice of sounds in isolation, which do not necessarily transfer to accurate production in real-life communication. Current approaches have thought of pronunciation as only one small piece of the language puzzle, and one that develops through exposure to language and practice. The fact is that many adult learners who receive no formal instruction or feedback on pronunciation may be highly unintelligible, even those who have been in an English-speaking environment for many years.

The extent to which pronunciation instruction becomes part of your curriculum depends on the needs and expectations of your students. Does their intelligibility affect their ability to communicate effectively; in other words, are there breakdowns in communication because of their pronunciation? If they are working, how important is intelligible pronunciation? Unintelligible pronunciation can affect one's ability to thrive or be promoted professionally, and immigrants and refugees can face discrimination on the job because of native speakers' unwillingness to adjust to a variety of accents. Students often report that native-English speakers judge their credibility, intelligence, and competence based on accent. It would be wonderful if, as ESL professionals, we could sensitize and educate employers, landlords, and other native speakers of English in our learners' lives. Given the unlikelihood of achieving that goal, we owe it to learners to help them achieve their highest level of intelligibility so that they can access a whole array of positions.

Some professions have higher linguistic demands than others and an employee who is highly unintelligible may not have adequate skills to meet those demands. The Equal Employment Opportunity Commission (EEOC 1995) has published guidelines that are used to determine whether or not a non-native English-speaking employee has been discriminated against because of his or her accent. The commission looks at the communication demands of a particular job in the following ways:

a the frequency and complexity of oral communication demanded by the job;

b the relative gravity of an episode of miscommunication;

c whether speaking is done under high-stress circumstances where time is of the essence; and

d whether communicative encounters typically exist with one-time listeners or, in contrast, with listeners who will have further contact with the employee so as to adjust to listening and comprehension patterns.

These criteria are useful for ESL teachers because they help us and our learners assess the language demands of a particular job. Using these criteria, let's look at the job of a nurse. How frequently does a nurse use English? How complex is the language? Would miscommunication have grave results? Is communication done under high-stress conditions? Is communication with one-time listeners, or would a listener have time to become accustomed to the speaker's accent? From the answers to these questions, we can see that being a nurse has very high linguistic demands and one would need highly comprehensible language skills in order to succeed in that job. Now ask yourself these same questions for each of the jobs below and see what you notice. Work with a partner or write down your answers if you are working alone.

Task 4.9

restaurant server	nursing assistant	receptionist	
supervisor in manufacturing	doctor	nurse	
dental hygienist	dishwasher	housekeeper	teacher
landscaper	truck driver	manufacturing line operator	

Which of the jobs have the highest linguistic demands based on the EEOC criteria? What types of jobs do many of your students hold? Did you discover that those jobs with the most minimal linguistic demands are also the least stable and low-paying? Helping learners achieve intelligibility is a way of advocating for them; it's helping them access the jobs they may very well be trained for already, or have the potential to attain.

4.3.2 Factors Affecting Pronunciation

There are a number of factors that can have an impact on one's ability to achieve intelligible pronunciation (Kenworthy 1987).

First language How phonetically different are the first and second languages? While this might seem like the most obvious factor, it is by no means the most important one. Learners whose first language is more phonetically similar to English will not necessarily have the most ease in acquiring the sounds of the new language. Other factors are equally important to consider.

Age The assumption that the younger you are the more likely you are to acquire a second language without an accent has come under increasing question. Studies on the effect of age on pronunciation in a second language have produced conflicting results (Jacobs 1988, Flege 1981). Generally speaking, however, learners exposed to English at a young age (before puberty) are more likely to achieve a native-like accent in a second language. Adult learners are capable of achieving comprehensible pronunciation, however.

Motivation It is often the case that adult ESL learners live in an environment where they can get by with limited English. Refugees may hold on to the hope that they will some day return to their country of origin, which might make them less motivated to speak clearly or be understood in English. Motivation that derives from negative reactions from family members or employers may be a cause for frustration rather than a positive motivator.

Expectations Along with motivation comes expectations about how one wants to sound in a second language, which are oftentimes unrealistic (Parrino 2001). Few adults ever attain a native-like accent in a second language, but some learners hold this as a goal of instruction.

Exposure to English Krashen's input hypothesis (1982) emphasizes the importance of adequate language input in language acquisition. While adult ESL learners may be living in an English-speaking country, they may not be immersed in English at home or work. It's imperative that teachers provide abundant exposure to spoken English in ESL classes, and encourage learners to seek opportunities to listen to spoken language outside of class as well (Celce-Murcia et al 1996).

Attitude and identity Accent has a strong impact on our identity, as first- or second-language speakers. Learners may have a stronger desire to sound like peers than to sound like the native-speaking population; this can result in a resistance to work on pronunciation in English.

Innate phonetic ability Some learners may be better than others at discriminating between sounds or mimicking sounds. As Kenworthy (1987) suggests, all learners have acquired one language, so they are capable of acquiring a second. They may go about it in different ways, using different innate skills and abilities.

These factors come into play in different ways and to different degrees for each learner. Recognizing these variables helps us to remember how complex the process of acquiring language really is. Understanding this complexity can help us to keep the goals of pronunciation instruction realistic.

4.3.3 What Should We Teach?

It is important to understand that the goal of pronunciation instruction is not accent-free English—that's neither realistic nor a necessity. Morley (1991) makes a distinction between pronunciation production and performance, suggesting that both have a place in ESL curricula, the latter being more important. Production refers to the understanding of discrete sounds as well as stress, intonation, and rhythm patterns—the traditional view of pronunciation. Performance refers to overall intelligibility (the ability to make oneself understood) and communicability (the ability to meet communicative demands). This view gives pronunciation a place within a communicative approach to teaching.

As ESL teachers, you need a basic understanding of the pronunciation features of English. Pronunciation is broken down into two areas: Segmentals, or the sounds of the language, and Suprasegmentals, or the stress, rhythm, and intonation patterns of the language. Segmentals consist of the phonemes of the language, or its smallest meaningful units. In English, /b/ and /v/ are phonemes because when one replaces the other in a word, the meaning changes:

bat/vat veil/bail

If two sounds are not phonemic in a learner's language, they may have difficulty differentiating between the two sounds in English. If a native-Spanish speaker uses English /b/ and /v/ interchangeably, which is possible in Spanish, the results can be problematic (*bowel* for *vowel*, for example).

There is more to English pronunciation than the individual sounds. In fact, various sounds used in combination, or sounds used in particular environments, are often more problematic for students learning English. Two examples of learner problems you may encounter in the production of English are the deletion and insertion of sounds. Many languages do not have consonant clusters (split, prompt). In attempting to produce the cluster, speakers might delete one of the consonants to make the cluster more manageable or, as with many Japanese speakers, they may insert a vowel (usually a schwa /ə/ sound) between the consonants: action /ǽkəʃən/[1]. Spanish and Farsi words do not begin with *s* + another consonant, so it's not uncommon for speakers of those languages to insert a short vowel sound '/ɛ/-Spanish' or '/ɛ/-special' (/ɛ/represents the vowel sound in 'met'). Learners whose first language does not have final consonants may omit final consonants in English. This can result in misinterpreting the causes of particular learner errors, in particular, plural endings and the *-s* in the third person singular of simple present verbs (She lives next door). Some learners omit final *-s* in speaking but not in writing, which may indicate that the omission is an issue of pronunciation rather than under-

[1] The symbols used here are from the International Phonetic Alphabet, or IPA. Each symbol represents the sound found in the word, regardless of spelling. *Met* and *meant* both contain the vowel phoneme represented as /ɛ/. It is very helpful for ESL teachers to learn the IPA in order to decipher phonetic transcriptions in ESL handbooks, articles, and textbooks. Some ESL students have learned the IPA in their country (Korean, Japanese, and Chinese students, in particular). I am not suggesting that you teach the IPA to students.

standing of a grammar point. A complete overview of phonetics is beyond the goals and scope of this book. There are a number of resources to guide you, however (see Recommended Reading). Your job is to identify those areas that affect intelligibility the most and to find ways to integrate practice of those pronunciation features into your lessons, which we explore in section 4.3.4.

Stress, Intonation, and Rhythm Depending on your learners' first language, inability to employ English-like stress, intonation, and rhythm can have an even greater impact on intelligibility than the mispronunciation of sounds. In fact, we can often derive a speaker's intended meaning from context when phonemic errors occur. Decide what the speaker means in each of these utterances:

I have 'lice' with all meals. (/lays/ in place of /rays/)

This shirt 'feets' me well. (/fiyts/ in place of /fɪts/)

I 'leave' in Gainesville. (/liyv/ in place of /lɪv/)

In each of these instances, the speaker is understandable through contextual clues. Now think of how intelligibility would be affected if a speaker used the wrong word stress on *committee* or *comedy* in these sentences:

What did you think of the **co**medy?

What did you think of the com**mit**tee? (Gilbert 1993:69)

What affects intelligibility more is a speaker's inability to stress the right syllable within a word (word stress), the right words in a sentence (sentence stress), or use intonation (changes in pitch) appropriately. These features of spoken language can be very difficult for native speakers of other languages to perceive. Below are examples that illustrate some ways in which suprasegmental features affect meaning:

1 Word stress:

a Now you need to add cold **cream**.

What would happen to the meaning of the sentence if you said '**cold** cream'? The first word of a compound noun is stressed: **book**case, **cof**fee table. Compound nouns are those combinations of two words referring to a specific item. '**Cold** cream' is a compound noun, whereas 'cold **cream**' is not.

b The pronunciation of teens/tens 13/30, 14/40, 15/50, etc.: In natural discourse the prominent difference between each is that the second syllable is stressed on the teens (thir**teen**) and the first syllable is stressed on the tens (**thir**ty).

2 Sentence stress:

I lost my **red** scarf. (not the blue one)

I lost my red **scarf.** (not my red hat)

3 The following examples illustrate how intonation affects meaning (Levis 1999:48):

She's my sister, Marcia. (Marcia is your sister.)

She's my sister, Marcia. (You're identifying your sister for someone else named Marcia.)

4 Another important feature of English is the use of thought groups, or semantically related groups of words within a sentence that are produced as chunks. These examples from Gilbert (1993) demonstrate the importance of developing an awareness of this feature of English. Were it not for changes in word groups and pauses, the pairs of sentences would sound the same:

Would you like the Super Salad? Would you like the soup or salad?

They have a house, boat, and trailer. They have a houseboat and trailer.

English is a stress-timed language: that means the time it takes to say an utterance depends on the number of stresses in that utterance:

I like movies. = 3 beats

I **went** to the **movie** with **Jane.** = 3 beats

Many of your learners will come from languages that are syllable-timed: the length of the utterance depends on the number syllables. When speaking English, those learners may have a tendency to stress every word in a sentence. Helping learners to recognize what kinds of words are stressed in English can improve their intelligibility (it also aids in their ability to understand key words when listening since those are the ones that are stressed). Table 4.3 illustrates those words that are stressed in a sentence, and those that are unstressed. Of course we can choose to stress any word for emphasis, contrast, or clarification: Are you coming to the party? No, I'm going to the **movies.**

TABLE 4.3

Content Words These are the words that carry the most meaning in the sentence. We stress these in natural discourse.	**Function Words** These are the small words that are the glue of the sentences. We tend not to stress these words.
Nouns	Articles
Verbs	Prepositions
Adjectives	Short conjunctions (*and, but, so*)
Adverbs	Auxiliary verbs
Conjunctions (*however, therefore*)	Pronouns

4.3.4 Approaches to Teaching Pronunciation

As the tide has turned back to including pronunciation instruction within learner-centered, communicative approaches to teaching, emphasis has been on making that instruction meaningful, i.e., teaching features of pronunciation in context and for communicative purposes. In the past, a good deal of instruction relied on repetition of **minimal pairs** (words with only one phonemic difference). So a student who had difficulty differentiating between the sounds /l/ and /r/ would practice pairs like the following: lice/rice; long/wrong; late/rate. Limericks, tongue twisters, and other texts that included multiple instances of the target sounds were also common. Anyone who spent time learning a foreign language in a language lab undoubtedly recalls hours of listen-and-repeat drills. While there is still a place for this focus on pronunciation production, and these kinds of exercises might give some immediate accuracy of sounds, that accuracy rarely transfers to extended, spontaneous speech produced outside of the classroom. That's where the need for a focus on pronunciation performance comes into play.

Celce-Murcia et al (1996:36) recommend the following progression in a pronunciation lesson: *description and analysis*, *listening discrimination*, *controlled practice*, *guided practice*, *communicative practice*.

1 *Description and Analysis/Listening Discrimination*

The goal of these steps is to raise learners' awareness of segmental and suprasegmental features through the use of visual charts, drawings, hand gestures—whatever means are within your learners' language abilities. Learners then need to take part in **listening discrimination** activities that allow them to demonstrate their ability to perceive sounds or patterns of the language. If learners are unable to hear sounds or patterns of stress, intonation, and rhythm, they will have tremendous difficulty producing them. In the sample discrimination activities that follow, learners need to listen to the teacher or fellow student and make choices about what they have heard. Completion of the **discrimination task** demonstrates their ability (or possible inability) to differentiate between sounds or among pronunciation patterns.

a. *Discriminating between /l/ and /r/*

In this activity, only Student A is given the Word Search handout below. Student B is given the list of words to call out to Student A. Instruct both students not to look at the other's sheet.

Student A: Circle the words that you hear from your partner. Words can go across, up, or down.

			R	I	C	K								
			O						L	I	C	K		F
			C											I
L	A	C	K		R			L	O	W				L
				L	I	G	H	T		R				E
					G				P	A	I	L		
R	A	C	K		H					P		I		
O					T		L	A	P			N		
W		W					O		A			K		
		R	I	N	K		N		I	F				
		O					G		R	I	D	E		
F		N								R				
A		G			L	I	E	D		E				
I														
L				F	A	I	R			L	O	C	K	

Student B: Your partner needs to find these words. Do not show your list to your partner. Read each word aloud clearly so that your partner can find them on the Word Search sheet:

light	rack	lick	low	file	wrong
ride	rink	pail	fair	lap	rock

b *Recognizing word stress*

Learning the word-stress patterns of new words begins with perceiving the patterns. In a lesson on jobs and places of work, learners listen to a list of words spoken by the teacher and sort them into the correct stress pattern:

Listen to these words and place them under the correct pattern below:

beautician carpenter plumber line worker

teacher server mechanic doctor

O o o	o O o	O o

c *Recognizing* -ed *ending variations*

This activity helps learners discriminate among the three different pronunciations of *-ed* endings in the past tense as well as recognize the rules that govern those variations:

Give each student a flashcard with one of these words on it and ask the class to move into three groups according to the way the *-ed* ending sounds in their word. The teacher allows the class to try the activity without her assistance and then says the words aloud that are causing difficulty:

studied	graduated	worked	lived
helped	decided	learned	

Students tape their cards to the board in the three categories they have chosen, and the teacher elicits what they notice: endings /t/, /d/, /ɪd/. When do we add an extra syllable? Only after /t/ and /d/.[2] (Depending on the learners' interest in or knowledge of phonetics, you can help them notice that we say /t/ after voiceless consonants and /d/ after vowels and voiced consonants).

2 *Controlled Practice*

Once your learners begin to perceive patterns, your instruction can turn to activities that provide opportunity to say the target sounds repeatedly, but in a meaningful context. Table 4.4 includes sample activities that provide this kind of practice.

TABLE 4.4 Sample Controlled Practice Activities

Strip stories: Write a story that contains numerous instances of the target sound or stress, intonation, or rhythmic pattern. Each learner receives a line of the story, which is practiced and recited for the group. As a class, students put the story in the correct order without looking at one another's strips. The stories can be generated by the class using picture prompts or realia.
Picture stories: Collect pictures of places and items that begin with a target sound. Tell the class the story and then have them recall the order and tell the story. Then have them shuffle the cards and change the story. Students may also find pictures of items in a magazine that use the sound and make up a new story to tell a partner.
Semiscripted skits/role-plays: In working on sentence stress and intonation, use semiscripted skits or role-plays (learners have to fill in some of the words). The context for these should relate to the content of the overall curriculum you're teaching: a job interview for work-readiness program; a mock interview with an INS agent for a citizenship class.
Chain activities: For sounds or word-stress patterns, collect a set of words or pictures around a theme (bookcase, coffee table, ironing board, light fixture, area rug). S1: *We're going to garage sales and we need* ________. Choose another student, who repeats the first item and adds one. This provides practice in stressing the first word of the compound noun.

[2] The three groupings are: /t/: helped, worked; /d/: studied, lived, learned; /ɪd/: graduated, decided. /p/ and /k/ are voiceless sounds and are followed by voiceless /t/. *Voiceless* means that there is no vibration of the vocal chords as the sounds are produced. /iy/, /v/, and /n/ are all voiced and are followed by voiced /d/. Only those words ending in /t/ or /d/ add the extra /ɪd/ or /əd/.

Table 4.4 Sample Controlled Practice Activities continued

Word search: The previous word search done in pairs provides controlled practice of the sounds. Different word search grids can be created for different learners in the same class. Minimal pairs are included in the activity, but because of the interactive format of the task, learners work on other communication strategies:

> Did you say *light* (pointing to the light on the ceiling)?
>
> Did you say *wrong*, as in not right?

3 *Guided Practice/Communicative Practice*

Finally, it is important that learners practice pronunciation patterns in unplanned, extended speech (much like "authentic use" activities mentioned in Chapter 3). The activities will not be completely spontaneous because you guide the students to use particular pronunciation patterns. Table 4.5 includes samples that move from guided to communicative practice.

Table 4.5 From Guided to Communicative Practice

Information-gap activities: Unreadable fax: Each student has a copy of a work document that is missing key figures (including teens/tens combinations). Pairs work together to complete their copy of the document.
Word association: Write a set of words that represent the pattern being taught. One student gives clues for a word and the rest of the class guesses which word they are thinking of. Example: a class working on the word-stress rule for words ending with suffixes (*tion/sion*) would be given words such as *education* and *tradition.*

Conclusion

This chapter has explored the areas of listening, speaking, and pronunciation within meaning-based, communicative approaches to teaching. Competent users of English employ a variety of skills and strategies to access spoken texts, interact with others, and make themselves understood. It takes time and practice to acquire these skills, and it is the ESL teacher's job to provide ample opportunities for these skills to develop.

Key Terms

Checklist of Key Terms	On your own, or with a partner, provide an example or brief definition for each concept:
schema theory	
prelistening	
listening for different purposes	
bottom-up processing	

top-down processing	
follow-up	
fluency	
intelligibility	
communicability	
phoneme	
word stress	
sentence stress	
minimal pair	
discrimination task	

Applying What You Learned

1 Listening Skills Development

If you are already teaching. . . choose an upcoming unit for which you haven't yet planned any authentic listening practice. Do one of the following: a. select an authentic taped segment (news report, weather report, commercial, song, etc.) that relates to the theme of your unit; b. tape record a brief interview of someone on that theme; c. check the resource library at your school for a commercial tape that contains a passage related to that theme. Using this listening passage, design a listening lesson. Include a prelistening activity, two listening activities (these could be listening for gist, specific information, etc.), and one follow-up activity.

Classroom Application

Now implement the lesson and answer the following questions:

How successful were students at achieving the tasks you prepared?

How well did your prelistening activity prepare them for the listening activities?

How did you know?

Is there anything you would do differently the next time you teach this lesson?

If you are not teaching. . . choose a theme (e.g., health, accessing community resources, getting ready for job interviews) and prepare a lesson as described in 1a. Show it to a partner and discuss these questions:

How well will the prelistening activity activate prior knowledge about the content of the lesson?

What listening skills do your activities enable students to practice?

2 Evaluating Fluency Activities

Choose three texts that your program uses for developing speaking skills, or choose three integrated-skills texts (if you are not teaching, find three texts to evaluate). Identify the activities that you think are designed to develop speaking fluency and evaluate those activities using this checklist.

	Yes/No	Strengths and weaknesses of the activity
Is there a true communicative purpose to the activity?		
Are there clear guidelines and outcomes for the activity?		
Does the activity allow for different learner strengths and abilities?		
Are there visuals that provide context and add authenticity?		
Does the activity allow for sustained interaction among students?		
Other features you're looking for in a fluency activity		

3a Your Views about Pronunciation

Respond to the questionnaire from 4.3.1 again and discuss, with specific examples, how your views have changed after reading Part III.

1 Most adults have extreme difficulty acquiring a native-like accent.

2 A pronunciation component should be included in almost every ESL curriculum.

3 Native-English speakers make negative judgments about people with a non-native accent.

4 Pronunciation drills are the best way to help learners acquire intelligible pronunciation.

3b Developing an Awareness of Intelligibility

The purpose of the learner pronunciation log is to raise your own awareness of what has the greatest impact on intelligibility.

Learner Pronunciation Log	
Sounds (individual sounds, clusters, insertions, deletions)	
Word stress (syllable stressed in a word)	
Sentence stress (words stressed in sentences)	
Intonation (rising and falling pitch)	
Rhythm (natural thought groups)	

If you are teaching. . . for one week, complete the learner pronunciation log for one of your classes. Listen for errors in the production of sounds, as well as stress, intonation, and rhythm that you believe cause breakdowns in communication (intelligibility). Also notice any compensation strategies your learners use (e.g., paraphrasing when they know they haven't been understood, using gestures, etc.).

After that week, prioritize the pronunciation problems affecting intelligibility that seem most prevalent for this group of students. This will help guide the choices you make about what are areas of pronunciation to include in your curriculum.

If you are not teaching. . . use the pronunciation log as you observe a class and as you interact with non-native speakers of English. What areas of pronunciation seem to have the greatest impact on intelligibility? From what you've observed, choose two to three areas you would most likely include in any ESL curriculum.

TRANSCRIPT OF INTERVIEW

David: Hi, Farid. I wanted to ask you about the holidays you celebrate from France and Iran. I know you grew up in Iran, but I know your mother's French. What's your favorite holiday in Iran?

Farid: My favorite holiday in Iran is called Nowrouz, which is . . . celebrates the Persian New Year.

David: Uh huh.What's the history of that holiday?

Farid: It's an old holiday that dates back to antiquity and . . . uh . . . it's the official start of spring. It's exactly at the equinox of spring.

David: What are some of the foods you eat at Nowrouz?

Farid: A variety of food. Fresh fruits that celebrate spring. But in particular a dish that is made of rice, herbs, and white fish.

David: What are some of the activities you do that day?

Farid: Typical activities that you do on New Year's . . . visiting families, eating out, and going on picnics.

David: Isn't there a special holiday a few days before Nowrouz, where you jump over fire?

Farid: Ah, yea, it's called the Holiday of Fire Wednesday and in that holiday, people make fires and jump over the fire. They say they would like to get good health from the fire and give their bad health to the fire.

David: What about clothing? Are there any special clothes for Nowrouz?

Farid: Nothing in particular except all the kids wear their brand new clothes.

David: OK, what about France? What's your favorite holiday in France?

Farid: One of my favorite holidays is the 14th of July, which is Bastille Day.

David: What's the history of that holiday?

Farid: That holiday celebrates the freeing of the prisoners of the Bastille prison, on the occasion of the French Revolution in 1789.

David: What are the special activities for that day?

Farid: It's a national holiday and there are some official celebrations . . . marches on the Champs Elysee, airplanes and military marches. At night there's music and dances in the street.

David: Are there any special foods?

Farid: You know, I don't know in particular, but I think people just like to eat outside because it's during the summer and people enjoy being outside.

David: Are there special clothes?

Farid: Not really. I'd say the red, white, and blue of the flag, anything with that theme.

Recommended Reading

Listening

Nunan, D. and **L. Miller.** (eds.) 1995. *New ways in teaching listening.* Alexandria, VA: TESOL.

This text includes close to 150 listening activities, plans, and ideas from practicing teachers all over the world.

Ur, P. 1984. *Teaching listening comprehension.* Cambridge: Cambridge University Press.

The author provides background in the characteristics of real-life listening, problems encountered by language learners, and ideas for planning successful classroom listening practice. The text contains a wide variety of exercise types that can be used as is or adapted for use with other materials.

White, G. 1998. *Listening (Oxford resource books for teachers).* Oxford: Oxford University Press.

The listening activities in this text are designed to help learners build confidence and independence in listening.

Pronunciation

Bowen, T. and **J. Marks.** 1992. *The pronunciation book: Student-centered activities for pronunciation work.* Burnt Mill, Harlow: Longman.

This book contains highly contextualized pronunciation tasks, many of which are designed to enhance learner awareness of their own pronunciation.

Celce-Murcia, M., D. Brinton. and **J. Goodwin.** 1996. *Teaching pronunciation.* Cambridge: Cambridge University Press.

This comprehensive overview of English pronunciation is highly accessible to new teachers and contains myriad suggestions for classroom application.

Morley, J. 1994. *Pronunciation pedagogy and theory: New views, new dimensions.* Alexandria, VA: TESOL.

A collection of articles on current pronunciation theory and practice of leading experts in the field.

Speaking

Bailey, K. and **L. Savage.** (eds.) 1994. *New ways in teaching speaking.* Alexandria, VA: TESOL.

A collection of oral communication activities compiled from practicing ESL/EFL teachers, it includes activities for fluency, accuracy, pronunciation, and speaking in particular content areas.

Klippel, F. 1984. *Keep talking.* Cambridge: Cambridge University Press.

A collection of highly interactive and personalized speaking activities, including surveys, discussions, and games.

McKay, H. and **A. Tom.** 1999. *Teaching adult second language learners.* New York: Cambridge University Press.

A teacher resource with a multitude of classroom activities appropriate for the adult ESL classroom.

Ur, P. and **A. Wright.** 1992. *5-Minute activities: A resource book of short activities.* Cambridge: Cambridge University Press.

The short activities in this book can be used for practicing particular language points, as ice breakers or warm-ups, or for supplementing a course book.

Useful Websites

Randall's ESL Cyber Listening Lab

http://www.esl-lab.com/

This site includes listening exercises and activities, including conversations and quizzes for high-beginning to low-advanced learners. (Real Audio is required to use this site—links for free downloads are provided.)

Pronunciation Skills and Activities

http://www.ohiou.edu/esl/english/speaking.html#PronunciationSkills

This site offers a variety of activities and links to activities targeting basic pronunciation issues.

5

Developing Reading and Writing Skills

Part I ◆ Integrating Reading and Writing Skills Development

5.1.1 Introduction

Print is everywhere. Imagine how difficult it can be for learners new to English to access the abundance of printed material that comes their way: bills, junk mail, school materials, advertisements, work instructions, schedules. Being an independent writer is a necessity for anyone who wants to go to school or attain and hold onto employment. In this chapter, we turn to the issue of literacy: the skills of reading and writing. We look at the varying purposes for reading and writing, the challenges students with no literacy in their first language face, and the most common approaches to teaching reading and writing to adult ESL students. It needs to be stressed that no one approach is used in isolation; a whole-language teacher may conduct a language experience to generate stories. A teacher using the Language Experience Approach may use phonics techniques to help learners recognize sound/symbol correspondences in a class-generated text.

The chapter begins with an examination of approaches for developing reading and writing skills together (LEA, Whole Language/balanced literacy approach), particularly with emergent readers and writers. Next, we turn to techniques for teaching reading and writing for learners who already have stronger literacy skills. Let's start by thinking about what we read and what is involved in reading.

Checklist

After reading this chapter and completing the activities, you should be able to

- describe various purposes for reading and writing.
- describe the difference between top-down vs. bottom up approaches to literacy development.
- describe processes used in the Language Experience Approach.
- develop a reading lesson that includes prereading, reading, and follow-up activities.
- explain the differences between product-oriented and process-oriented writing tasks.
- create a writing activity that is form-focused; create a process-oriented writing lesson.
- explain considerations for deciding when and how to correct learner errors in writing.

Getting Started

Task 5.1

Read the following real-world case and answer these questions with a partner, or write answers in your journal:

1 What are Choua's literacy needs? What kinds of texts does she need to read?

2 What unique challenges does she face?

Paseng goes to the university in Eau Claire, WI, about a five-hour drive from his mother's home in Milwaukee. He returns to his mother's home every weekend. Aside from his desire to see his mother, his primary reason for returning home each week is to help her go through all of the mail she received the previous week. Paseng's mother, Choua, is not literate in English or in her first language. She can't tell the difference between the Publisher's Clearinghouse ad and a request to visit the Social Security office to go over her benefits. When Paseng speaks to her on the phone before each week's visit, he can hear the panic in her voice.

This is a common scenario for many immigrant families. For now, Choua is not enrolled in an ESL class and the likelihood that she'll acquire the literacy needed to maneuver independently through the barrage of text in our culture is small. There are many students like Choua in your classes, who have had little or no experience with literacy, yet they are bombarded with written texts every day in our very print-dense culture. Just think about all the things you need to read each day.

Task 5.2

Working with a partner or on your own, think of *everything* you read in a given day. Write your answers in this box:

Daily Reading

Now look at your list of items and put them into one of these two categories: **Everyday** or **Intensive Reading.** I've included some examples to get you started.

Types of Reading Material

Everyday Reading	Intensive Reading
menus	novels
billboards	poetry
packaging	

1 What types of reading texts do you encounter most often?

2 *How* do you read the things in column 1 vs. those in column 2?

3 Which of the two do you think your learners encounter most often?

Follow-up As you read about reading principles and practices in the chapter, reflect on how the items you brainstormed above could best be integrated into ESL lessons. What reading skills does a reader employ when reading these different types of texts?

5.1.2 Views of Literacy

A variety of terms describe the different types of texts we encounter and the ways we read them. Everyday reading includes **environmental print:** billboards, signs, packaging, menus, etc. It also includes **functional texts** (forms, applications, bills, etc.). All of these can be considered **instrumental,** that is, we read them for an immediate purpose (Harmer 2000). We look up a number in the phone book because we need to call someone; we read a menu in order to make a choice at a restaurant. On the job, we read a manual in order to operate a machine. Reading these types of texts often involves reading very selectively, for example, when you receive your phone bill, you look directly at the amount due, due date, and probably the long distance calls made to assure that no mistakes have been made to your bill. You **scan** the text, or read for specific information; you probably do not read all of the fine print.

In her work on competency-based literacy instruction, Lynn Savage (1993) describes four types of reading:

Survival Literacy Literacy which revolves around learners' immediate day-to-day needs, e.g., recognizing prices, forms of identification.

Document Literacy Literacy needed to decipher charts and tables, labels, bills, advertisements.

Quantitative Literacy Literacy needed to use and understand texts with numeric information, e.g., pay slips, schedules.

Prose Literacy Literacy that requires an ability to understand more extensive texts, e.g., manuals, rental agreements, etc.

These descriptions illustrate the enormous range of text types learners need to access. In the process of conducting a needs assessment at a company concerned about cross-cultural issues, I noticed that many of the problems supervisors cited were related to issues of literacy. The examples below illustrate the different types of literacy identified by Savage:

1 *Some of our workers don't punch out on the new computer system we use for that, even though we've shown it to them again and again.* (Document and Quantitative)

2 *We have workers who are highly skilled and have been employed here for several years. We're a medical device manufacturer and can be audited by the FDA. This means that our line operators can be asked at any time to show exactly where in the production process they are on a manufacturing instruction. While the workers have fairly strong oral skills, it has become apparent that their literacy skills are lacking and they can't always respond accurately to the auditors.* (Document and Prose)

3 *I requested a schedule (verbal request), and the schedule was provided, but not in the format I expected.* (Document and Quantitative)

4 *Sometimes a worker won't mark down that a defective part was thrown out. We have a form to use, but sometimes they won't even know where to mark it down. They don't seem to understand why this is a problem.* (Document)

In these workplace examples, literacy involved reading and writing schedules, knowing the conventions of a particular workplace, reading manuals, reading and using online time cards, and reading and completing forms. Literacy involved the ability to perform these tasks as well the ability to use new technology to complete the tasks, what we could call 'technological' literacy. Added to this list is 'graphic' literacy, or the ability to understand symbols. How do you organize information on your computer screen? How do you know what restroom to go into, even if you are in a different country where you do not know the language? You use **graphic literacy** to read symbols like these:

Task 5.3

Think back to Choua and her lack of experience with text-based literacy. Can she read or write a story? Yes, she can, but the symbols she uses for conveying meaning are not with written words. What story does this *pa ndau* (Hmong quilt) tell? Can you 'read' the story? Share your interpretations with a partner.

(Photo by Mark Eifert, reproduction courtesy of Michigan State University Museum)

Follow-up Read the story on page 161 and compare it to your own interpretations.

Hamilton (1999), and Kress and Van Leeuwen (1996) suggest that we differentiate uses for literacy in different cultural contexts, including not just print literacy, but mass media and electronic literacy. Literacy is **situated** in different contexts, or domains, in our lives, for example home, work, or school (Barton and Hamilton 2000), and the skills we use to access print in these different contexts vary. Also, activities that involve literacy do not happen in isolation. Look at the following daily tasks learners may encounter along with the literacy skills that may be used for each one:

Daily Tasks	Literacy Activities
Preparing meals	Reading packaging; measurement/numeracy
Food shopping	Making lists; reading labels and pricing; reading signs in the store
Getting to work	Reading bus schedules, street signs

(Dyck, S., Battell, E., Isserlis, J., and Nonesuch, K. 1996:192)

In reviewing this task analysis, we can see the ways in which literacy is situated in everyday tasks, and how its uses combine with other language and life skills. It becomes evident that literacy activities occur as part of other daily tasks; therefore, educators need to look beyond reading and writing as a skill set taught in a classroom, to the actual uses for these various forms of literacy used in learners' lives.

Defining literacy more broadly acknowledges the strengths a learner brings to the task (a strength-based vs. deficit-based view is discussed in 2.2.6). Given her experiences with literacy, Choua may have an easier time reading icons that convey manufacturing instructions on a computer screen than a learner who is dependent on text-based literacy. Likewise, teachers need to have a view of literacy that encompasses multiple purposes for reading and writing; there are reasons other than survival and work that motivate adult ESL learners to attain literacy in English. Parents want to understand and help their children with homework, and correspond with school administrators and teachers. Literacy is also a vehicle for recording and passing on culture and traditions from one generation to the next (Crandall and Peyton 1993).

5.1.3 How Do We Read?

Reading and listening have many parallels and are referred to as the **receptive skills** (writing and speaking, the productive skills). There are, of course, many differences as well, one being the permanence of written text, allowing the reader time to go back to reread as needed. In real-world listening situations (i.e., the teacher is not replaying a tape), the listener has one opportunity to access the information or seek clarification. One of the key similarities between reading and listening is the important role **prior knowledge** plays in order to understand and use written or oral texts, or what is called **schema**

theory (for a complete discussion, see 4.1.3). As with listening, an efficient reader is one who can draw the information they need from the whole text, using top-down processing. Task 5.4 illustrates the powerful role prior knowledge plays in helping us access the meaning of written texts.

Task 5.4

Look at the following text and answer the questions that follow:

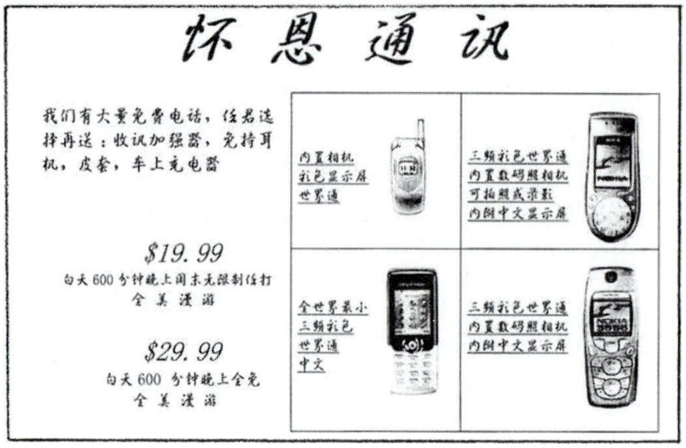

(Courtesy of Grace Su)

What is the purpose of this text?

Where might you find this text?

What information is given in this text?

Who is the audience for this text?

Even if you don't know any Chinese, what could you decipher from this text? Were you able to identify the purpose for the text? Could you guess the kind of store that placed this ad? Could you "read" the words? No, but you could gain a preliminary understanding of what the text was about, what it would be used for, and the places where you'd find certain types of information. Top-down approaches to teaching literacy are based on the premise that any reader brings knowledge and experiences from the world and their life experiences, and that is where literacy development needs to begin. Had I asked you to decipher individual characters in the text, you would have gotten nowhere in your understanding. Starting with a bottom-up approach to reading with your ESL students will have the same effect. That's not to say that working on letter/sounds, word and sentence level decoding is not part of what we do; it is just *one* part of the picture.

Reading, like listening and speaking, is interactive in nature and open to various interpretations. A text does not just transmit information, as shown in Figure A. It involves information going from the text to the reader and back. A text means something different to each of us because of what we bring to it. The ways we read a text depend on prior knowledge, our needs, expectations, the context in which we are reading, as well as our own interpretations, experiences, and culture. This interaction is depicted in Figure B.

FIGURE A **A one-way view of reading**

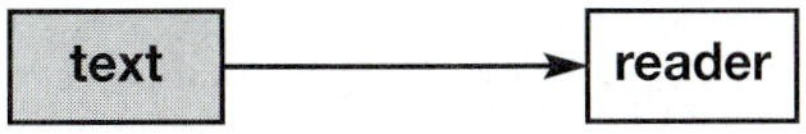

FIGURE B **An interactive view of reading**

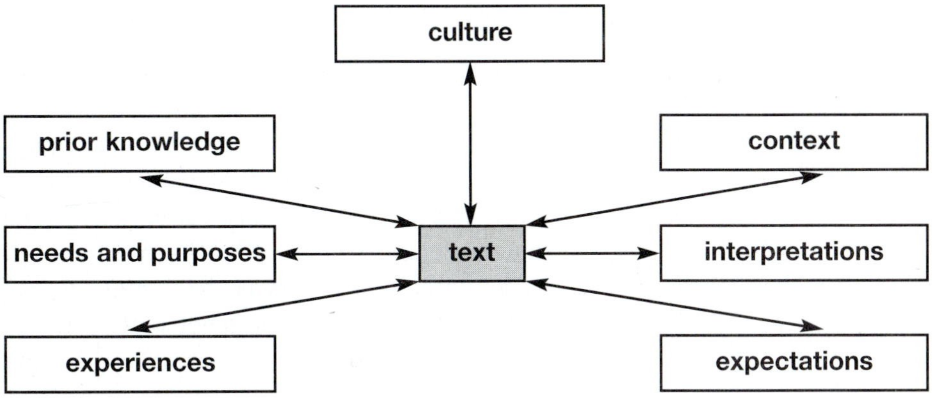

Bottom-up approaches that rely heavily on decoding letters, words, and sentences are one-way approaches to reading. Holistic, top-down approaches allow for these multiple interpretations and experiences that a reader brings to a reading text.

5.1.4 Teaching Literacy Skills: Working with Learners with Limited Literacy

ESL teachers help learners develop literacy skills in just about any type of ESL program. What differs is the themes or content of instruction. For example, a family literacy class might focus on parenting and school systems, while a vocational English class would use work-specific manuals and documents. Another key difference is the approach to literacy development a teacher chooses, and this depends largely on the learners' level of proficiency and experience with reading and writing. Throughout this book, I have made reference to students with "few literacy skills" or "limited literacy." These emerging readers may fall into one of the categories seen in Table 5.1 (Haverson and Haynes 1982).

TABLE 5.1 **Types of Emergent Readers**

1 Preliterate	Students speak a language that does not have a written form, or has a form that is rare or has developed very recently (e.g., Hmong).
2 Nonliterate	Students speak a language which has a written form, but the students don't read or write that language themselves. This is often the case of refugees whose education was interrupted due to war (e.g., Somali, Sudanese).

TABLE 5.1 Types of Emergent Readers continued

3 Semiliterate	Students have some formal education or are able to read and write but only at an elementary level.
4 Literate in a non-Roman alphabet	Students are literate in their first language, but need to learn the sound/symbol correspondences of English. Because these students are already literate, their acquisition of literacy skills in English will generally come much more easily than for the three other groups described above.

The approaches we use with preliterate, nonliterate, and semiliterate learners differ from those used with more proficient readers, even those literate in a non-Roman alphabet. You learn to read once, and reading skills and strategies learned in the first language transfer to reading in a second language (see Chapter 1 (1.2.8) for the discussion of Cognitive Academic Language Proficiency). An approach that has been successful with preliterate, nonliterate, and semiliterate learners is the Language Experience Approach (LEA) because it begins with what language learners are able to produce orally and uses that language as the basis for creating written texts.

A. Language Experience Approach

The Language Experience Approach has been used for decades in elementary schools for first-language literacy development. Because the texts used in this approach are student-generated, it is ideal for any age learner and has found great success as an approach for emergent adult ESL readers and writers. LEA is based on the assumption that if the words we read describe our experiences, we are far more likely to understand them. Far too often the reading texts found in even beginning-level ESL materials are beyond the level of the learner audience and the content is disconnected from their life experiences, being outside their frame of reference.

So how does LEA work? A teacher who uses LEA begins by having the class take part in a group experience; this may be a field trip or a hands-on activity such as cooking, planting, etc. (for examples of activities students can take part in, see Taylor 1993). In cases where this is impractical, a set of pictures for describing a sequence of events or learners retelling an event from their lives can be used as the starting point. After taking part in the activity, the teacher elicits orally from the class what happened during the experience, which she or he then transcribes on the board. There are divergent views on what the teacher transcribes. Many educators transcribe the text verbatim, with all of the learners' errors. This is based on the idea that in order for learners to make meaning of the written word, it needs to be connected to what we know they can already say and understand orally. The teacher will make corrections offered by other classmates as she or he is recording the story on the board, but other corrections to the text become part of an extension activity in a later lesson. The other approach is to make corrections to the text as it is being written, but those corrections need to be accessible to the students in class, i.e., no changes in vocabulary or additions of complex grammar forms. The teacher taking this approach would add a plural *–s*, perhaps, or *–ed* verb endings, for example.

In Laura Lenz's family literacy class, some students are reordering the LEA story generated the day before, while others copy the story.

Once the class has created the text, the students can take part in any number of activities, many of which are used in any reading lesson (see Table 5.2).

TABLE 5.2 Language Experience Activities

- Give the story a title.
- Illustrate the story.
- Match lines from the story with a visual representation.
- Copy the story.
- Cut words in sentences up and have student reorder them.
- Cut the sentences up and have student reorder them.
- Have students create comprehension questions to ask a partner.
- Make a **cloze text** (leave out all the verbs, or every fifth word, for example, which learners fill in).
- Collect stories and create a class text for other groups at school to use as their reading text.
- Do phonics work: find all of the words that start with the letter ____.
- Practice with sight-word recognition: How many times can you find the word *there*?

The Language Experience Approach by no means needs to be used as a stand-alone approach to teaching ESL literacy. The principles of LEA have become standard practice as part of many ESL classrooms. This may take the form of learners with limited literacy reporting to a fellow student what they did over the weekend, and having the more capable writer transcribe the story. In project-based learning, a language experience may be part of a project, for example a book of folktales told by students in class and transcribed by the teacher, students with more literacy skills, or volunteers.

B. Whole Language/Balanced Literacy Approach

In Chapter 2, we looked at the core principles of the **Whole Language approach.** It is often thought of as an approach to literacy development, particularly because it replaced phonics-based, bottom-up approaches in many school systems. Whole Language principles related to literacy development are the following:

- It is a top-down approach.
- It works with whole, authentic texts (not adapted, simplified books).
- It encourages the use of inventive spelling so that learners can begin to write without first worrying about mechanics.
- It is process oriented; learners create texts in steps including prewriting and multiple drafts.

While Whole Language has its critics, it represents much of what we know to be best practice with adult learners, namely, a focus on meaningful and relevant material, a valuing of prior knowledge and experience, and an emphasis on using reading and writing skills and strategies to understand texts (predicting, using contextual clues, etc.).

More recently, ESL and mainstream educators have used what is called a balanced literacy approach. This approach encompasses Whole Language principles while acknowledging the need for developing phonemic awareness or, with some adult learners, the ability to hold a pencil or write the alphabet. This leads us to phonics, a bottom-up approach to literacy development that is used for first and second language learners.

C. The Place of Phonics

Phonics views literacy development as a linear process whereby learners first acquire **sound/letter** (or sound/symbol) **correspondences,** with which they create words and then sentences. It is based on the assumption that the learner has acquired oral language, which is the case for children learning to read in their first language. This is not necessarily the case for adult ESL learners, however. In cases where adults have minimal or no oral skills in English, this bottom-up approach is problematic for ESL literacy development. Phonics does not encourage readers to make meaning of what they are reading, or to use contextual clues, predicting, or other top-down, holistic processes that are all used by efficient readers. There is no question that we use both top-down and bottom-up processing as we read, but the two are best used in combination, and always with the goal of creating meaning out of what we read.

A more promising place for phonics within adult ESL literacy development may well be as one of many tools a teacher employs with her students as part of a balanced literacy approach. Let's look at a text created through a language experience, along with examples of phonics-based activities that help emergent readers recognize sound-spelling correspondences and sight words.

Planting a Seed Put dirt in a pot. Make a small hole in the dirt with your finger. Put one seed in the hole. Cover the hole with more dirt. Pour some water in the pot. Be careful—don't pour too much water. Wait for one week. You will see a small green plant.
a Circle all the words that start with 'p'.
b Now point to other things in class that start with this sound.
c Find all the words with silent 'e' at the end of the word.
d Can you find words around the classroom that end in silent 'e'?
e Underline all the words that end in 't'; practice saying those words out loud.
f How many times can you find 'the' in the story?

(Thanks to Julia Reimer for sharing this LEA story from her class.)

By starting with a class-generated text to work on phonemic awareness, you can be assured that the learners understand the meaning of the words they are working with in a text. Contrast this with the following example from a phonics-based program. As you look at this example, ask yourself these questions: What is helpful about this activity? What is not as helpful? Why?

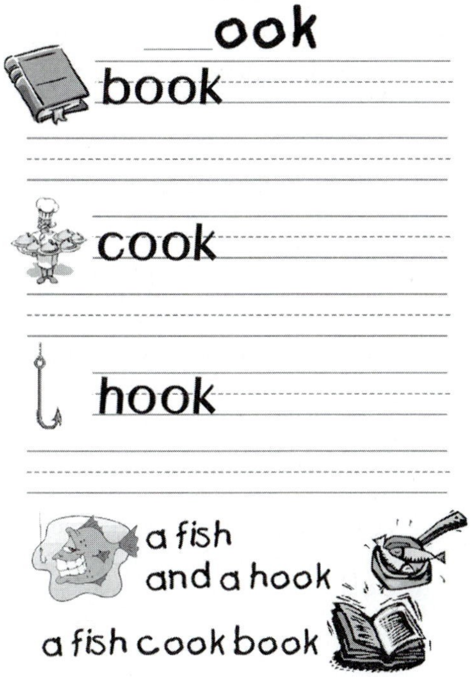

From Boggle's World (http://bogglesworld.com/phonics.htm)

Fluent readers can decode words quickly (Van Duzer 1999), so there are benefits to learning to recognize patterns like the one practiced above. The question is: How meaningful is the language commonly found in phonics activities? These activities are best used in conjunction with holistic approaches, using words that are familiar to learners. Sentences generated from a language experience like the *Planting a Seed* story are more meaningful to adult learners than sentences that can be generated from a set of decontextualized rhyming words such as *book*, *hook*, and *cook*.

5.1.5 Other Strategies and Techniques for Emergent Readers and Writers

The approaches outlined in this chapter so far can be used with learners who have limited literacy skills. In using these approaches, teachers need to draw on an array of techniques to help learners develop the most basic skills, some of which are purely mechanical. Imagine the learner who has never held a pencil, or who has never flipped through the pages of a book. There is much work to be done before such a learner is comfortable with reading and writing. Table 5.3 outlines some of the basic literacy skills emergent readers and writers may need to work on, along with sample activities.

Table 5.3 Literacy tasks for emergent readers and writers

Basic Literacy Skills	Sample Activity
1 Hold a pencil	Practice tracing shapes and letters.
2 Write from left to right	Copy class-generated stories.
3 Write the letters of the alphabet	Display alphabet in room; practice copying alphabet; play concentration with letter flash cards.
4 Alphabetize letters and words	Learners stand in alphabetical order by first letter of name, and gradually go to second and third letters of names.
5 Recognize upper and lower case	Circle all the upper case letters in a text. Sort nouns (proper and common) into two sets. Elicit what learners see in each set.
6 Recognize sound-spelling correspondences	Match sounds to pictures; bingo; find all the words with a particular sound in a text; find all the ways to write a particular sound; same/different activities (do these words start with the same sound or different sound?).
7 Recognize sight words	Label everything in the classroom; match pictures to words.
8 Develop numerical literacy	Practice with phone numbers, addresses. Put numbers in increasing order; listen and respond to simple addition facts, e.g., How many children do you have? How many does Elena have? How many do you have all together?

(Basic Literacy Skills adapted from Vinogradov 2000)

Conclusion This section has focused on approaches that integrate reading and writing instruction, particularly those used with students who have limited literacy. Next we turn to activities and lessons that help learners access the print that they encounter on a daily basis, for example, environmental print, work documents, or newspaper articles.

5.2.1 Preparing Students for Functional Reading

All learners need practice in understanding environmental print (labels, signs) and functional texts (forms, applications, IDs), which often follow set conventions. The size, fabric type, and place of origin of an article of clothing are usually found on the label sewn to the neck or waistband of a garment. For washing instructions, we need to look at the back of that label, or perhaps on an inside seam of the clothing. The nutritional value of a food item is displayed in a format that is consistent from one product to the next. These conventions are not universal, so teaching functional reading goes beyond reading words; it includes knowing where to find information, and knowing which information is helpful and necessary to the reader. Within an integrated curriculum, functional reading tasks are commonly incorporated within thematic units, or situated in contexts that relate to what learners need to do outside of the classroom.

In this section, two examples are presented to illustrate how a teacher can incorporate practice with functional reading texts in ESL lessons. The first example is from a beginning-level basic skills class that has been working on clothing, colors, and basic shopping vocabulary. The teacher includes a functional reading task on recognizing sizes on clothing labels. Students first match the sizes (small, medium, large, extra large) with the abbreviations used on labels (sample clothing labels are displayed on a handout or on the overhead projector). Then clothing items are passed around the room and students work in pairs to find sizes and complete questions like those below:

Small	Medium	Large	Extra Large
1 M			
2 L			
3 XL			
4 S			
What size is the green shirt?			
What size is the orange shirt?			
What size is the white shirt?			
What size is the dark blue shirt?			

(From Patsy Vinogradov, personal communication)

The theme of health and wellness is found in many ESL curricula. In the following example from an intermediate-level integrated-skills general English class, the teacher brings in over-the-counter medications students may need to use, which are distributed to each class member. The purpose of this task is to give learners practice in finding key information on medicine labels. Each student has the grid and mingles to gather information from classmates to fill in the instructions for each product.

Gathering Information about Medicine

Product	Directions: frequency and amount of dose	Helps the following symptoms	Warnings
aspirin			
antacid			
cough syrup			
decongestant			
nonaspirin pain relief			

Functional reading tasks like the two presented in this section can be created for any type of functional reading text (e.g., washing instructions in clothing labels) or environmental print (e.g., advertisements, signs). It is important that you identify the types of texts that follow set conventions within our culture so that learners gain the skill of reading selectively to find the information they need within a written text. Here are some examples of those types of texts. Can you think of any others? Look back to your list of reading texts that you generated in Task 5.2 on page 126 for ideas.

- Unit pricing at the grocery store
- Pharmacy labels
- Product quantity and measurements
- Bills
- Pay slips
- Classified ads
- ______________________________
- ______________________________
- ______________________________

As you choose content and develop lessons for your learners, pay attention to the types of print around you that are associated with the themes you are teaching in class: street signs and store names for a unit on getting around the neighborhood; pharmacy labels and intake forms for a unit on health and wellness. Analyze the tasks that learners need to complete each day and identify the literacy needs within those daily tasks.

5.2.2 Developing Reading Lessons

Learners at every level encounter longer texts, for example, authentic articles, short stories, or work manuals. They need practice in employing effective reading skills such as anticipating content, inferring meaning of words from context, and interpreting and analyzing the meaning of what they read. A reading lesson unfolds in a series of stages, similar to those described for listening lessons in Chapter 4 (see Table 4.1). Table 5.4 summarizes the reading skills that are typically practiced in a reading lesson, beginning with prereading to activate learners' schema, followed by reading-skills practice, and ending with a follow-up/postreading activity which allows learners to make use of the knowledge gained from the reading text. While lessons should always begin with prereading and end with follow-up, the number of activities in between will vary depending on the level of the learners and type of text used.

Table 5.4 Reading Skills Development: Reading tasks that can be included in a lesson

Reading Skills	Purpose of Activities
1 Anticipating content (prereading)	Activate prior knowledge (schema) and make predictions about the content of the reading.
2 Reading to confirm predictions	Confirm predictions made during prereading.
3 Reading for gist (skimming)	Read for main ideas.
4 Reading for specific information (scanning)	Pick out specific information in a text without understanding every word.
5 Reading for detail	Read more intensively for details of the text. Move from identifying short, factual information, to interpreting the meaning more deeply.
6 Finding meaning of words through context	Use contextual clues to determine meaning of new words.
7 Making inferences	Analyze, interpret, and evaluate the meaning of a text.
8 Transferring knowledge (follow-up/postreading)	Give further practice using the content of the text; check understanding of the text through another medium.

While beginning-level learners will be challenged enough in determining the gist and finding specific information in a reading passage, intermediate to advanced-level students need practice with making inferences and going beyond the factual information presented to them.

The following sample lesson demonstrates the stages common to reading lessons in which learners are working on longer texts and practicing multiple reading skills. The teacher has chosen an article entitled "Border City Goes to

All-Spanish Policy," (see full text on pages 161–162). As you look at the activities, notice the ways in which the teacher helps students to anticipate content, allowing them to connect their prior knowledge about the topic to the article.

Sample Reading Lesson

CLASS DESCRIPTION 22 high-intermediate level learners from a variety of countries

SETTING Pre-academic/Transition English Program

Objectives	
Learners will	• research the English-only movement. • make use of Internet resources. • anticipate content. • read to confirm predictions. • read for specific information. • exchange information they have learned from the text. • express opinions for and against Spanish-only policy. • prepare and conduct city council meeting. • make a decision for or against the policy.

Stage I: Prereading

Objective	To generate the learners' schemata. Prereading tasks serve to get the learners thinking about and talking about the content of what they are about to read. This will enable them to anticipate content and facilitate comprehension of the reading passage.

1 Assigned the day before: Do a search on the Internet to see if you can answer these questions:

What is English Only?

What do supporters of English Only believe?

Do you have English Only policies at your workplace?

2 Report answers to Internet research in small groups and as whole class.

3 These words and phrases are from an article about a group of immigrants. Look at the words and discuss what you believe the article will tell you:

Spanish	English	INS
illegal immigrants	city council	Mexican border
safe haven	official language	

4 Discussion: Do you agree or disagree with the following statements?

a It's a good idea to have 'safe havens' for illegal immigrants.

b Non-native speakers of English should be able to use their first language at work and public meetings.

c In a mostly Spanish-speaking community, government documents and transactions should be done in Spanish.

d City employees should be allowed to ask about anyone's immigration status.

e The INS would never allow a safe haven for illegal immigrants.

Stage II: Reading to confirm predictions

Objective	To enable learners to confirm predictions made during prereading

T Look at the article quickly to check your predictions.

(Give learners article face down and give them one minute to check predictions, then turn article over again).

How many of your predictions were correct? Did you find anything that surprised you?

Stage III: Reading for specific information

Objective	To give learners practice in picking out specific information in a text without expecting them to understand every word

Student A Now read the article to find out if these statements are true or false:

a T/F El Cenizo has made Spanish the town's official language.

b T/F City workers are encouraged to uncover city workers.

c T/F The mayor of El Cenizo doesn't speak English.

d T/F Written ordinances will be in both English and Spanish.

Student B Now read the article to find out if these statements are true or false:

a T/F El Cenizo has a high population of first-generation immigrants.

b T/F The mayor thinks city council meetings should be in English.

c T/F City employees cannot ask about anyone's immigration status.

d T/F Government transactions must be done in Spanish with English translations within a week.

A students answer their questions and help each other; **B** students do the same. **A/B** pairs get together to share the information they found.

Stage IV: Postreading/Follow-up

Objective	To give learners further practice using the content of the text; to further check understanding of the text through another medium

Have students prepare a mock city council meeting to debate the pros and cons of Spanish-only policy.

One team develops list of 'pros' and the other brainstorms list of 'cons.'

Conduct mock meeting.

Debrief: Which team had the strongest arguments?

In this lesson, a substantial amount of time is dedicated to prereading activities. Then students take part in two reading activities, each one approaching the text in a different way. The follow-up activity allows learners to go beyond reading only for factual information; they reflect on the pros and cons of the Spanish-only policy, connecting the reading to their own lives and opinions. Through this lesson, they discover the ways in which English-only and other language policies affect immigrants.

5.2.3 Using Learner-produced Texts

> Students who publish their writings within and beyond the classroom experience many benefits. They discover that the realities of their own lives are worth thinking about, getting down on paper, and sharing with others. When they see their thoughts and concerns and those of others like them in print, they find they have a powerful voice and play a vital role in their new culture (Peyton 1993:60).

Joy Peyton, an expert in adult ESL literacy, makes a strong case for using student-written texts in the ESL classroom. As an offshoot of LEA, ESL teachers and textbook writers have published student-written materials that can then be used as the basis for reading instruction. Doing so has many advantages:

- The texts are simply written and easy to understand.
- The content is relevant to new immigrants as the themes are those chosen by other new immigrants.
- Using stories written by other new immigrants, especially those that have been published, is very motivating for ESL learners.

In her family literacy program, Laura Lenz used project-based learning to create the following learner-produced publications: a cookbook, a world travel book, a family stories book, as well as a video on telling children stories. In the world travel book, students from the same country took responsibility for writing about different topics. Three different students from Liberia wrote these excerpts from the world travel book.

Liberia

People	In Liberia people don't have money, clothes, food, or good water. People make farms before they eat and sell some food at market. They buy clothes at market. In Monrovia our people have businesses and electricity and rent refrigerators. There are different languages like Mano, Gio, Bassa, Kpelle, Vai, Kru, Grebo, Kissi, Loma, and English.

History	Liberia is in west Africa near the Atlantic Ocean. Guinea, Ivory Coast, and Sierra Leone are next to Liberia. Liberia was named by slaves from America who returned to Liberia in 1816. Monrovia is the capitol of Liberia. Monrovia is a city on the west coast of Liberia.
Food	In Liberia in the morning we eat potatoes, cassava with gravy, or doughnuts. Cassava grows on the ground and is big and long. You take off the peeling and boil it or eat it raw. For lunch or dinner we eat rice with meat. We eat goat, chicken, or beef. We also eat fufu with palm butter. Fufu is made out of cassava. Some types of food that grow in Liberia are plaintains, potatoes, eddoes, plums, oranges, coffee, and cocoa. Many people grow their own gardens. They plant potatoes, greens, cabbage, bananas, eggplants, rice, and cassava. When the food is grown, people eat it or sell it.

Excerpts written by three Liberian students from the World Travel Book

In producing these texts, Laura took learners through multiple activities and learners created numerous drafts before publishing their work. (See section 5.3.3 for more ideas on developing written texts like these. For a complete discussion of implementing learner writing/publishing, see Peyton 1993.) The results show the care students take in completing their work as well as the rich content of learner-generated texts. The texts are authentic, yet the level of language in the stories is accessible for other learners with beginning-level literacy skills. Now these texts can be used as the basis for a reading lesson like the one following:

Sample reading lesson with learner-generated texts

I. Prereading

Task 1

Teacher asks class these questions:

T Where is Liberia?
Who can find it on this map?
Do you know anyone from Liberia or other country in Africa?

Task 2

T Let's see how much you know about Liberia. Don't worry if you are not sure. You will read what other students wrote about this country later in the lesson.

Are these sentences true or false? Circle True or False.		
True	False	Most people in Liberia have electricity.
True	False	People speak many languages in Liberia.
True	False	Liberia is on the east coast of Africa.
True	False	Many people buy and sell food at the market.
True	False	Liberia was named by slaves who returned to Africa.

Compare your answers with a partner.

II. Reading activities

The reading on Liberia with the multiple sections makes it ideal for the technique called jigsaw reading. **Jigsaw reading** consists of assigning different reading texts and tasks related to one topic to different groups of learners in a class. Jigsaw reading allows learners to become 'experts' about one topic, which they can then present to their peers. In sharing what they have read, there is a genuine information gap among students since each group member has read something different, i.e., everyone has something new to learn.

T Now you can learn more about Liberia. Some of you will learn about food, some about people, and some about the history.

- Three groups (A, B, and C) are created and each one is given only one section of the reading about Liberia (A: People, B: History, C: Food).
- Each group (A group, B group, C group) is given the worksheet below and must work together to find answers to only their questions.

Work with your group to find answers to these questions.

Group A People	How do people make money? Where do they get clothing? What languages do they speak? How is life in Monrovia?
Group B History	Where is Liberia? How was it named? What is the capitol?
Group C Food	What do people eat in the morning? What do people eat for lunch and dinner? What foods grow in Liberia?

- Once each group has answered the questions for their section, the teacher creates new groups made up of one member from each of the original groups (ABC, ABC, etc.).
- Students in the new groups present the information found in their section on People, History, or Food.

As students listen to their classmates, they write answers to the questions for the sections they did not read.

T Now go back to the true and false questions to see if your guesses were correct.

FOLLOW-UP/ POSTREADING Now interview your classmates to learn some things about the history, people, and foods from their countries. Use the same questions you used for the reading activity.

	People	History	Food
Name Country			
Name Country			
Name Country			

This lesson contained the same stages as the advanced-level reading lesson using an authentic article. The activities for beginning-level reading lessons serve the same purposes: activate prior knowledge, read selectively, and apply the knowledge gained in other contexts.

Conclusion Whether a teacher is working with preliterate students or learners with highly developed literacy skills, all instruction should have some key elements in common. Activities need to reflect the ways in which literacy is situated in learners' lives and teachers need to draw on learners' prior knowledge about the content of the lesson. Learners should be given opportunities to go beyond the information provided in the text and interpret it through their unique experiences, knowledge and interests.

Part III ◆ Teaching Writing to Second Language Learners

5.3.1 Introduction

The Language Experience Approach, Whole Language, and balanced literacy approach all integrate reading and writing instruction. In this section, we look at instructional strategies that focus specifically on developing writing skills for both everyday and academic purposes, including those for the emergent writer as well as more proficient writers.

Getting Started

Task 5.5

Take a few minutes to brainstorm what you have written in the past week. Work with a partner or on your own.

What have you written in the past week?
checks
a note to a friend

Now place the items from your list in one of these two categories: Everyday/Functional Writing or Extensive Writing.

Everyday/Functional Writing	Extensive Writing

Now answer these questions:

1 Which type of writing do you do more often?

2 How is the writing process different for these two types of writing?

5.3.2 Product-oriented vs. Process-oriented Writing

Writing takes on many forms in our lives, everything from jotting down phone messages to writing research papers, and the processes we use to write vary greatly depending on the purpose of the writing task. As you saw in Task 5.5, much of what we write is highly **instrumental,** writing for an immediate, **functional** need such as writing a check or filling out a credit card application. Other types of writing require more planning and revising, for example, a letter to the editor. Table 5.5 provides examples of both functional and extensive writing tasks. How does this compare to your own categories in Task 5.5?

Table 5.5 Types of Writing Tasks

	Functional Writing Tasks	Extensive Writing Tasks
Work-related	Filling in forms to report defects of parts Filling in accident reports Writing resumes	Writing a thank-you letter to a visitor Responding to e-mail requests Writing letters of apology
Academic	Completing registration forms	Writing lab journals Writing essays Writing research papers
Personal	Addressing letters Writing checks	Writing essays for an ESL class Writing a letter to a teacher at school Writing a letter of complaint to a landlord

In teaching writing to ESL learners, there have been two divergent approaches to writing instruction: **product-oriented** and **process-oriented.** In many ways, these two approaches have parallels with the types of writing we do (see Table 5.6).

Writing tasks that follow set conventions and for which the reader has specific expectations, for example, checks or time cards may merit a more product-oriented approach to teaching. These types of functional tasks are not open to interpretation by the writer and often follow conventions that are specific to our culture. Extensive writing tasks, on the other hand, can benefit from the stages of brainstorming, drafting, editing, and rewriting in a process-oriented approach.

TABLE 5.6 Product-oriented and Process-oriented Approaches to Teaching Writing

Product-oriented	• Focus on "getting it right" • Controlled tasks following models • Final product evaluated
Process-oriented	• Focus on the steps that go into writing • Giving and receiving feedback and creating multiple drafts • Initial focus on ideas/content

Task 5.6

Look at this list of writing needs identified by two different groups of ESL students. Which writing needs might benefit from a product-oriented approach, a process-oriented approach, or a combination of the two?

Group I: Intermediate-level adult ESL	**Group II: Advanced pre-academic ESL**
Completing vacation slips	Writing responses to readings
Writing notes to teachers	Writing short essays
Filling out applications for jobs	Writing a research paper
Taking phone messages	Writing lab reports
Writing monthly reports at work	Taking short-answer tests
Writing resumes and cover letters	

Write your answers here:

Product-oriented	**Process-oriented**	**Product-oriented/ Process-oriented**
Taking phone messages		

Follow-up If you are in a class, compare your answers with those of another group. Which of the examples might benefit from a combination of the two approaches? An application form typically contains sections where personal information is recorded: name, address, phone number, work histories. Learners would benefit from the fairly mechanical practice of filling in personal information following a model. What about open-ended questions found on applications? Here learners may benefit from brainstorming possible responses, reviewing their personal strengths, organizing ideas, and then writing, all of which is more process-oriented (Price-Machado 1998).

5.3.3 WRITING FROM THE VERY BEGINNING

At the very beginning levels of instruction, learners need practice in handwriting, spelling, basic grammar structures (tense, word order, subject-verb agreement), punctuation, among other things. These skills should not be taught in isolation, but rather they should be integrated throughout instruction. This section contains an array of writing activities that can be characterized as form-focused and primarily product-oriented. We begin with writing tasks for emergent writers, those with extremely limited experience with writing.

Working with Beginning-level Writers and Beyond

Copying words, making lists, or labeling objects have great benefit for emergent writers, provided that practice is motivating and helps learners to strengthen their writing skills. **Vanishing letters** (Brod 1999) helps learners to build confidence in writing words on their own. Learners begin by copying a complete word. Then the teacher removes one letter at a time until the students write the word on their own:

Street	**S __ r e e t**
	S __ r __ e t
	S __ __ __ e t
	__ __ __ __ e t
	__ __ __ __ __ t
	__ __ __ __ __ __

This technique works equally well with sentences or short paragraphs using vanishing words.

Many of the everyday writing tasks that involve simple prose, for example, writing notes to school or leaving a message for a co-worker, can be developed through **scaffolded writing** (Brod 1999). With this technique, the teacher provides a sample text with key information left out:

	Date: ____________________
Dear ____________________,	
____________________ needs to leave school early today for	
____________________. I will pick her up at ____________________.	
Thank you.	
Yours truly,	
____________________	

Similar to scaffolded writing is the use of **sentence starters,** which provide a framework for developing short prose pieces. In the student-produced World Travel Book (see 5.2.3), the teacher provided students with sentence starters such as these:

I come from ____________________.
____________________ is in ____________________.
In my country, people ____________________.
We eat ____________________.
The capital is ____________________.

The sentences generated through this task were then combined to develop simple paragraphs. Each piece of work was reviewed by the teacher or a volunteer and then the students typed the final drafts during computer class time.

Parallel writing (Raimes 1984) begins by providing students with a written model, after which learners write a text using similar vocabulary, structures, and organization on their own. In *Idea Exchange 1* (Blanton 2002), learners read stories written by other immigrants:

Please read about Lien's family:

> **MY FAMILY**
>
> There are six people in my family: my grandmother, my parents, my older sister, my younger brother, and I. We are from Taiwan, but we live in New Orleans now. We are very close. In the Chinese culture, children live with their parents for a long time. Daughters live with their parents until they get married. After the children are married, parents live with their oldest son. My parents have only one son. They will live with him.
>
> In Taiwan, my father was a sea captain. Now he works in a Chinese restaurant. My mother was a teacher. She doesn't speak enough English to teach in the United States. Now she is a seamstress. My sister, my brother, and I are students. I am an art student at the University of New Orleans. My sister is a business student at the same school. My brother studies biochemistry at Tulane University. My grandmother stays at home. She cooks for us and takes care of the house.

(From Idea Exchange *p. 21, Blanton 2002)*

After completing a variety of reading and grammar activities, students work toward writing a similar story. Activities to prepare them to write their stories include conversations with a partner, drafting, reading to a partner and getting feedback, and rewriting. Parallel writing is used at all levels of instruction; models simply become more complex and varied as learner level increases.

Dictations have been used throughout the ages in language teaching. Provided that the content of sentences or passages that are used is meaningful and related to the content of instruction, dictation is an excellent way to help learners build confidence in their writing, and to check their ability to transfer what they understand orally to writing. Dictation is commonly done in pairs, making it an interactive task as well, as students check for understanding and ask for clarification. Here are just a few ways to make dictation meaningful:

- In a lesson on telephoning, dictate name and phone numbers to a partner.
- To practice pronunciation of number pairs 13/30, 14/40, etc., dictate phone numbers, addresses, or simple equations that use those numbers.
- Dictate short passages that, once checked for accuracy, are used for reading or further writing practice (parallel writing, vanishing words).
- Dictate vocabulary words that have been covered in class for review and to practice spelling.

An alternative to strict dictation is a guided writing technique called **dicto-comp**. The teacher reads a short text, for example, a paragraph, story, or even a short article depending on the level of the learners. After reading the text aloud two or three times at normal speed, the teacher writes key words on the board and has the students write what they can recall from the text. The story and key words provide learners with content while giving them practice at writing in their own words.

These form-focused activities can be used within any teaching approach or type of lesson, for example, with the Language Experience Approach, class-generated texts become the starting point for parallel writing. Vanishing letters or words can be used for portions of the text, or the text can be used for pair dictation. In a contextualized language lesson, students can use scaffolded writing or sentence starters to practice writing short letters or notes, for example, phone messages or letters of complaint to a landlord. Vanishing letters can be used to practice new vocabulary in the lesson (foods, clothing, colors, shops, etc.).

5.3.4 Extensive Writing

Extensive writing tasks generally benefit from a process-oriented approach, which entails pre-writing, planning, drafting, and revising. Table 5.7 outlines stages common to a process-oriented approach.

Table 5.7 A Process-oriented Approach to Writing

1 Identify the purpose	Relay information to a friend in a letter. Academic purposes for writing (essays, research papers, scientific reports).
2 Identify the intended audience	An office worker reading a form. A friend reading a letter. An employer reading a report.
3 Prepare for writing	Brainstorm key ideas alone or with a partner.
4 Organize ideas	Organize ideas using graphic organizers, word webs. Make outlines.
5 Write multiple drafts	Write ideas first, worry about mechanics later. Write multiple drafts. Share drafts with a peer. Self/peer edit.
6 Revise	Revise and write final draft.

The following sample lesson demonstrates how a teacher can employ a process-oriented approach, while at the same time integrating product-oriented activities. This teacher is working on writing resumes with a group of high-intermediate level students in a work-readiness program.

Sample Writing Lesson

1 Prewriting

A Whole class: T: Did you have a job in your country? How did you find that job? What did you need to send to the employer? What do you need to do in the U.S.? (Send in an application or write a resume.)

B Brainstorm information to be included (students work in pairs and then one student gathers and writes information on board).

Things to include on a resume		
work experience	hobbies	age
family situation	education	sports
training	languages	

C Learners look at three sample resumes written by former students who have found jobs. Learners are asked to identify the categories and the types of information included in each. Teacher elicits similarities and differences between what the class predicted and what they found on the samples (e.g., we don't include age and family-status in the U.S.).

2 Organizing information: Creating word webs

A With a partner, students write what they have done in each category and create a word web for each one: personal information, education, jobs, etc.

Example

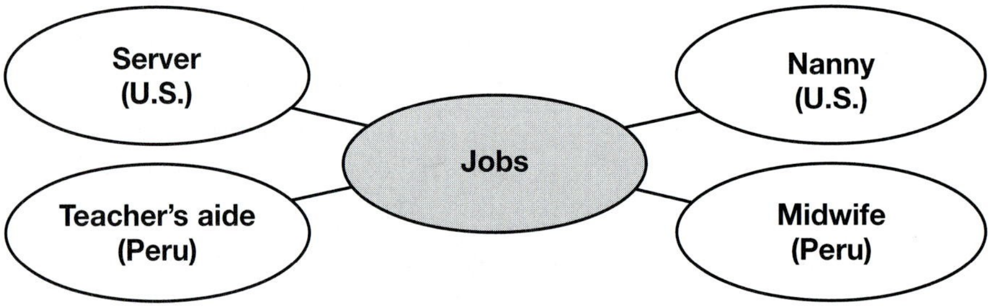

B Transfer information from the word webs to a timeline to organize the information chronologically.

3 Writing first draft

Create first draft of resume.

4 Peer-reading: Classmate Revision Checklist

Classmate Revision Checklist		
Writer's name:		
Checker's name:		
1 Is the resume complete? (If you circled *no*, highlight the incomplete portions.)	YES	NO
2 Did you understand everything your classmate wrote? (If you circled *no*, ask him or her to revise the unclear portion.)	YES	NO
3 Are the verbs in the correct tense? (If you circled *no*, help the writer correct them.)	YES	NO

(Sample questions from Price-Machado 1998)

5 Revision
Revise draft using feedback from peers

This sample lesson serves as one example of the ways in which teachers can implement a process-oriented approach, starting with a brainstorming stage, followed by planning, organizing, drafting, editing, and revising. There are also elements of a product-oriented approach, showing sample resumes that learners can use as one model. There has been a long-standing tradition of using a process-oriented approach in academic ESL courses. The process of planning, organizing, drafting, and revising allows for a clearer and more accurate product. There are many learners who appreciate the opportunity to see examples of what a particular type of writing should look like, for example, a lab report or literature review (Kim Koffolt, personal communication), so even in academic settings, there may well be a place for both approaches to writing instruction.

5.3.5 Using Dialogue Journals with Adult ESL Learners

Developing fluency in writing is just as important as developing oral fluency, and **dialogue journals** are an ideal way of promoting written fluency. A dialogue journal is a regular written conversation between teachers and learners (or among learners) without the constraints of controlled, product-oriented tasks. Learners read and write for a genuinely communicative purpose—the content is real; the teacher response is authentic. Teachers may get a glimpse of what a learner is facing at home or with family, as the following exchange between a teacher and learner illustrates (Isserlis 1996b:58):

Oct. 2

> . . . (my son) is better because He take medice. Thank you for you answer. I and my family are well. And we had a good weekend. Thank my dear teacher . . .

Oct. 23

> . . . How old is (your son) now? Does he sometimes watch TV in English? I think he's lucky, because he is growing up hearing 2 languages-he'll be able to know Spanish and English. Do your other kids speak both languages, too?

Oct. 23

> . . . (my son) have 2 1/2 year old. When He Born he weingh 2 Pounds now he have 27 pounds. he Barn from only sixth month. Some times he watch cartoons But he liked played with her toys. He Can said some words in English. Yes my other Kids speak English and Spanish.

In later exchanges, the student shares problems she is having with high blood pressure. Janet and her student are communicating about topics that may not come out in the more 'public' classroom setting. Isserlis (1996b), Peyton (1996), and others have highlighted many of the benefits of dialogue journals, which are outlined in Table 5.8.

TABLE 5.8 Benefits of Dialogue Journals

1	A focus on communicating personal ideas, thoughts, and feelings can free learners from the fear of making mistakes.
2	Learners are writing for an interested and attentive audience.
3	Rapport and, hopefully, trust is built between/among learners and teachers.
4	Learners can recognize the progress they are making as their entries become longer and more complex.
5	Learners can articulate issues and problems they face in safe, private manner.
6	Common learner issues emerge, which can then shape the curriculum.

Reading and responding to dialogue journals is very time consuming for the teacher and learners. There are a number of ways to make this valuable learning tool manageable for everyone.

- Provide designated class time for journal writing.
- Have peers or volunteers respond to journals every other week.
- In large classes, have half the class hand in journals one week, and the other half the next.

Teachers need to realize that dialogue journals are not intended to be a form-focused endeavor, and the response should be first and foremost about the content of what learners have written. This is not a time to correct learner errors, but rather an opportunity to recognize areas for growth in learners' written language, which can then become the focus of later lessons. For those teachers who want to make corrections or give feedback about learner language, limit the corrections to one or two areas, for example, verb tenses or verb agreement. Another option is to let learners know that for one entry a week, you will respond to their grammar. As learners become more proficient, they may ask that the teacher make more corrections. When teachers get a glimpse of learners' lives and concerns, teaching may become more learner-centered, and dialogue journals are an ideal vehicle through which this can happen.

5.3.6 TECHNOLOGY AND WRITING

Many of the technological tools available to adult education programs provide excellent vehicles for developing writing skills (see full discussion of uses of technology in Chapter 8). In project-based learning, the final product can be displayed online, which can then be viewed by other ESL learners throughout the country. Teachers at Lao Family in St. Paul, Minnesota describe their project that culminated in a Life Stories book, which was produced in print and online.

In September 2001, the students of Lao Family English School were given disposable cameras. "Take pictures of your life," they were told. "Show us your family, your home, your work, anything that's important to you." After some practice shots, they were off and running. Two weeks later, the cameras were returned.

In the weeks that followed, students used their photos in class for a variety of learning activities. They shared their photos with their classmates and teachers, wrote stories, read to each other, and joined in countless conversations about the people and things they'd photographed.

At the end of October, each student was asked to choose three photographs to write about for a "whole school book." Students wrote their stories in class and then typed and printed them in the computer lab.

Cindy Bestland ◆ Tylyn Harper ◆ Patsy Vinogradov
English Instructors ◆ November 2001
http://www.laofamily.org/lifestories/index.htm

Classes can connect with other programs by establishing e-pals to practice writing fluency. E-mail can be used for conducting peer reviews and providing feedback of written drafts. For those students with developed keyboarding skills, e-mail can be used as the vehicle for dialogue journals.

5.3.7 Responding to Learner Writing

An initial response to writing normally focuses on the content of what has been written rather than the form. From there, a teacher needs to ask him or herself: What is the purpose of the writing task? In responding to a journal entry, the teacher may not give any corrective feedback at all since the purpose of the task is simply to gain fluency and unblock some of the inhibitions learners may have in completing more structured tasks. In the case of emergent writers, getting words down on paper is a great achievement in and of itself, as in the following sample. This learner came to class with no literacy, and to the teacher, the entry (Figure 9.10), which was produced more than a year into the program, represents tremendous progress on Elizabeth's part. The teacher, Laura, responds with an encouraging statement about Elizabeth's education, but she does not correct any errors. She focuses on form in writing through other types of activities in her class such as sentence starters, LEA, and parallel writing.

FIGURE 9.10 **Sample journal entry with teacher response**

Name Elizabek
Date 05-14-02

Journal Topic Countries

What i like about my country. the Food,
weather. Sontime Friend Family sit down
together and eat.
oneThing i enjoy about my country is
every Sunday wy go to Church on sunday
NO Wark.

I like the U.S. because i get
help with my education.
my comeing to the us is a bless to i and
my Family. I like every thing about tis
country. Thanks to the U.SA.

Elizabeth,
It is good to have
things about Liberia and the
U.S. that you like.
you are doing so well with
your education!

If a learner were writing a resume or a cover letter, the approach to feedback would be different given the audience for the writing. Many of the considerations in Chapter 3 (Table 3.6) apply here as well, particularly who the learner is and what the purpose of the task is. Feedback to writing begins in the same way oral feedback is given: indicate where the errors are, but don't correct them for the student. The following are some guidelines for teachers to keep in mind:

- Always begin with a response to the content of what learners have written. Provide feedback on what is clear in their writing: *I like the way you described your family members with so much detail.*
- When responding to longer pieces of writing, consider content, organization, discourse (e.g., topic sentences, transitions), syntax, vocabulary, and mechanics (e.g., spelling, punctuation) (Brown 2001).
- Develop consistent conventions that your learners can understand: *sp* for spelling, *T* for tense, underlining for wrong word choice. There are many editing conventions, but it is often best to develop a set of editing marks with your students so you know the marks are understood.
- Provide opportunities for peer review and revision through conferences or group time.
- Develop a realistic sense of what a given learner is capable of producing and do not expect perfection or try to rewrite their work.

Like so many teaching processes and routines, responding appropriately to learner errors takes practice. Teachers need to have a clear idea of what a learner is capable of, and then provide encouragement and feedback that is accessible to that learner. Patience should prevail... language isn't learned overnight!

Conclusion

Attaining literacy in a second language means far more than learning to decode and write words. Literacy involves activities that are conducted in rich social contexts between and among individuals. Attaining literacy in English broadens learners' opportunities in their communities, homes, and jobs. It allows them to attain certain jobs, help their children with schoolwork, and correspond with teachers and others in the community. ESL educators have the task of determining their learners' literacy needs and selecting approaches and contexts for teaching reading and writing that are the most suitable for them.

Key Terms

Checklist of Key Terms	On your own, or with a partner, provide an example or brief definition for each concept.
environmental print	
functional texts	
scanning	
graphic literacy	
schema theory	
receptive skills	
top-down processing vs. bottom-up processing	
preliterate, nonliterate, semiliterate	
Language Experience Approach	
balanced literacy approach	
phonics	
sound/letter correspondences	
skimming	
jigsaw reading	
process-oriented approach	
product-oriented approach	
scaffolded writing	
parallel writing	

graphic organizers	
prewriting	
word webs	
dialogue journals	

APPLYING WHAT YOU LEARNED

1 Reading Skills Development

If you are already teaching and work with pre- or nonliterate learners. . . conduct a language experience with your students. Implement activities suggested in section 5.1.4 and reflect on the benefits the Language Experience Approach has for your learners. Also reflect on any difficulties learners experience and think of alternatives that you might try the next time you use this approach.

If you are working with learners with more developed literacy. . . choose an authentic text (environmental print, a short reading, learner-written materials) that relates to an upcoming unit you are teaching, but for which you haven't integrated reading practice before. Using this text, develop and implement a reading lesson including prereading, two reading activities, and a follow-up activity. After you teach the lesson, reflect on the successes learners had as well as any difficulties they experienced. What would you do differently the next time you teach a lesson like this?

If you are not teaching. . . choose a theme commonly covered in basic skills ESL classes (e.g., shopping, transportation, opening a bank account, describing people—talk to an experienced teacher for ideas).

1. Collect examples of functional reading texts that are associated with the theme you chose (e.g., labels, packaging, schedules).
2. Analyze the skills needed to understand the texts you chose, for example, reading nutritional information requires understanding of numeracy and charts.
3. Create two different activities that would give learners practice with reading these functional texts (see section 5.2.1).

2 Helping Learners with Writing

If you are already teaching. . . reflect on and discuss (or write about) these questions:

1 What are your learners' writing needs?

2 Do their needs involve functional or extensive writing tasks?

3 What would be the best approach for preparing them for those needs: product oriented, process oriented, or a combination of the two?

4 Choose one writing need and develop and implement a writing lesson that addresses it.

If you aren't teaching. . . look at integrated-skills ESL textbooks for three different levels of instruction.

1 What reading and writing practice is provided?

2 Is the focus on functional reading and writing or on intensive reading and extensive writing?

3 What approach is used to teaching writing: product-oriented, process-oriented, or a combination of the two?

RECOMMENDED READING

Anderson, N. 1999. *Exploring second language reading: Issues and strategies.* Boston: Heinle and Heinle.

This accessible text on reading theory and principles provides new and experienced teachers with a framework for teaching reading strategies to ESL students.

Campbell, C. 1998. *Teaching second language writing: Interacting with text.* Boston: Heinle and Heinle.

This text presents key issues in writing and invites the reader to explore his/her own practice.

Crandall, J. and **J. Peyton.** (eds.) 1993. *Approaches to adult literacy instruction.* McHenry, IL: Center for Applied Linguistics and Delta Systems, Inc.

A collection of articles on current approaches to teaching literacy, including competency-based education, Whole Language, the Language Experience Approach, student publishing, and the Freirean, or participatory, approach.

Wrigley, H. and **G. Guth.** 1992. *Bringing literacy to life: Issues and options in adult ESL literacy.* San Mateo, CA: Aguirre International.

A comprehensive introduction to the connections between theory and practice in adult literacy development. The authors provide information on methods and approaches, assessment, technology, and teacher development as well as promising practices from literacy programs across the country.

Useful Websites

National Institute for Literacy (NIFL)

http://www.nifl.gov/

This federal organization offers information about literacy and supports the development of high-quality literacy services.

The Learning Edge

http://thewclc.ca/edge/

An online, interactive literacy project for ESL learners.

ProLiteracy (Laubach Literacy and Literacy Volunteers of America)

http://www.proliteracy.org/

This site has information about domestic and international programs including, Women in Literacy, New Readers Press, and News for You. It also includes a searchable database that can be used to find local programs.

Appendix

Story of Hmong Quilt

In the upper half of this cloth there are scenes of harvesting corn, pounding rice, and feeding animals. The third tier of images shows shamanistic ceremonies and the bottom tier shows traditional courting customs. The mother of the bride is furious when she learns from a messenger that her daughter has been seduced by her would-be husband and threatens the messenger with a stick.

Article for Sample Reading Lesson

Border City Goes to All-Spanish Policy

By Madeline Baro Diaz, Friday, August 20, 1999
Associated Press Writer
El Cenizo, Texas (AP)—Habla espanol?

If not, you might walk into an El Cenizo city meeting and wonder what side of the Rio Grande you're on.

Two weeks ago, commissioners in this small working-class community along the Mexican border passed an ordinance declaring that all city meetings and functions would be held in Spanish. They also passed a measure forbidding city employees to turn in illegal immigrants.

El Cenizo is believed to be the only U.S. city with an all-Spanish policy. English translations of meetings are available but must be requested 48 hours in advance.

"It's not because we don't speak English," said City Commissioner Flora Barton. "It's because we're doing it for those that speak only Spanish, and we want everybody to be comfortable and to understand and to be aware of what's going on here in El Cenizo."

El Cenizo is a largely blue-collar town of 7,800 about 10 miles outside Laredo. Its main streets are paved, but dirt roads also run through the city. Well-kept, modest houses exist side by side with ramshackle homes and buildings. For years, the city had no garbage or ambulance service.

Ms. Barton estimates that more than 90 percent of El Cenizo's residents speak Spanish, though many also speak English. A few people, particularly younger ones, speak only English.

For several years, meetings have been bilingual, since residents routinely asked commissioners to explain things in Spanish, she said. But some Spanish-speakers wouldn't attend city meetings because of the language barrier and were surprised by commissioners' decisions.

The most recent city council meeting, on Aug. 12, was conducted in Spanish after passage of the measure. Ordinances and resolutions still will be written in English, but the city will translate them upon request.

El Cenizo's new policy apparently violates no state laws.

"The attorney general's office is unaware of any state statute or court case or attorney general opinion which directly addresses this question," said Andrea Horton, a spokeswoman for the Texas Attorney General's Office.

English First, a Virginia-based organization working to make English the official language of the country and to undo bilingual education, was troubled by the city's actions.

"El Cenizo is the canary in the mine," executive director Jim Boulet Jr. said Thursday. "I think this is a wake-up call to this country, where in a land where 328 different languages are spoken, that we either are going to speak in one language in this nation of immigrants or we are going to be speaking in many."

In addition to the language measure, El Cenizo passed a Safe Haven Ordinance, forbidding city employees and officials to ask residents whether they are legal immigrants or citizens or to help an agency like the Border Patrol and the Immigration and Naturalization Service find illegal immigrants. City employees who violate the ordinance can be fired.

Ms. Barton said the city will still cooperate with the Border Patrol on other matters, such as stopping drug smuggling.

She said the ordinance is not aimed at making El Cenizo a haven for illegal immigrants. She said residents simply resent constantly having to prove their status to the Border Patrol.

INS spokesman Tomas Zuniga warned: "If there comes a time when we come into conflict with the city ordinances, we would pursue the matter at that time. I don't foresee it going that far, but the extreme level would be where we take action through legal means."

Jessika Silva, director of the El Cenizo Community Center, which offers a basic English class taught by a volunteer, said the Spanish-language ordinance reflects a harsh reality for many people in El Cenizo: "They have to work hard all day so they don't have time to learn English."

But Virginia Salazar, an El Cenizo resident who teaches nutrition at a community clinic, believes the ordinance is wrong-headed.

"We want our children to get educated," she said. "We want them to have better jobs, to progress. It looks like we're going backward instead of progressing."

6

Planning for Teaching and Learning

Part I ◆ Lesson Planning

6.1.1 INTRODUCTION

Planning for teaching and learning is a complex process that needs to take numerous variables into account: Who are the learners? What is the context for learning? What are their needs? What are my own beliefs about teaching and learning? These are among the questions teachers ask themselves as they plan lessons day-to-day. This chapter focuses on the decisions teachers make within their courses and from one lesson to the next. *How can I connect the lesson to learners' lives? What are the objectives of the lesson? What materials will I need? What do I need to review from previous lessons?* These are just a few of the issues addressed in this chapter on planning for teaching and learning.

This chapter covers three important areas of planning for teaching and learning. In Part I we explore the processes teachers use in day-to-day lesson planning as well as the ways careful planning can help promote learner successes in a lesson. In Part II we turn to the importance of planning for some of the key interactions that take place in all lessons, including introductions, directions to activities, and comprehension checks. You will see that those are not elements of a lesson to be left to chance, especially for those new to teaching ESL. Finally, in Part III we explore the importance of developing learner autonomy through the development of learning strategies so that students can continue to progress in their language development outside of the classroom.

CHECKLIST

After reading this chapter and completing the activities, you should be able to

- enumerate lesson-planning considerations.
- identify and articulate learning objectives for lessons.
- describe the characteristics of a balanced lesson.
- describe how to achieve consistency from one lesson to the next.
- use teacher language that minimizes extraneous talk.
- create checking questions that allow learners to demonstrate their understanding of concepts.
- define learning strategies and integrate practice of them in lessons.

Getting Started

There are just as many ways to plan lessons as there are teachers planning them. Planning takes on many forms for different teachers: some carefully script their lessons, while others keep key questions in mind as they choose activities and materials, simply writing reminders for themselves. From my own experience, those teachers new to ESL benefit from detailed lesson plans with objectives that are clearly articulated, a list of materials, descriptions of activities and interactions, and prepared questions to be used in introductions to a topic, directions, transitions and comprehension checks. This is not to imply that the plan should dictate every twist and turn the lesson takes—a good teacher is one who takes the learners' lead. From my observations, however, it is clear that learners who feel that there is purpose and direction in a lesson are more likely to participate in class and contribute to discussions. Careful planning also builds teacher confidence, which in turn inspires confidence in the learners.

Task 6.1

I asked several teachers to describe how they plan for their ESL classes. Some of the teachers responded in terms of long-range planning, and others talked about what they do day-to-day to plan each lesson. Read excerpts from their responses below and write examples of things these teachers consider related to each of the areas listed in the table. Think of other considerations and add some of your own to the table as well:

Lesson Planning Considerations

1 Learner needs	
2 Choosing and organizing content	
3 Objectives	
4 Review	
5 Learner involvement	
6 Materials	
7 Activities	
8 Flexibility	
9 Evaluation	

Patsy (Adult Literacy): Here are some of the things I keep in mind and ask myself constantly as I plan:

How will the students get a decent mix of literacy and oral skills during this lesson? How will I make the new information relevant? By this I mean, how is this topic/skill related to their lives—how can I help them understand that it is both important and achievable? How can I incorporate authentic materials into this lesson? This is so important for adults, but it's not always easy with lower levels. It requires LOTS of time to find pictures, make manipulatives, haul in realia and props, etc. But, it's always worth it. How can I make this lesson more interactive? How will the students talk/write with each other and share real information/thoughts with me and each other during this lesson?

Suzanne (ESL section of Freshman Literature Course)

For each of the topics or themes or texts (literature class) I cover, I try to assess or determine the students' knowledge/background and familiarity about the topic in both their own culture and the U.S. Based on that, and on the syllabus/course objectives, I redefine or set new objectives for what I hope the students get from the topic. I evaluate their work and response, and I also evaluate/review the topic or text to consider if or how I would use it in the future.

Bonnie (General English Integrated-skills with international students and adult immigrants)

I try to plan my lessons immediately after class ends as I'm most aware then of anything that needs review or additional practice. It's pretty sketchy—as I've usually done them all plenty of times before—but I think it's important to link them and the time planned for each to the students' needs and the objectives for the day. I guess that's what's most important for me in lesson planning —adapting much-used plans and activities to meet the needs of the students in the current class.

Celeste (Intensive EL Civics and Lifeskills Class)

For an academic year (four quarters) each teacher develops a curriculum map. The map is divided into three sections: Civics, Lifeskills, and Grammar. Per quarter we set an outline [changeable based on student need] of Civics (elections, community info, holidays, cultural readings) objectives and activities, Lifeskills (CASAS competency-based) objectives and activities, and Grammar objectives and activities.

Per Week: I plan for a quarter in week chunks. For each week I set a Civics topic to cover, a lifeskills topic (maybe they overlap), and choose a grammar topic to cover (or continue covering for hefty topics like simple past). Then I plan the 15-hour week around the three areas.

Beth (Transition Class)

The whole spectrum of planning ESL classes, from choosing course content to how each day progresses, is ideally an ongoing dialogue between myself and my Advanced Level D class. At this level, students are deeply involved in goal-setting and self-assessment. Currently each student is involved in creating a folder of various tests and assessments of their interests, learning styles, strengths, challenges, specific learning strategies, and so on. This helps students learn what their specific goals and needs are, and they can negotiate with me and the others in class to get their needs met. Since this is the final stage before mainstream work or higher education, each student knows his or her task is to become fully responsible for learning, with the instructor present as informant and facilitator.

Follow-up These excerpts illustrate the range of considerations that go into planning lessons. While each of these teachers answered the question *What goes into planning the ESL classes you teach?* differently, there are some common themes and considerations in their responses, particularly in regard to organizing the lesson in relation to learners' needs and previous learning.

In her work on course design (Graves 2000), Kathleen Graves suggests that the process teachers use to plan for learning is best represented as a system of interconnected variables, which includes assessing needs, formulating goals and objectives, defining the context for learning, articulating beliefs, conceptualizing content, developing materials, and designing an assessment plan. While her work focuses on the larger process of designing whole courses, her emphasis on planning as a cycle, not only a set of steps to follow, is echoed in many of the teachers' thoughts on lesson planning above. In the discussion that follows, we examine these key areas of lesson planning:

- Determining learner strengths, needs, and expectations
- Identifying clear learning objectives
- Connecting lessons to learners lives and needs
- Choosing materials that are relevant to the learners
- Balancing activities and content in a lesson
- Connecting one lesson to the next
- Assessing whether students have mastered content

We will see that all of these factors come together as a system for planning that is flexible and responsive to learner needs, rather than a linear, step-by-step process.

6.1.2 IDENTIFYING LEARNER NEEDS

In order to ensure instruction meets the needs of learners whose motivations and expectations vary greatly, a teacher needs to collaborate with learners to identify the goals for instruction. That does not mean that every time you teach a class, you need to create a completely new curriculum. In fact, often times an ESL teacher comes into a program that has previously determined and articulated **goals** and expected **outcomes** for each level. If there is an assigned textbook, that, too, helps to shape the curriculum. Celeste uses a curriculum map for planning each term, which includes civics, life skills, and grammar; then she modifies the map each term based on learner needs. Suzanne does the same thing; her literature course may cover the same topics and themes each time, but she modifies class activities based on her learners' prior experience with and reactions to the materials. State or national standards also influence the goals and content of classes, especially in programs that serve large numbers of students and offer multiple levels of instruction (Chapter 10 includes a discussion of those types of standards). Regardless of established goals for a course, each group of learners is unique and needs to take different pathways to meet the goals and outcomes of the curriculum.

There are a number of ways students can have a voice in shaping instruction. The teacher's job is to develop tools and techniques for eliciting learner input that are manageable for the learners. For students with developed literacy skills, brainstorming, and writing down and ranking their wants and needs are manageable tasks. Low-literacy learners can articulate and prioritize their wants and needs as well by using pictures and drawings that represent their ideas. At a family literacy program I visited, the teacher had students create collages with photographs from magazines that depicted learner wants and needs. These learners had minimal literacy skills, but they were able to orally present their collage to the teacher and to the class. A teacher at the same site asked mothers to articulate parenting and language goals, and then had them create visuals using photographs and drawings, which were posted throughout the room (see Maria's representation below).

Many programs use individual learning plans and goal setting as part of the intake process. These processes should not be one-time events that occur only at the beginning of a course. Learners should revisit and rearticulate there needs on an on-going basis, which means that needs assessment becomes an integral part of day-to-day planning. Beth sees on-going self-evaluation as a way of building her learners independence and autonomy as they prepare to move from her transition course into higher education.

6.1.3 Sitting Down to Plan

The steps a teacher takes to plan each lesson vary depending on the teaching context, program curriculum, and even the approach or philosophy to teaching. While program goals and outcomes are there to guide your planning, each class develops its own road map to meet its destination. Lesson plans become the teacher's road map. If you are using a textbook, sometimes the themes and activities in the book determine the **objectives** for the day. In a class using the Language Experience Approach, the class-generated text becomes the focus of many of the teacher's decisions about what areas of language to practice, and/or might supplement other texts and topics being used. Some components of lesson planning logically precede others, for example, researching a grammar rule and patterns before designing an activity that practices that grammar point, or choosing the context or theme before collecting visuals and realia. Table 6.1 outlines the areas a teacher needs to consider in planning.

TABLE 6.1 Lesson Planning Checklist

1	What will the students accomplish in this lesson? The answers to this question become the learning objectives for the day or rationale for the lesson: Why are we doing this?	Identifying and articulating clear **objectives** for the day helps to guide learning. There are many types of objectives, but what they all should have in common is a focus on what the learners will accomplish through the lesson, not on what the teacher does in the lesson. These objectives may relate to skills, competencies, functions, grammar, culture, learning strategies, or civic involvement. Here are some examples: • Students will be able to greet others and introduce themselves. • Students will be able to make requests over the phone. • Students will learn about after-school services provided for their children. • Students will choose an appropriate free after-school activity for their child.
2	What specific target language do I want the students to produce? Is there any vocabulary they'll need?	The **target language** is the linguistic focus for the day. Is the objective for students to produce phrases for making polite requests? Perhaps you want to focus on simple past tense. You need to identify the language students need in order to accomplish real-world tasks.
3	If this is a grammar or functional lesson, what do I need to know about the form and meaning of the language?	If you are talking about life circumstances, you may be teaching the present perfect tense: *Subject + have/has + past participle (I have lived here for 7 years).* Do you know what a past participle is? Do you know when to use *for* or *since* with this structure? Do you know when we use this tense in English instead of the simple past *(I moved here in 1997)*? Even if you don't teach explicit grammar rules to your students, you need to do your homework about the forms (see suggested grammar resources).
4	If this is a reading, writing, listening, or speaking lesson, what sub-skills do I want learners to practice?	In an LEA lesson, students may use the class-generated text to practice sequencing or recognizing sound-spelling correspondences. In a listening lesson, students may listen for gist or specific information.
5	What contexts or themes could I use that are relevent to my students, the objectives, and the target language?	Many times your program has identified a set of competencies as the outcomes for the level you are teaching (ask for, give, follow, or clarify directions; recognize and use signs related to transportation; interpret transportation schedules and fares; use maps relating to travel needs). Contexts or themes you choose in order to meet these outcomes can vary depending on your students. What forms of public transportation do they use? How do they get around their neighborhood or the community? Use their life circumstances as the context for presenting and practicing the competencies. How do you know about their life circumstances? Continually embed assessment of this into lessons.
6	What are some authentic materials, visuals, realia, etc. that I could use related to the context?	In a basic skills class, you need to support learning with realia (real objects, for example fruit and vegetables) or visual aids. Use circulars from the newspaper for lessons on shopping. In a lesson on accessing schools, bring in school bulletins, conference forms, etc. In a lesson on calling in sick to work, bring in telephones. Check to see what resources are available at the school.

7	How does this lesson relate to previous lessons? What do students already know? What can I recycle?	Constantly review and recycle language and themes from one lesson to the next. We do not learn something after one try. Sequence language forms in terms of what you have already covered, e.g., the present continuous *(I am studying English)* typically follows and is contrasted with simple present *(I work at a hospital).* ESL textbooks usually do the sequencing for you, or can provide models to consider/adapt.
8	What activities best serve to move learners towards meeting the lesson objectives?	Choose activities that naturally generate the target language that is the focus for the day. For example, in a lesson on the passive forms *it is made of/ it is used for,* have learners role play looking for an item for which they don't know the name at a hardware store. Shopper: I need a tool that's made of metal and wood. It's used for hitting nails. Clerk: You need a hammer. Also, choose activities that allow learners to use the language they need to know in *their* lives.
9	How will I evaluate learner success and the success of the lesson?	Include activities that enable learners to *demonstrate* their level of comfort and ability with a particular language point, skill, or strategy, and observe them using the language. Take note of areas that are most difficult for them to review and recycle in later lessons. Ask learners to reflect on what they learned each day.

(Many of the questions were drawn from Julia Reimer's Lesson Planning Grid, *TEFL Certificate Course Reader, Hamline University)*

I have found that many teachers new to ESL put too much emphasis on activities before considering learner needs, objectives, context, and connections to previous learning. I always remember the time when a student teacher in our Certificate Program came to my office for advice about her upcoming lesson in the practicum. Our conversation went something like this:

Betsy So what theme or language area do you have in mind?

Chris I really want to do a find-someone-who mingle about personal interests.

Betsy Well, that might be an activity you could use at some point, but it all depends on the objectives you have for the lesson. What have you noticed the students need more work on as you've observed the class these past weeks?

Chris Well, I know that a lot of them want to talk about jobs, but I really thought that activity you demonstrated on personal interests was fun.

What is guiding Chris's decision about what to teach in the lesson? Like Chris, many teachers think of teaching as a series of activities when, in fact, the activities should be among the last things to consider in planning. As the conversation continued, I urged Chris to look at the theme of jobs and to articulate some skills and language around that theme that might be useful for these students. She ended up doing a lesson on reading job announcements, which led to mock interviews the next day. She included a personal and professional interests survey as one of her prereading activities.

Equally important in the planning process is ensuring that your lessons have a balance of interactions, language skills, and learning modes. McKay and Tom (1999) compare a balanced lesson to a balanced meal, where a lack of balance will make the lesson less than satisfactory for many of the learners. They suggest that teachers evaluate their choices of activities in a lesson in terms of groupings, skills, difficulty, and learning modes (see Table 6.2 for a detailed outline of these factors). It has been found that learners may exhibit variation in accuracy across different language tasks; they may do extremely well on a discrete-point, fill-in-the blank activity, yet show minimal accuracy when using the language in an open-ended task; the communicative demands of a task may affect performance (Tarone and Parrish 1994). These findings underscore the importance of providing an array of activity types to practice particular language points within each lesson.

TABLE 6.2

Factors to Consider	Some Questions to Ask Yourself
Groupings: whole group, small groups, pairs, and individuals	Is there a balance between whole group, small group, and individual work? Is the grouping appropriate for the task at hand?
Language skills: reading, writing, listening, and speaking	Have I integrated a variety of language skills?
Difficulty: Easy, medium, and hard	Do I have some easier activities that build to more difficult ones? Do I include familiar language? In an evening program, do I want to start with more demanding activities before the students become tired?
Learning modes: seeing, hearing, saying, doing, thinking, feeling, and interacting	Am I promoting a variety of learning modes? Will this lesson appeal to a variety of learning styles?

(McKay and Tom 1999:20)

Task 6.2

In Chapters 3, 4, and 5, a number of sample lesson plans were provided. Now examine two of those lessons from a lesson planning perspective. Look at these two contextualized language lessons in Chapter 3: Telephoning on page 58 and Sharing Life Stories on page 64. Evaluate them using these questions:

1	Is there a balance between whole group, small group, and individual work? Is the grouping appropriate for the task at hand?
2	Has the teacher integrated a variety of language skills?
3	Are there some easier activities that build to more difficult ones?
4	Does the teacher promote a variety of learning modes? Will this lesson appeal to a variety of learning styles?
5	Do the activities move learners toward meeting the objectives of the lesson?

6 Are the activities and materials connected to the learners' lives?

Follow-up Compare your answers with others in your class. Is there anything that you would do differently in the lessons you evaluated? You can use this checklist to reflect on and evaluate your own lessons and those that you observe.

This section has examined the many considerations teachers need to take into account as they plan lessons from one day to the next. How does all of this relate to the lesson planning requirements of a school? What does the final lesson plan look like? Is there a set convention for lesson plans? Many districts provide teachers with templates for lesson plans. The problem with that is that no one template could possibly account for every type of lesson; that is why I have presented lesson planning as a process that brings multiple considerations together. Table 6.3 illustrates a range of lesson types and designs:

TABLE 6.3 Sample Lesson Plan Templates

Reading Lesson Class Description: Setting: Time: Materials: Assumptions:	**Objectives** Learners will: (These objectives will be related to reading skills: anticipate content, read to confirm prediction, scan for specific information, etc. Depending on the pre- and postactivities, there may be listening, speaking, writing, or vocabulary objectives as well.)	**Lesson Stages** Prereading: Reading activities: Follow-up/Postreading:
Contextualized Language Lesson Class Description: Setting: Time: Materials: Assumptions:	**Objectives** Learners will: (These will be related to the competencies and functions presented and practiced in the lesson as well as linguistic competence: grammar, vocabulary, spelling, and pronunciation.)	**Lesson Stages** Language used in real-life context: Practice in meaningful contexts: Application/Extension:
LEA Lesson Class Description: Setting: Time: Materials: Assumptions:	**Objectives** Learners will: (These will start with completing the experience and the other objectives will relate to developing basic literacy: copying the text, identifying sounds/letters, etc.)	**Lesson Stages** Conduct experience: Generate story: Multiple language activities that revolve around class-generated text:

Clearly, there are a multitude of possibilities when it comes to lesson-plan formats. Find out what the expectations are of your program and design lessons in keeping with those expectations, while at the same time acknowledging that there is no 'one size fits all' plan.

6.1.4 Building Continuity from Day to Day

Teachers need to think beyond day-to-day planning in the choices and decisions they make about their lessons. Celeste refers to planning in one-week chunks, and within those chunks she makes sure to include life skills, civics, and grammar. The teacher for the class depicted in Table 6.3 plans her Adult Basic Education Level 1 class in much the same way, viewing one-week blocks as the time frame for her lesson plans.

Table 6.4 A One-week Plan for Adult Basic Education Level 1 Class

Each class period: 3 hours				
Monday	**Tuesday**	**Wednesday**	**Thursday**	**Friday**
Finish lesson on greetings and introductions. Preview vocab. for bank realia (deposit slips, etc.). Make predictions about experiences class will have at bank. Field trip to the bank for language experience.	Brainstorm questions about bank; use those to generate LEA story. Write language experience story together. Copy story; give story a title.	Sentence scramble (reorder words in sentences from LEA story). Sequence sentences from story.	Cloze activity with text (leave out all verbs in past tense). Co-construct dialogue for opening a bank account.	Role-play opening a bank account. As class, preview forms for opening accounts.

At this level, learners take part in only one or two activities a day, so a teacher needs to think of balancing learning not only within a lesson, but also across lessons over an extended period of time. If we look at only one class session in the one-week plan above, there is not a lot of variation of skills, modes of learning, or interactions. But if we look at the whole week, we see a very balanced plan that includes reading, writing, listening, and speaking as well as civics education, and the competency of opening a bank account.

Another way to build continuity in ESL classes is to establish **curricular routines.** Celeste shared with me that planning for 15 hours a week with the same group of learners was, at first, a daunting task. She decided to build some routines into her weekly plan: a life skills listening lesson every Wednesday after the break, a reading lesson on Thursday, Fridays for the computer lab. Here is an outline of the reading routine she uses every Thursday:

1. At the beginning of class, each table is given one word used in the context of the reading and has to create a simple definition and picture for their word. (Celeste chooses words that build schema for the reading.)
2. Each group sends a member from their table to the board to write the definition and draw the picture.
3. Each group shares their word with the whole class.

4 Based on these key words, Celeste elicits predictions about the story and writes them on the board.

5 Learners read to confirm those predictions.

6 Learners read for more detail with specific questions that are assigned as homework.

Celeste chooses short readings that relate to themes she is covering that week. I observed her class on two separate Thursdays and was struck by how quickly the groups engaged in these prereading activities. No time was lost in trying to explain the tasks and the learners took control of the entire process.

Another way to ensure continuity in lesson planning is to choose topics and themes around which learning is organized for an extended period of time (a week, a month, even a term). Woodward and Lindstromberg (1995) refer to these themes as **threads** for lesson planning. Adams and Ferlet (2002) report on the way they use the theme of food to teach multiple skills to a group of preliterate Somali women. They begin an extensive unit by teaching the vocabulary of food items common to their culture, as well as fruits and vegetables available in the area in which they are now living. The flow chart below illustrates the ways they branch out and expand the theme throughout an entire term.

Theme-based Teaching

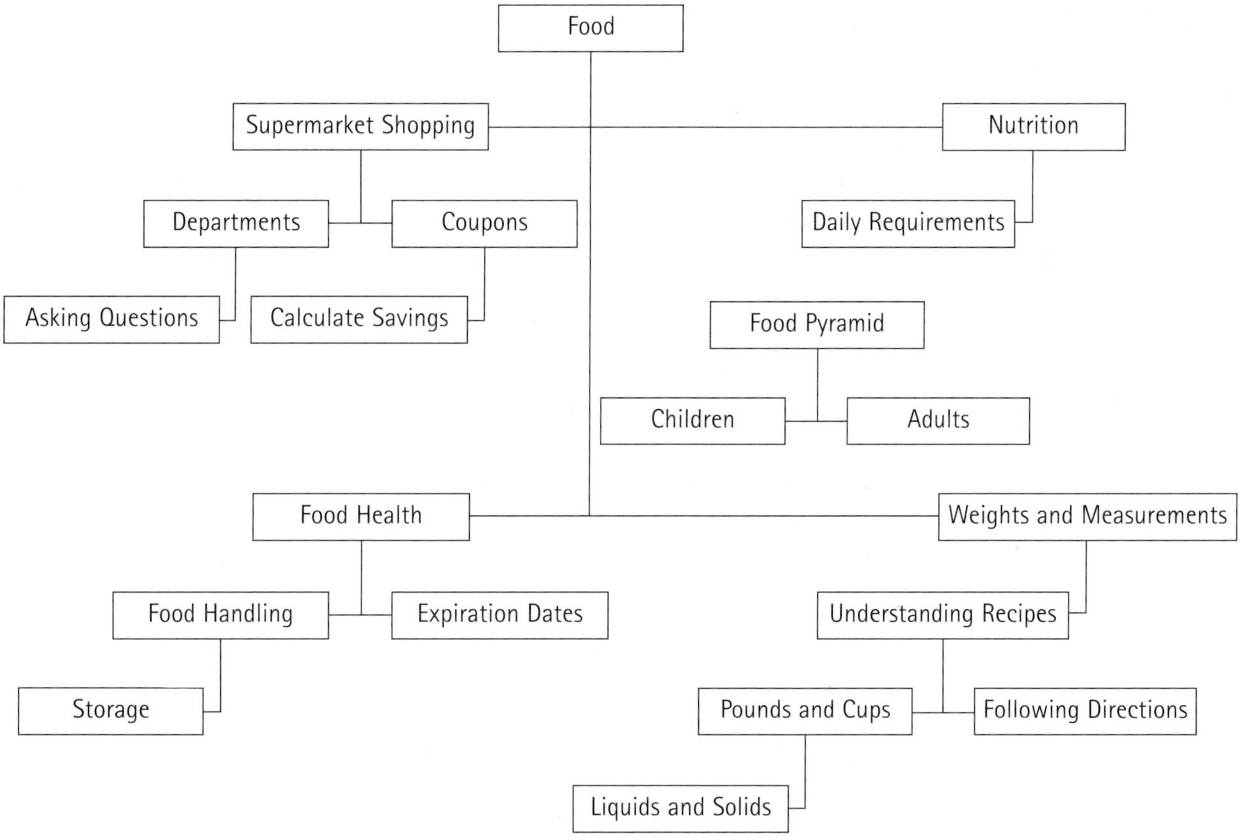

Project-based learning (2.1.10) is yet another means of providing a strong thread for learning. Themes and activities within PBL provide rich language practice that is continuous and connected to learners' lives. Susan Gaer (1998c) reports on successful folktale and cookbook publishing projects that emerged from learners' concerns about passing on cultural traditions to their own children. The World Travel Book project presented in Chapter 5 was the basis for extensive, interconnected lessons that integrated reading, writing, listening, and speaking as learners planned, wrote, read, and presented their stories to one another and to others in the community.

6.1.5 Setting Objectives that Challenge Learners

A final consideration in lesson planning is the degree to which the lesson truly challenges students. Scogins and Knell (2001), in a large study of adult education classes, found that teachers tend to seek mostly factual information from learners rather than interpretive information. Often they do not promote higher-order thinking skills such as inference, analysis, evaluation, or application to learners' lives or the outside world. Teachers use many **display questions,** which are those for which the teacher knows the answer, e.g., *What happened to Alex at the end of the story?*, rather than questions that elicit learners opinions or analysis of material, e.g., *How do you think Alex felt at the end of the story?* In evaluating a lesson, a teacher can ask himself or herself the following questions:

- Do the activities challenge learners to create extended and meaningful responses, rather than one-word utterances?
- Does the lesson move learners beyond gathering factual information to analyzing and interpreting information?
- Have I included questions that elicit deeper analysis of material, even with beginning-level learners?
- Does the lesson allow learners to see application to their lives?

Conclusion Planning lessons is a complex process that needs to take into account the learner's strengths, needs, and expectations. Teachers then identify learning objectives that are achievable and related to what the *learners* will do in the lesson, not what the teacher will do. Those objectives need to promote higher-order thinking skills and challenge the learners to go beyond basic skills development. Using themes, projects, routines, and review helps to establish continuity and build learner confidence. All of these considerations work together to inform lesson planning, resulting in lessons that are flexible and responsive to what happens on any given day, at the same time guiding the learners and teachers on the best path possible to meet the learning objectives. In the next section, we turn to the importance of planning for interactions that occur within every lesson so that teacher language, directions for activities, and questions that check comprehension enhance rather than get in the way of learning.

6.2.1 Teacher Language

The language that teachers use in class, or **teacher talk,** can have a tremendous impact on the success of interactions they have with their students. This teacher talk falls in to several categories:

- Directions for activities
- Direct instruction
- Warm-up chats
- Transitions
- Feedback
- Checking understanding

All of this discourse is appropriate in an ESL class provided that it is conveyed using language that is accessible to students. In Chapter 1 you learned that input should be just beyond the level of the learners (Krashen's i+1); teacher talk that is i + 10 will not be helpful, and will get in the way of learning. Which of these teacher instructions in French can you understand?

a Écoutez et répétez, s'il vous plait.

b Ouvrez vos livres à la page 76.

c J'aimerez que vous m'écoutiez et que vous répétiez les phrases suivantes après moi.

d Si vous voulez, vous pouvez ouvrir vos livres à la page 76.

I am guessing that many of you could ascertain the meaning of items a. (*Listen and repeat, please*) and b. (*Open your books to page 76*); they are direct and to the point, and within the reach of most learners, especially when combined with gestures. But what about c. (*I'd like you to listen and to repeat the following sentences after me.*) and d. (*If you would like, you can open your books to page 76*). Unless you've studied French, I imagine that many of the words were out of your reach. Items c. and d. include extraneous teacher talk, i.e., the majority of the words are not needed to convey the intended message. Not only that, but the language used is indirect and grammatically complex. It may seem that no teacher would use language like samples c. and d. with learners new to English but, as you read the examples below, you may be able to imagine yourself saying these things:

e Would you mind moving over there next to Alexis?

f Who can tell me what is happening in this picture?

g What kind of weekend did you have?

h The first thing we're going to do today is a dictation.

In fact, many teachers new to ESL fear that by simplifying their language too much, they will talk down to students, which is a valid concern. Minimizing teacher talk does not mean dummying down language to the point of using incomplete, unnatural utterances. On the other hand, using indirect, polite language can make the directions ineffectual to the learner who hasn't acquired polite modals or indirect questions. "*What did you do this weekend?*" is much easier to understand than the question: "*What kind of weekend did you have?*" Giving a step-by-step account of each stage in your lesson (*The first thing…, Now I'll give you a handout…*) adds no value to the instruction. All of the items above represent the way we naturally interact with other native-English speakers; in an ESL class, excessive words can clutter the air, making it difficult for the beginning-level learner to pull out what is truly important.

6.2.2 Maximizing Learner Involvement

In Part I of this chapter, I talked about the importance of learner input in shaping the content of instruction. Learner involvement is also about the roles students take on in the class. With every decision you make about a lesson, you need to think about the roles and responsibilities learners take on so that they are doing most of the work and taking the lead. When teachers in our program reflect on their lessons, I ask them a question that I learned from Jack Richards at a TESOL convention session on teacher reflection:

What did I do in this lesson that my learners could have done?

This question has become something of a mantra for me because far too often I see teachers doing all of the work for the learners.

Task 6.3

Read each of these excerpts from adult ESL lessons plans and answer these questions:

What are the roles of the students and teacher in each one?

What does the teacher do that the students could be doing?

How can you change the scenario so that the students take on more of a teaching role?

1 Review of sequence words and imperatives

T gives each student an ingredient for a recipe.

T gives each step of the recipe: *First, put the butter in the bowl.*

Learners come to the front of the room and add an ingredient as their step is called out.

2 Correcting a listening activity on store announcements

After completing a listening activity, T displays the grid learners completed for the listening task on an overhead transparency and elicits correct answers from the whole class to fill in the grid.

3 Practice of numeracy using grocery ads

T calls out the names of two items in a newspaper circular.

Students scan to find items.

Students tell teacher which item is a better deal, taking into consideration the number of ounces, price per pound, etc.

Follow-up The instructional choices the teachers made in these lessons are sound in terms of the content they have chosen and the activities they have prepared. But what is lacking is an awareness of learner responsibility and involvement in these segments. If these teachers asked themselves the question *What did I do in this lesson that my learners could have done?*, they may have come up with some of the solutions you found in the task above. As you plan your lessons, look at them critically *before* you walk into class and evaluate the roles and responsibilities you've given your learners. The more they take responsibility for activities the better; the more you are talking and leading, the more they are only listening and following.

6.2.3 Giving Directions

One of the most important (and most difficult) things for new teachers is learning how to give clear directions; after all, if the students don't know what they are supposed to be doing, they won't get very far. My mottos have always been "Just do it!" and "Less is more."

"Just do it!" represents the need for teachers to demonstrate, or do an activity, rather than explain it. Once having demonstrated the activity with a student, have two students try one item for the whole class.

"Less is more": The fewer words used, the better. Lengthy or multistep explanations are difficult for beginning-level learners to follow. Identify the steps to the activity and demonstrate each step, one at a time, as it is needed to complete the task at hand.

Task 6.4

Look at the sample activity.

Talking about interests and hobbies

1 How do you like to spend your time after work or on the weekend? Circle three things you like to do. Cross out three that you never do. Write three other things you like to do in your free time.

swim	visit family	listen to music	go to the library
garden	cook for friends and family	visit friends	read
sew	watch television	take walks	exercise

Three other things you like to do: ________________________________

2 Now talk to the other students in class and find the person who has the most things in common with you. Ask that person the following questions:

How often do you do that activity?

What do you like about that activity?

What are some things you did in your country that you can't do in the U.S.?

Now read two versions of directions for completing the activity. Which directions are more effective? What is it that makes them more effective? Talk to your partner or write your answers in your journal.

Sample directions for activity: Talking about interests and hobbies

<table>
<tr><th>Version A</th><th>Version B</th></tr>
<tr><td>Teacher distributes handout to class.

Teacher: Now you are going to talk about things you like to do after work or on the weekend. I want you to circle three things you like to do, cross out three you don't like to do, and add three more things you like to do. After you finish, talk to people in class and find the person who has the most in common with you. Ask them the questions at the bottom of your handout.</td><td>**Teacher:** Mai, what do you like to do on the weekends?

Mai: I like to read.

Teacher: So do I. (T places sample handout on overhead and circles 'read'.) Do you ever sew?

Mai: No.

Teacher: Neither do I. (T crosses off 'sew'. T distributes handout to class.) Marco, what do you do on the weekend?

Marco: Play soccer. (T uses questioning look.) Do you see soccer on the list? (T points to overhead.)

Class: No. (T asks Marco to write it in on the blank. T and class now read instructions together.)

Teacher: What do you circle?

Class: Things we do on the weekend.

Teacher: What do you cross out?

Class: Things we don't do.

Class completes part 1 individually and then T gives instructions for part 2 through a similar demonstration.</td></tr>
</table>

Follow-up What is the key difference between the two versions? In Version A, the teacher describes the activity, but doesn't demonstrate what learners need to do. She doesn't check for understanding or have learners interact with her. While Version B might seem longer, there are no lengthy explanations. The teacher is having a meaningful conversation with her students as she demonstrates the activity. The teacher and students walk through a sample of the activity together, she asks checking questions that allow learners to demonstrate their understanding and, most importantly, she models what they need to do.

6.2.4 Checking Learner Understanding

A family literacy instructor who was new to working with immigrant families shared the following incident with me:

> We organized a special after-school meeting with families in our program. I told my students that we would be meeting from 2:30 until 4:30 in the school cafeteria. I arrived at 2:20 to set things up and waited for the families to arrive. Two of the families came at 2:30, but the others arrived between 3:00 and 4:00. One family came right before we were finishing up the meeting. I was so surprised and quite disappointed. I asked the families why they came so late, and they appeared confused, saying they came between 2:30 and 4:30 as instructed.

As an ESL professional, this story did not surprise me at all. For one thing, in many cultures, coming between 2:30 and 4:30 means arriving *any* time between 2:30 and 4:30. I also know that many people who have not had experience working with immigrants do not check for understanding when they give instructions. Or, if they do, they often ask *Do you understand?* or *Is that clear?*, to which the students say *yes* or nod their heads. In this case, what the learners understood was quite different from what the teacher intended.

Understanding can be about:

- Language: The learners misunderstand the words used by the teacher.
- Culture: The students' cultural concepts may be different, e.g., the use of *from_ to _* to denote a time frame.
- Background: The learners' understanding and interpretations of events are shaped by their own life experiences, which are different from the teacher's and from their classmates'. This means that everyone in the same room can have different interpretations of the same events.

Why do people say they understand when in fact they may not? There are a number of reasons, many of which are true for all of us:

- The learners believe they have understood.
- They want to show respect for the speaker; in some cultures, saying "I don't understand" means *You weren't clear so I couldn't understand you.*
- They want to save face (as we all do).

Given these factors, teachers need to check for understanding in ways other than asking "Do you understand?". Had the family literacy teacher used **checking questions** like the following, there may not have been confusion about the start time of the meeting:

T The meeting is from 2:30 to 4:30. So what time do you need be in the cafeteria?

Class 2:30 (If they reply that they can arrive between 2:30 and 4:30, you can clarify and check again. The checking question reveals the holes in comprehension without intimidating the students.)

T How long is the meeting?

Class Two hours.

This same approach can be used when teaching language points. You have been working on the present perfect (I *have lived* here for 12 years), which the students confuse with the simple past (I *lived* here for 12 years).

T I have lived here for 12 years. When did I move here? Do I *still* live here?

If you need to check understanding of a vocabulary item, use the same approach.

T I need to hire a babysitter for my kids. I want someone who is *prompt.* Does a prompt person come late or on time? My kids get off the bus at 3:00. What time does the babysitter need to be at my house?

Notice that these checking questions allow the learners to demonstrate their understanding. This kind of checking can be done in nonverbal ways as well, for example, yes/no cards that are held up in response to a question. Asking students to complete simple tasks can serve to check understanding as well, for example, placing words on a continuum to show degrees:

Least to most frequent: never, rarely, sometimes, often, always

Strength of likes/dislikes: hate, don't like, like a little, like a lot, really like, love

Task 6.5

The following phrases were used in a family literacy class. Many of the vocabulary words were new for learners. With a partner or on your own, choose the question that would best check a non-native English speaker's understanding of the word in italics, or write a checking question of your own. The first has been done for you.

1 You'll need to bring a record of your child's *vaccinations.*

a Who gives vaccinations?

b Do you understand vaccinations?

c What do vaccinations stop?

In number 1, a and c allow the learners to demonstrate that they understand that a doctor or nurse gives vaccinations and that vaccinations stop diseases. Question b could elicit a yes with no guarantee of actual understanding.

2 Make sure to prepare *nutritious* meals.

a What does *nutritious* mean?

b Give some examples of nutritious foods.

c Which of these foods are nutritious: candy, an apple, whole grain bread, cheese, potato chips?

d ______________________________

3 *Transitions* can be difficult for young children.

a When do transitions happen?

b What is a transition?

c Do you know what *transition* means?

d ______________________________

Follow-up There may be some variation in your responses, but what is important is that the question you chose or wrote allows learners to demonstrate their understanding of a concept. The questions themselves need to be comprehensible to learners as well, and taking the time to plan these questions in advance benefits everyone.

Some Important Reminders

Whether you are giving directions, organizing activities, eliciting language, asking checking questions, or giving feedback, Robin Scarcella (1992) provides these important reminders for interacting with any non-native speaker of English:

- Use plenty of **wait time.** It can take many seconds (10–15) to retrieve the information from our memories and then produce a response. All teachers are guilty of giving far too little wait time after asking students a question.
- Do not always expect students to volunteer answers to your questions. Use techniques to call on students that are not intimidating, calling on more proficient learners first to provide more models of language, for example. Use ball or beanbag tosses, in which the students select the next person to speak.
- Students may come from cultures where students do not question teachers. Let them know that requests for clarification, simplification, or repetition are welcomed and expected. Teach the phrases they'll need to ask for clarification, e.g., *Could you please repeat that?*
- If verbally demanding open-ended questions are received with a blank stare, try yes/no and choice questions. They can be easier to answer, yet they still demonstrate the students' understanding.

Part III ◆ Promoting Learning beyond the Classroom

6.3 LEARNING STRATEGIES DEVELOPMENT

Learning shouldn't stop when students walk out of the classroom.

While this statement might seem obvious, helping learners to recognize and use learning strategies to learn outside of class takes conscious effort on the part of both teachers and learners. What are **language learning strategies?**

Task 6.6

Suppose you are in another country and you need to buy a fingernail clipper. You speak some of the local language, but you have no idea what the word is for fingernail clipper. How could you ask for this item without using the name for it? Talk to a partner or write your ideas below:

____

____

Follow-up In order to make yourself understood, you probably used one of the following **compensation strategies:**

- Using mime or gesture
- Defining the word or explaining its function
- Using a synonym
- Getting help from someone who speaks the native language and your language

All of these represent ways of being resourceful and getting what you need in another language, rather than giving up and leaving the store. Compensation strategies are just one type of language learning strategy that can be taught within any type of ESL curriculum. Teaching them empowers learners to progress and actively learn on their own. These strategies are any tools or tactics that learners employ to learn more effectively and more autonomously. Different strategies serve different purposes, but they can be used in any combination. Rebecca Oxford proposes two classes of strategies: direct strategies and indirect strategies. Table 6.5 summarizes the different types of language learning strategies she proposes, along with examples of each.

TABLE 6.5

Direct Strategies	Indirect Strategies
Memory Strategies Those that help you to remember language Examples • Sorting words into logical categories • Use sounds and images to remember words	Organizational Strategies* Those that help you plan for and organize learning Examples • Setting goals and objectives • Seeking opportunities for practice • Connecting new information with known information

*Oxford calls these metacognitive strategies. For a full description and discussion of language learning strategies, see Rebecca Oxford 1990.

Cognitive Strategies Those that enhance understanding Examples • Recognizing and using phrases • Repeating new language • Summarizing	Affective Strategies Those that improve your emotional state for learning Examples • Using relaxation techniques • Rewarding yourself • Keeping a language learning diary
Compensation Strategies Those that help you overcome limitations Examples • Guessing intelligently through visual or other clues • Asking for help • Using mime or gesture	Social Strategies Those that promote learning cooperatively Examples • Asking for clarification • Asking for correction • Interacting with proficient users of the language

Good language learners employ strategies that make them more conscious about how they learn, that allow them to monitor the success of learning, and to manage their time, affect, and effort. Developing effective language learning strategies is a goal that merits attention in any ESL class, regardless of the focus of instruction. It is important to be explicit about the strategies learners are using in class and to tell them how they can employ them on their own. The following examples illustrate how that can be done:

Sample A In this class, the students do regular listening activities, both from the textbook and from authentic sources such as news reports and taped interviews. The teacher always begins with prelistening activities, which allow the learners to anticipate content and check their predictions as they listen. Each time she does that, she makes it explicit to her students. The teacher then shares how she uses that same strategy at home to practice listening to the news in German on the local cable channel:

Making the strategy of predicting and guessing content explicit *Just as you need to improve your English, I am working on my German because my family and I are going to Germany this summer. Luckily, my local cable channel shows the news in German each night. I don't know much German yet, but before I listen, I write down all the events I heard about that day, either in conversations with people, on the radio, or in the newspaper in my language. Then when I listen in German, I try to hear some of those key words. I can always understand some names of countries and people, and some other words that sound like English. I want you to try doing that with the news in English every day.*

Sample B The class has been doing an activity on names of household objects (tools, appliances, etc.). Each student gets a picture of an object and the class is asked to make three logical groupings. She leaves it up to the students to decide what those groupings should be (likely choices are the kitchen, basement or garage, outdoors). After they form groups, she asks what they called their groups and writes the group names in circles on the board:

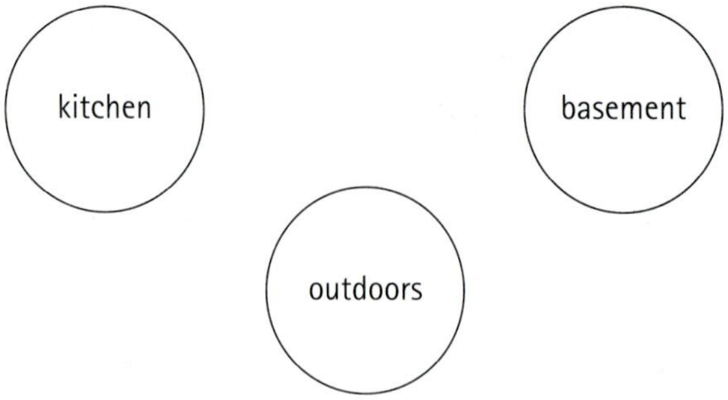

Now she invites them to create a **word web** by placing their words around the correct circle, as shown in this example:

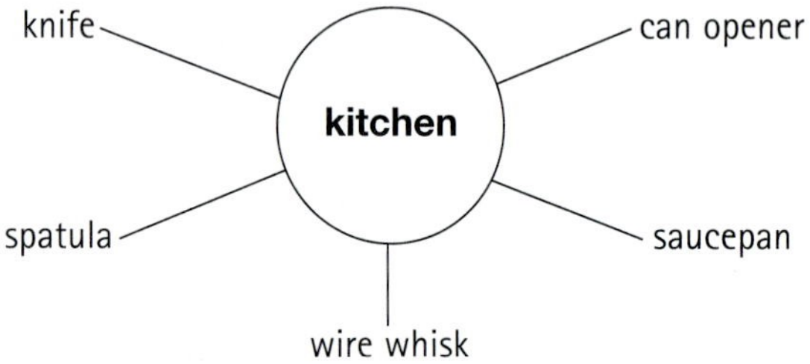

Making the strategy of using word webs explicit *This is a good way to organize new words that you learn. It helps you to remember them better if you put them in groups like the ones we made on the board. Each week, keep a list of new words you learn and hear. At the end of the week, draw word webs like these and organize all of your new words.*

Integrating learning strategies development into your lessons is one more way that learning and teaching can promote successes and accomplishment for your students. Just as with teacher-student interactions, the teaching of learning strategies should not be left to chance or taught haphazardly. They should be presented, practiced, and made explicit throughout instruction as an integral part of your lessons. In fact, research indicates that more positive results are shown if strategy training is taught in connection with specific content (O'Malley and Chamot 1990, Weinstein 1988).

CONCLUSION

In this chapter, the discussion of planning for teaching and learning has included far more than writing a lesson plan before walking into an ESL class. Teachers need to prepare for classroom interactions and integrate learning strategies instruction into lessons. They need to find ways to build continuity from one lesson to the next. While many of these teaching routines become second nature for experienced ESL teachers, those new to the profession need to be mindful of the importance of all of these elements to assure that learners have an optimal learning experience.

Key Terms

Checklist of Key Terms	On your own, or with a partner, provide an example or brief definition for each concept.
course goals/outcomes	
objectives	
target language	
curricular routines	
threads	
project-based learning	
display questions	
teacher talk	
checking questions	
wait time	
language learning strategies	
word web	

Applying What You Learned

1 Lesson Planning

If you are already teaching. . . use the lesson-planning guidelines below to plan an upcoming lesson (see pages 168–169 for the questions you need to ask yourself for each section). Afterward reflect on the ways that using these guidelines helped your planning. What areas had you overlooked before? In what ways did using the guidelines affect the outcomes of the lesson?

Lesson Planning Considerations	
1 Learner needs	
2 Choosing and organizing content	
3 Objectives	
4 Review	
5 Learner involvement	
6 Materials	
7 Activities	
8 Flexibility	
9 Evaluation	

If you are not teaching. . . talk to an ESL teacher about the class she or he teaches and write a class description based on the information given to you. Choose a unit from the textbook that class is currently using and prepare a lesson plan using the lesson-planning guidelines above. Write a lesson plan according to the type of lesson you create (i.e., a reading, listening, or contextualized language lesson plan will look different). If possible, ask the teacher for feedback about your plan.

2 Giving Instructions

If you are already teaching. . . audiotape a portion of your lesson when you are giving instructions to your students. Transcribe your instructions and answer these questions:

a Do I demonstrate or describe the activity?

b Do I provide sufficient modeling of what needs to be done in the activity?

c Do I break the activity down into logical steps and give learners only the information they need to complete each step?

d Do I check for learner understanding?

e Do I have students try the activity before the whole class undertakes it?

How did you do? Are you satisfied with your instructions, or did you discover some areas where you might improve? Rewrite the instructions to reflect any changes you would like to make the next time you use this activity.

If you are not teaching. . . choose an activity in an ESL textbook and script the instructions you would give for the activity. Think of how you would demonstrate the activity as well as which techniques you would use to check that learners understand what they need to do. Practice giving the instructions to a classmate, friend, or family member, and ask for feedback about your instructions using the questions above.

3 Checking Understanding

If you are already teaching. . . identify key vocabulary and grammatical or functional language in an upcoming lesson and prepare checking questions to use with your learners. Remember that good checking questions allow learners to *demonstrate* their understanding. Avoid: *Do you know. . .?, Do you understand. . .?, What does _______ mean?* After the lesson, reflect on how successful you were at checking learner understanding. Is there anything you would do differently if you were teaching this lesson again?

If you are not teaching. . . choose a unit in a textbook and do the same exercise. Practice your checking questions with a partner in class.

Recommended Reading

Grammar References for Teachers

Azar, B. 2000. *Chartbook*, 3rd Edition. Prentice Hall.

This book draws on the classic Azar grammar series with concise explanations, timelines, and examples of grammar points, particularly the tense/aspect system of English.

Celce-Murcia, M., and **D. Larsen-Freeman.** 1999. *The grammar book: An ESL/EFL teacher's course.* Boston, MA: Heinle and Heinle.

This comprehensive volume provides a detailed overview of the systems of English grammar. It contains sample activities at the end of each section.

Firsten, R. and **P. Killian.** 2002. *The ELT grammar book: A teacher-friendly reference guide.* Burlingame, CA: Alta Book Center Publishers.

This reference provides teachers with grammar explanations and examples that can help teachers communicate about and explain grammar effectively.

Lesson Planning

Nash, A. 2001. *Civic participation and community action sourcebook.* Boston, MA: New England Literacy Resources Center.

The volume contains numerous teachers' accounts of how they applied project-based learning to promote civic participation with learners in their programs. The examples in the book can serve as models for developing an emergent, project-based curriculum in adult ESL programs. This book can be found online at http://hub1.worlded.org/docs/vera/index1.htm.

Woodward, T. and **S. Lindstromberg.** 1995. *Planning from lesson to lesson.* Essex: Pilgrims.

This guide focuses on developing lesson threads that allow learners to recognize continuity and progress.

Learning Strategies

Ellis, G. and **B. Sinclair.** 1989. *Learning to learn English: A course in learner training.* Cambridge: Cambridge University Press.

This text helps learners to recognize and develop effective learning strategies.

O'Malley, J.M., and **A. Chamot.** 1990. *Learning strategies in second language acquisition.* Cambridge: Cambridge University Press.

This text provides an overview of learning strategy theory and describes instructional models for learner training in the classroom.

Oxford, R. 1990. *Language learning strategies: What every teacher should know.* New York: Newbury House.

This comprehensive overview of learning strategies theory includes a multitude of practical ideas on how to help learners develop learning strategies.

Useful Websites

OTAN for Teachers English as a Second Language Lesson Plans

http://www.adultedteachers.org/content/browselessonplans.taf?function=list&from=&doccatid=3

Part of the Outreach and Technical Assistance Network (OTAN) Website, these pages contain lesson plans for ESL teachers on community resources, health, employment, and government and law.

7

Managing ESL Classes

Part I ◆ Meeting the Challenges of Teaching Adult ESL

7.1.1 Introduction

An ESL teacher can have an excellent lesson plan with a variety of activities and relevant material, yet things in the classroom can still fall apart. There are a multitude of factors that influence the success of a lesson that are less tangible than the written plan, textbook, or handouts that the teacher has prepared. Identifying those factors and accounting for them in the planning stages can have a tremendous impact on learning. In the first part of this chapter, we examine the impact factors such as multilevel classes, the classroom environment, open-enrollment, or pairing/grouping students can have on learning, with a focus on turning challenges into opportunities for learning. In Part II, we turn to suggestions for working with learners with particular needs, for example, students with learning disabilities, physical handicaps, or those who have experienced trauma. Let's start by looking at Lynn's class, which may resonate with many experienced adult ESL teachers.

CHECKLIST

After reading this chapter and completing the activities, you should be able to

- describe the characteristics of the multilevel classroom.
- explain how to elicit common class goals.
- develop strategies for differentiating instruction in multilevel classes.
- describe a number of considerations and techniques for pairing and grouping students.
- describe special needs groups and know where to get support and information for assisting those students.

Getting Started

Task 7.1

Read the description of Lynn's class and answer these questions with a partner or in your journal:

1. Identify issues that could have an impact on learning and teaching.
2. What could Lynn do to turn some of these challenges around? Think in terms of learner roles and responsibilities, tasks, teaching and learning strategies, and the classroom environment.

Issue	Possible Solution

Lynn teaches a class of 26 adults enrolled from a variety of cultures: Liberia, Laos, Vietnam, Russia, Mexico, Ukraine, and Bosnia. She is frustrated by the challenges she faces each day in trying to meet their varying needs. Attendance varies from 12 to 26 students. The Vietnamese and Russian students are most interested in long grammar explanations and written activities.

The Liberian students have highly developed oral skills, but have limited literacy skills. The classroom is used by other programs at her school, so she hasn't been able to make use of the space as she'd like. She knows her students would benefit from more interaction with one another, but she's not sure how to organize pairs and group activities. Her program has an open-enrollment policy, which means that students are joining the class weekly. Lynn has always been very forthcoming in helping her students with personal issues (calls to landlords, rides to appointments). Lately, she has felt that they ask too much of her.

Follow-up Lynn faces numerous challenges, among them handling a multilevel/multicultural class, dealing with varying experiences and expectations, and managing open enrollment. These are just a few of the issues we will look at in the chapter. As you read the chapter, look for other possible solutions to the challenges you identified above.

7.1.2 Working with Multilevel Classes

When I asked Lynn what her greatest challenge was, she expressed great frustration with having to deal with the multiple levels of her learners. It is not only teachers like Lynn who are frustrated; learners are as well. In a study of learner attrition (Brod 1990), learners cited "classes so multilevel that those with no literacy skills are mixed with those quite literate (or those with very high oral skills are mixed with those with very low oral skills); lack of peer support and reinforcement; and instructional materials that are not relevant to learners' needs and lives" as among the reasons for leaving programs. The fact is, multilevel classes are a reality of almost every ESL program, and should not be seen as a deterrent to learning. Many would argue that multilevel classes allow for richer interaction among students, promoting multiple perspectives, peer teaching, and multifaceted learning. The question is: What are some effective ways to make multilevel classes rich and productive learning environments for all students? This discussion needs to begin with an understanding of what multilevel actually means. Is it only a question of language proficiency?

Task 7.2

Take a few minutes to brainstorm as many characteristics of a multilevel class as you can.

What are the characteristics of a multilevel class?	
variation in proficiency levels	*different school experiences*

Follow-up The simplest view of multilevel classes is that some learners are very proficient and participate all the time, and others are noncommunicative, leading the teacher to think they lack skills in English. Teachers often cite variations in literacy level as a key obstacle to learning as well. In fact, the outward behaviors students exhibit in class have as much to do with experiential and affective factors as they do with language proficiency. Jill Bell (1991) proposes four broad categories of factors contributing to a multilevel class: previous experience with education, country and culture of origin, individual factors, and situational factors. Table 7.1 presents those four categories along with some of the factors teachers need to consider when planning for multilevel classes.

TABLE 7.1

What does Multilevel Mean?	
1 Previous experience with education	Some factors to consider
Formal vs. informal education	• Number of years of schooling, if any • Experience learning other languages • Comfort with sitting in a classroom
Expectations about learning/teaching	• Content, e.g., grammar, speaking, civics • Student/teacher roles • Amount of written work vs. oral/aural work • Approaches to teaching; group/pair work
Literacy skills	• First and second language literacy • Preliterate, nonliterate, or semiliterate (Table 5.1)
2 Country and culture of origin	Some factors to consider
Classroom behaviors and expectations	• Degree of willingness, comfort, and ability to speak up in class • View of teacher as expert • Discomfort with pair/group work • Differing norms of student-teacher interactions, inside and outside of class • Roles related to gender and age
Tensions among groups in the class	• Political unrest between students' countries of origin • Tension between different clans from the same culture • Status within country of origin
Native language	• Similarities or differences with English or other first languages in class, e.g., Spanish has far more in common with English than does Chinese.
3 Individual factors	Some factors to consider
Personality	• Introverted vs. extroverted • Preference for individual vs. group work • Analytical vs. intuitive
Motivation	• Reasons for learning English: personal, professional, or academic • Voluntary learning vs. compulsory learning

Attitude to new culture	• A refugee's desire to return to country of origin • Circumstances which precipitated immigration • Degree of acclimation to new culture
Age	• Effects of age on language acquisition • Degree of flexibility with trying new ways of learning • Effects on attention span, eyesight, hearing • Physical stamina—ability to sit, stand, move about
Learning-style preferences	• Visual, aural/oral, kinesthetic, tactile • Preference for saying and doing things • Preference for writing everything down
4 Situational factors	Some factors to consider
Situation in the new culture	• Length of time in the country • Legal status, workload, family demands • Part-time or full-time student • Socioeconomic condition
Access to English outside of class	• Time and effort available and devoted to learning English outside of class • Amount of input in English from television, radio, family, friends, or co-workers • Opportunities for interaction in English with family, friends, or co-workers

(Adapted from Bell 1991:4–8)

Given the tremendous number of variables at play in a multilevel class, creating lessons that meet so many diverse needs may seem impossible. The fact is, we can never meet everyone's needs all of the time; what we can do is be aware of these variables and plan instruction accordingly.

7.1.3 Establishing Goals in Multilevel Classes

Students in multilevel classes need to feel that their needs are being addressed, and individual learning plans are essential. However, one way to bridge the gap between learners' diverse needs is to identify and negotiate shared goals, which results in more realistic expectations for the whole group (Balliro 1997). Lynda Terrill (Shank and Terrill 1997) reports on a technique of illustrating and posting each skill (listening, speaking, reading, writing) in the corners of the classroom and having learners stand next to the area that is most important to them. The teacher then writes the names of the students next to the skill area and leaves them posted throughout the term. She also suggests using pictures of themes and situations learners may encounter and having them work collaboratively to choose those that are the most important to them, then tallying the group results. These techniques give all students a voice in the needs assessment process, and they build cohesion and cooperation among the group members from the very start of the class.

Balliro (1997) highlights the importance of students taking responsibility for their own learning in the multilevel class. She cites an approach used by Andy

Nash in a workplace setting, which could be used in any ESL program. The learners take part in a discussion using these sentence starters:

*A good teacher*____________. *A good student* ____________.

The responses become the ground rules for the class, which are written and displayed in the classroom:

*We (the students) will*____________. *The teacher will* ____________.

This activity allows learners to articulate their expectations about areas such as homework and class participation. Making these expectations public allows learners to recognize the variation in expectations of the group.

A technique used for personal needs assessment in one-on-one teaching settings called 'scattergrams' (Wilberg 1988) is ideal for establishing goals within multilevel classes. Students create personal goal sheets like the one below. Each student creates a number of sheets addressing different areas of their lives (Language I use at home, work, school, in the community, etc.):

Language I need at work. . .		
follow written instructions	*complete defect reports*	*talk to co-workers*
understand spoken directions	*take certification tests*	
1		
2		
3		
4		

This student works in manufacturing as a line operator. A student who works in food service in a hospital will have very different needs. Each student prioritizes his or her needs and revisits them every month to identify progress. Needs can be added to the box and priorities reorganized each month (or more often). Learners share their 'scattergrams' with others in class and identify common goals that become the basis of a group scattergram. The class can post this in the room and revisit and revise it on a regular basis. This process addresses both the individual and common goals of the group.

Some ESL textbooks include goal-setting tasks that are ideal for negotiating common goals in a multilevel class. The following samples from the *Collaborations* series (Intermediate 1) demonstrate approaches that could be used at the start of any class. Learners with more literacy could read and transcribe the goals for less literate students in the class.

4 Doing It in English: Expressing Long-Term Goals

A. Read what two of Marianna's classmates hope to do in the future.

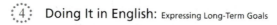

I hope to find a great job.
I really want to go back and help my country.

Arelette Tabpe and Yolette Jean-Louis are students at Bergen Community College. In this photograph, Arlette is sitting at her computer, and Yolette is standing on the right. They are talking about their long-term goals.

B. Below are some other goals of Marianna's classmates. Which ones are your goals too? Check (✔) them.

____ find a great job
____ go back and help my country
____ buy a house of my own
____ give my children a good education
____ live in a safe place
____ start my own business

C. Brainstorm with your class. Make a list of your classmates' long-term goals.

Our Long-term Goals
____
____
____
____
____

10 Ideas for Action: Reaching a Common Goal

A. Work in a small group. Talk about your long-term goals. Find one goal you all have in common. Write it here.

____

B. Brainstorm with the group. Think of some things that will help you reach this common goal. Make a list of your group's ideas below.

1. ________________
2. ________________
3. ________________
4. ________________
5. ________________

C. With your group, choose one idea you all like best. Tell the class.

(From Collaborations, *Huizenga and Bernard-Johnston 1995)*

7.1.4 Strategies for Working with Multilevel Classes

Teaching multilevel classes does not mean preparing multiple lesson plans each day, rather, it's a question of providing multiple options within the same lesson plan. The overall goals for the lesson are the same for the whole group; it's the path learners take to achieve those goals that differs (for a full discussion of classroom options, *Teaching Multilevel Classes in ESL* by Jill Bell is a must-read for both novice and experienced teachers). What follows are some practical strategies for adapting lessons, including ways to vary tasks and learner roles, multiple options for activities, and using self-access materials.

A. Allow for learner choice and use open-ended tasks that don't have a definite end

Classroom activities that have one set outcome can be frustrating for learners who are unable, for whatever reason, to complete the task in the allotted time frame. One way to avoid this is to provide learners with a choice of items to complete within a given time frame, allowing for variation from one student to the next. The following example illustrates this strategy, which can be used when learners are practicing any language function or workplace competency. Assume that the instructor has already presented the language needed for making requests and asking permission at the workplace. The following scenarios are cut up and passed out to students, with extra copies left on a table in the room. Students mingle and make polite requests or ask permission of others in class; students can choose to grant or refuse the request. When a student is finished with one scenario, he or she chooses another one on the table and continues the task. This activity gives all learners a chance to practice at their own pace. Students are also given the choice of scenarios allowing them to choose those for which they feel most prepared. Whether students complete one or eight scenarios, they can feel the accomplishment of completing the piece(s) of the activity they select. In order to motivate learners to take on greater challenge, suggest that they complete at least one more item than they did during the previous class.

Sample scenario strips:

It is stuffy in the room.
You want to open the window.
You are in the lunchroom and want to look at someone's newspaper.
You forgot your wallet at home and need to borrow $1.00 for a soft drink.
You don't feel well and want to leave work early.
You need time off for a doctor's appointment.
You want a co-worker to help you understand an employee announcement.

B. Assign different tasks to different ability-level students

Teachers I have worked with through the years have shown concern over assigning different tasks to learners within the same lesson. They often ask: Won't some groups wonder why they aren't being asked to do the same thing? This concern may come from our own experiences in school with being assigned to different reading or math groups according to level. No one wants to be in the 'low' group. I believe that learners appreciate the effort put into creating specific tasks for different groups. They are in class to learn English, not to worry about what another group is up to. It does take more time to plan multiple tasks, which can be an obstacle for part-time teachers who have limited paid preparation time. Consider developing materials like those below cooperatively with other teachers. A file of multilevel tasks can be created and shared by all the teachers at your site.

In a vocabulary lesson on jobs, different groups are given one of the following tasks:

Option A: Prepare a set of visuals on cue cards like these:

1. taxi driver

2. housekeeper

3. parking attendant

4. hairdresser
barber

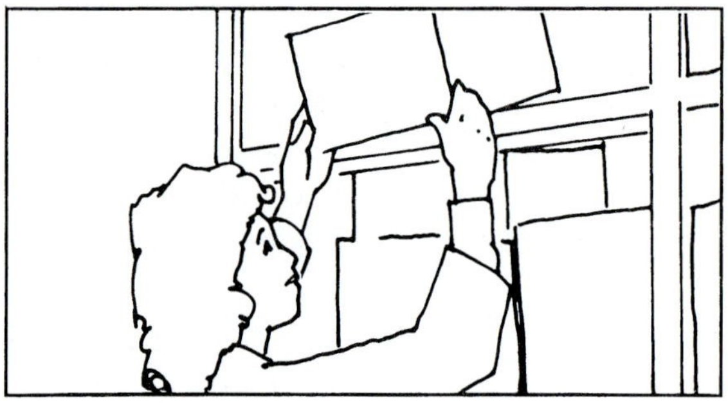

5. stock clerk

6. waitress
waiter

Match each job to the appropriate duty. Work with a partner.

_______ cleans houses	_______ serves food
_______ drives passengers	_______ stocks shelves
_______ cuts hair	_______ parks cars

(Brems, Working in English, Book 2, *McGraw-Hill Contemporary)*

Have learners sort the jobs according to whether they are indoor/outdoor; typically held by men/women in your country; require special training/no special training.

Option B: Prepare a set of cue cards with names of professions written on them and do the same as Option A. Sort words into these categories as well: jobs people in the group have done; jobs they'd like to try.

Option C: Small group discussion with these questions (name of profession written along the side of page):

What jobs do people do outdoors/indoors?

Which are typically held by men/women in your culture? What about in the U.S.?

Which of the jobs would you be interested in and why?

What experiences have you had in your daily life with any of these workers or occupations?

All three options allow learners to practice the vocabulary in ways that are accessible to them. In Option A, learners with limited literacy skills can rely on the visual representations of the jobs. The categories for sorting the words are factual and completing the task does not require extended use of language. However, successful completion of the task demonstrates that the learners understand something more than just the job title. Option B requires that learners can read the names of the jobs and sorting the words into categories requires more discussion than in Option A. Option C allows more advanced learners to discuss the jobs in more depth, bringing personal experiences and interpretations to the discussion.

Multilevel Listening Tasks

Any time you use a listening passage in a lesson, there are a variety of ways you can have learners work with the same passage. One routine I have often used in my ESL and EFL classes is to record the daily news headlines from radio or television to expose learners to authentic language. News broadcasts are delivered very quickly, as are most truly authentic listening passages, so the challenge is to prepare tasks that are accessible to varying ability levels. The alternative tasks below serve to illustrate the types of activities you could do with any passage, one from an assigned textbook, an interview, or a taped dialogue.

Record the morning news headlines from radio or TV and prepare materials to do any of the following tasks depending on the levels in your class:

Option A: Give a visual cut-out of the country and have the students hold up their card if their country is mentioned. If there is a large map in the room, students can stand by the map and point to countries they hear mentioned. This could be done on a local or national scale as well.

Option B: Hand out pictures of things mentioned in the news. Students hold up their picture as the item or person is mentioned (you often find corresponding photos in the newspaper for the same day).

Option C: Give a list of countries (or cities and states), key words, or names that are covered in the news. Students check off the words as they hear them.

Option D: List news topics on a handout and have students circle the topics that are covered in the news as they listen.

weather	crime	sports
national	international	local
government	people	business

One recording can be used to accomplish all of these activities, with different learners taking part in different activities. The tasks require minimal preparation and the places and names would likely appear in later broadcasts, allowing the teacher to recycle the tasks in later lessons.

Teachers can vary the degree of difficulty of listening and reading activities in textbooks by assigning only half of the items to some students, who then share their answers with students who completed the other items. Different prereading/listening and postreading/listening activities can be assigned depending on ability level. I recently taught a listening lesson based on a video clip about a controversial language teaching method used in China. I provided two options for follow-up, the first for the learners who had very high oral proficiency and had expressed their desire to have more discussions in class. The second option was designed for learners at the low-intermediate level, who sometimes struggled with tasks that were too open-ended.

Option A: Learners worked though a set of discussion questions about language learning and teaching preferences, followed by a ranking activity whereby students rated the degree of importance of different elements, e.g., pair/group activity; use of visual aids. They prepared a list of what they agreed they wanted in a language class, which they presented to the whole class.

Option B:

What is the best way to learn a language?

Write words or draw pictures for each of these things:

The classroom	The teacher	The students	The activities

The categories made the task more concrete than an open-ended discussion; those who had limited literacy skills could use pictures or symbols, or others in the group simply transcribed their contributions. The final outcome was to create a poster representing the ideal language class. This alternative to a discussion activity proved very successful for the low-intermediate level learners.

Providing two options allowed for multiple outcomes (each group chose the language to include and the ways to present information), and the options appealed to a much greater array of learning styles.

C. Assign varying roles

One of the core principles of cooperative learning is that each member of a group needs to have a clear role and purpose in order for the cooperative learning task to be successful. In a multilevel class, more advanced students can quickly dominate, leaving little room for participation by less advanced or quieter students. Here are some possible roles that can be assigned to students with particular strengths:

- Students with stronger literacy skills can be scribes during group activities, particularly those that have an outcome to report to the whole class.
- Learners who are hesitant to speak can be timekeepers; if they have developed literacy skills, give them cue cards with sentences like these: *We have 10 more minutes. We need to finish in 5 minutes.*
- Students who tend to dominate discussions could act as facilitators with some set ground rules; their job is to make sure everyone participates a set number of times. This allows the more verbal, and perhaps more advanced, students to participate while making them aware of the need for others to have a chance to speak.

These roles are interchangeable, i.e., everyone can be the timekeeper or facilitator. The idea is that each person knows what his or her role and purpose is as a group member, in addition to the responsibility of completing the activity itself.

D. Use different versions of the same dialogue or text: scripted; semi-scripted; discourse chains

Many textbooks have dialogues designed to present or provide opportunities to practice language; teachers and learners can also create dialogues collaboratively. The following variations demonstrate what you could do with one dialogue for learners with varying ability levels. Some learners may feel safest simply practicing a written dialogue, while others are ready to move on to something far more challenging. Learners with limited literacy will have difficulty reading a dialogue, but may be ready to practice based on visual cues (see Bell (1991:122–126) for even more ways to adapt dialogue activities).

Version A: Scripted dialogue

Worker	I'd like to report an accident.
Supervisor	What happened?
Worker	I cut my hand.
Supervisor	How did it happen?
Worker	Someone left a broken glass container in the sink and I picked it up.

Supervisor Is it bad?

Worker I don't know, but it hurts.

Supervisor You'd better fill out an accident report and get it checked.

Version B: Semiscripted dialogue

Worker I'd ____________ an accident.

Supervisor What ____________?

Worker I ____________ my hand.

Supervisor How did ____________ ?

Worker ____________ a broken glass container in the sink and I ____________ it up.

Supervisor ____________ bad?

Worker I don't know, but ____________.

Supervisor You'd better ____________ and get it ____________ .

Version C: For students with limited literacy skills

Show a picture of the problem (cut hand/broken glass container; watery eye/broken goggles)

Students create their dialogue based on those visual cues.

Version D: Discourse chain

Worker	Supervisor
Report accident →	Find out what happened
Explain what happened →	Find out how it happened
Explain how it happened →	Find out if it is bad
Tell if it's bad →	Tell worker what to do

(Original dialogue from ESL for Action, *Auerbach and Wallerstein 1987)*

E. Use role-plays with very complex to minimal roles; use picture prompts with no words

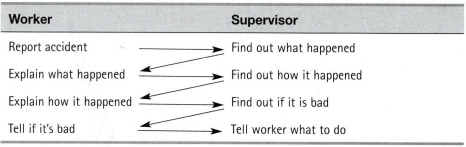

Role-plays can be used successfully with learners at all levels provided that the directions and role descriptions are understandable to students. In a multilevel class, there may be students for whom written role descriptions are too complex and incomprehensible. An alternative to role-plays with prescribed roles is to provide a picture of a scene and allow learners to choose who they want to be and what they want to say (Ladousse 1987). A scene on video with the sound off can also be used, played through one time and then freeze-framed for reference by the students as they prepare their role-play. Upon showing the scene, let each group work together to choose their parts and prepare and practice their role play. Find pictures, take photographs, or record scenes of:

- A visit to the doctor
- An accident scene
- Customers at a checkout in a grocery store
- Customers returning something to the store
- A parent-teacher conference

F. Language Experience Approach

The Language Experience Approach (for full discussion, see 5.1.4) is generally viewed as an approach for working with emergent readers, but it can be used very effectively in a multilevel class as well, even with high-level reader/writers. As the teacher elicits stories orally from the group, the advanced learners can make corrections and spell words for the class, taking on the teacher's role (Bell 1991). Bell also suggests starting the story with contributions from the emergent reader/writers, and ending it with contributions from the more advanced students. This way, follow-up activities can be done that are appropriate to each level using different portions of the story.

Another option is to pair students to create texts (Bell 1991). Teachers in our program have used the following sequence of steps successfully with mixed-ability pairs:

- Set up an event that could be used for language experience.

  or

- Have students think of an important event in their lives in the last (week, month, year).
- Practice telling the story silently to themselves; ask students to think through the beginning, middle, and ending, as well as key points in the story.
- Pair more literate learners with those with limited literacy skills. Have them tell their story to their partner.
- More literate learners write the story as it is told to them. Those with limited literacy skills can draw pictures or verbally recount what they have understood. These verbal accounts could be tape-recorded and used for other class activities.
- Student-generated texts are then used by the whole class for other practice activities.

G. Self-access materials and computer labs

A national study of adult education found programs with computer-assisted learning labs or independent-study components to have higher retention rates

(Fitzgerald 1994). These self-access options can range from thematic classroom stations with activities that can be completed individually or in small groups, to self-access centers and computer labs. The choices a program makes depend on its size and resources. What is clear is that providing learners with multiple options meets a wider range of needs in the multilevel classroom. In this section, the focus is on classroom self-access materials (computer software and distance learning materials are discussed in Chapter 8).

In preparing self-access materials, clear instructions and answer keys are crucial in order that the work can be done autonomously. Activities and tasks should be ones that are familiar to learners so that they can get started without teacher assistance. Note that a number of the activities listed practice and review grammar points. Thinking back to Lynn's class at the beginning of the chapter, her Russian and Vietnamese students expressed a desire to have more grammar practice. By providing grammar activities in self-access centers, she can meet their needs while continuing to work on other areas of language with the class. The options in Table 7.2 are easy to develop and can be used over and over by different groups of learners.

TABLE 7.2 Classroom Self-access Options

• Prepare sets of vocabulary words that have been covered in class and have learners sort words into logical categories, create word webs (see 6.3), and then create a story using the words.
• Create sentence strips using language taught in class, class-generated stories, or functional dialogues that students need to put in a logical order. Provide all possible orders in the answer key.
• Cut up sentences and have students put them in the correct order. This is a good way to highlight word order in questions and in negative and more complex grammar structures.
• Provide book/stories and tapes (commercially produced or ones you've recorded). Short stories or high-interest articles that can be completed in one or two class periods are ideal.
• Have students create their own tapes of stories to share with family or others in class.
• Provide grammar review activities with answer keys (see Recommended Reading for good sources).
• Develop listening lessons using listening passages from commercial ESL textbooks, news broadcasts, or short interviews. Provide students with preview questions, comprehension questions to answer while listening, and follow-up questions that can be answered in a journal.
• Provide listening fill-in activities to practice grammar or vocabulary. There are many commercial textbooks for this purpose. Provide texts of listening passages (songs work well for this activity), and white out the structure of focus or vocabulary for students to fill in as they listen to the tape.
• Create an in-class reading corner with graded readers, high-interest articles, and short stories. Have students keep a reading log (stories read, record of main ideas/summary and reactions).
• If doing project-based learning, have a permanent station where learners can complete portions of the project the class is currently working on.

In situations where the ESL teacher shares the classroom with other programs, these self-access materials can be stored in small crates and brought in and out of classrooms.

7.1.5 The Classroom Environment

Take a few minutes to visualize what you would want to see when you walk into a language classroom. What do you see on the walls, what objects are in the room, how are the seats arranged? All of these features have an impact on learning, particularly for learners new to English. Everything from wall charts with the alphabet, common phrases, and vocabulary to student-produced work displayed on the walls enhances learning. Unfortunately, sharing classroom space in large institutions can make covering the walls with visual aids impractical. Many of the items below could be moved in and out of a classroom if necessary.

- Create bulletin boards with language experience stories, student writings, drawings, photographs; in sites with shared classrooms, display these in school entrances or hallways.

- Display projects completed by previous classes and the current class.
- Display helpful phrases around the room: *What does ______ mean?; Can you repeat that, please?*
- Label objects around the room: chalkboard, door, window, table, chair, and any other visual aids.
- Post visual aids/charts around the room with common vocabulary, e.g., body parts, services and stores, neighborhood maps.

It is important that classes be as inviting and comfortable as possible. Create seating arrangements *before* students arrive, or ask students who arrive early to class to help you. Make sure the seating arrangement is appropriate for the mode of instruction you will be using. It may be that a horseshoe with seats facing the front is best for a teacher-led presentation. Perhaps the class starts with small groups checking homework together, which would require seats arranged in clusters. The classroom arrangement should be part of your planning process and not left to chance.

7.1.6 MANAGING LARGE CLASSES

The participatory and learner-centered practices described in this book include extensive learner interaction and input, which some teachers find daunting with a class of 30 to 40 students (not to mention classes of 50 to 200, common in many overseas settings). Some teachers shy away from communicative activities all together because they are concerned that it will be too chaotic or unmanageable. Pairing students and using cooperative learning, however, are among the ways you can assure that learners get ample opportunities to practice language and receive feedback and support from peers. Relying on teacher-directed tasks would mean almost no practice time for students. Another common concern for teachers with large classes is difficulty keeping up with individual student progress as well as lack of time to correct student work or respond to dialogue journals in meaningful ways. All of this points to the need to promote learner autonomy so that students do not rely solely on the teacher for guidance throughout the lessons, as well as the need to build peer feedback and support into instruction.

- Create activities with built-in peer feedback and/or correction. For written tasks, provide Student A with half of the answers completed and Student B the other half. Ideally, make copies on different colors to make the distinction between the two versions of the activity more obvious. After completing their items, learners read their responses and receive feedback from their peers. For speaking practice, use information-gap activities, which allow for immediate feedback from peers. Provide answer keys for homework (on an overhead projector or on handouts that you collect for later use) that pairs or small groups can work through together. Some weeks have peers read and respond to dialogue journals.
- Give answer keys to selected students around the room and have them become the experts who provide feedback to others in class. This role can be assigned to students at any level.
- Model and thoroughly check for understanding of activities *before* students begin to work in pairs or groups, otherwise you will find yourself with multiple groups or pairs in need of help once the class has started an activity.
- Make yourself available to the pairs or groups in class; monitor progress, take notes for individual students or small groups that can be distributed to students after an activity. There may not be time to give everyone feedback at the end of the class.
- Learners may be more reluctant to speak up in front of a large group of peers. When practicing language points, provide ample models and then let students practice in pairs before calling on individuals. This gives them time to rehearse their responses.

- Use **think-pair-share** as a class routine: Pose a question and let students think about it; then pair up and talk about it to a partner; finally, have students share answers with the whole class. Think-pair-share can be used any time in class: when brainstorming vocabulary, answering prereading or prelistening questions, or practicing a particular language point. It allows all students the opportunity to use the language, even if they do not volunteer to speak in front of the whole class.
- Establish class routines for starting and stopping activities—switching lights on and off, clapping—or decide as a class what that signal will be. Avoid shouting over the students to get their attention.
- Establishing rapport in a large class takes time. Teachers can assign **base groups** who spend time together each class period to check homework, answer questions, or complete particular activities. Designating base groups can provide learners with a support system. In advanced-level classes that include a significant amount of discussion and debate, try creating groups who stay together over a set time period (2–3 weeks).
- Students in large classes complete their work at different times, so it is important to promote learner autonomy. Provide reading corners with books, newspapers or magazines, self-access materials, or ongoing dialogue journal assignments. Have multiple options ready or extension activities focused on the same materials.
- Assign student mentors to new students to help them feel that they are a part of the class.

The suggestions above are useful for any class, large or small, but serve to enhance student interaction in those situations where the teacher cannot be accessible to all of the students all of the time.

7.1.7 OPEN ENROLLMENT

Many ESL programs have an **open-enrollment** policy, which means that learners are allowed to enter a program at any time throughout the duration of a course rather than only at the beginning of a term. There are many legitimate reasons for using open enrollment:

- Immigrants and refugees arrive in communities throughout the year and need to be able to enter a program right away.
- Adult learners' life circumstances can change dramatically, requiring that they step in and out of programs.
- It is thought that due to high attrition rates, classes would be far too small by the end of a term if closed enrollment were used. Keeping classes full partially fulfills state and federal funding requirements.

The result for teachers in some programs is that students come in and out of classes on a daily, or even hourly, basis. This presents the teacher and the class with a number of challenges (Scogins and Knell 2001):

- Goal setting with individuals when there are no volunteers or intake personnel available.
- Keeping track of learner progress.
- Knowing who the learners are and how many learners to plan for each day.
- Building a sense of community and cohesiveness.
- Making sure new learners don't feel left out when entering a group.
- Helping learners catch up to the rest of the class.

While the challenges are great, there are a number of things that teachers can do to improve learner involvement in an open-enrollment program:

- Use peers as tutors. Learners at a higher proficiency level benefit from teaching others. As with volunteer teachers, instruct them on how to give a brief orientation to incoming students and assign them to the new arrivals.
- Take full advantage of volunteers. Instruct them on how to give a brief orientation to incoming students and assign them to the new arrivals.
- Develop a simple introductory task that learners can complete if they arrive in the middle of a class: a simple goal-setting task (*In this class I want to . . .*); a simple survey of needs and interests; a set of visuals depicting needs and interests that they can choose from.
- In large classes, understand that you can't and shouldn't interrupt the lesson each time new students arrive. Greet them and have them introduce themselves to the class, and assure them that you will talk to them during the next break.

It is not uncommon for programs with open enrollment to have retention rates of only 25%–50% by the end of a term, and a national evaluation of adult education programs revealed that one third of ESL students leave programs within two months (Fitzgerald 1994). Of course there are many personal factors that influence this, but there are things programs can do to improve retention. A study on outreach and retention of adult ESL learners (Brod 1990) showed that learners who set and discuss realistic goals with their teachers are less likely to leave programs. The program then needs to give regular feedback on learner progress in relation to these goals. Silver (as reported in Brod 1990) underscores the importance of outlining with learners what a program can (or cannot) do for them at the time of enrollment. In the national evaluation cited above (Fitzgerald 1994), it was found that those programs that assist learners with child care, transportation, and job skills had considerably higher retention rates, as do those with computer-assisted learning labs or independent-study components. These are lessons that all programs may be able to draw on to minimize the revolving-door climate of many ESL classes.

7.1.8 Managed Enrollment

While there are a number of strategies and techniques that a teacher can employ for making open-enrollment classes more manageable, some programs have gone even further, implementing a policy of **managed enrollment.** In using managed enrollment, a program determines a set time period during which learners can enroll in classes, most often at the beginning of each term. There are programs that allow enrollment only one day or evening per week, which is an improvement over those that have students entering every day, or even throughout a given class period. The programs described below permit students to enroll at the beginning of short terms (8–9 weeks), ensuring that those students who are on waiting lists will not need to wait an indeterminate amount of time to enter classes.

A managed-enrollment pilot program at the Metropolitan Adult Education Program (MAEP) in Santa Clara County, California, showed significant improvement in both student retention rates and learning gains (School Services of California 2002). With managed enrollment, the retention rate rose to 70% from 38% the year before when open enrollment was in place, test scores rose an average of 15%, and the teachers reported that the new procedures made teaching and learning more organized and focused.

When MiraCosta College's noncredit ESL program had an open-enrollment policy, there were as many as 300 students on a waiting list each term. Their records showed that only 25% of students attended regularly for a complete semester, which is representative of many programs. Changes in grant requirements for federal funds used learner gains on standardized tests as the basis for funding rather than student attendance (Ramirez 2001). All of these factors led MiraCosta to pilot a managed-enrollment program, which proved to have tremendous success.

MiraCosta now offers five 9-week sessions per year, with enrollment allowed only during the first two weeks of class. Those not admitted are placed on a waiting list for the next session. Students who miss more than three to five classes are dropped and put on the waiting list for the next session. The pilot program had the following outcomes:

- A rise in retention from less than half to over 80%.
- Promotion to the next level at end of each session rose from 3% to 25%–30%.
- All students on waiting lists were admitted to the following session.

Equally significant is the response from teachers and students who were involved in the pilot. Faculty reported that because students were promoted in a more timely fashion, there was a greater incentive to study. This statement sent to Sylvia Ramirez (ESL Coordinator) from one of the instructors in the program, Lynn Morgan, speaks volumes about the benefits of managed enrollment:

> *Just wanted to mention that the students in room 12 are very happy with the new sessions program. I think it's wonderful too! We are able to accomplish so much more when we have the same students attending regularly. And I think the students can really see measurable progress in eight weeks. They all told me they learned a lot. In fact they were so pleased with their progress that they wanted to go out and celebrate the completion of the session. Short-term goals do allow the students more frequent successes.*

Ramirez reports continued success with promotion rates now at 50% every nine weeks and FTES (full-time equivalent student for state apportionment) up by 23% over the previous year. "It has changed the whole culture of our program" (Sylvia Ramirez, personal communication). At present, few programs have managed enrollment in place, but as the word of successes like the one above gets out, managed enrollment may become a common practice in the years to come.

7.1.9 Pairing/Grouping Students

Task 7. 3

Most of us have had experience working in pairs or groups at work, in classes, or at conferences with varying degrees of satisfaction and success. Think of a pair or group activity you recently took part in and reflect on what made the activity successful (or not successful). Think about the assignment of group members, roles of members, the purpose of the task, and anything else that had an impact on the success (or lack of success) of the activity and write your answers in your journal or talk to a partner in class.

Pair/Group activity: ______	
Assignment of group members	
Roles of members	
Purpose of the task	
Other factors?	

Follow-up What do you think had the most impact on the success or failure of the pair/group activity in which you took part? How much do you think the facilitator or teacher planned the groupings and the activity? As we turn to the discussion of pairing and grouping students, try to relate your experience to the recommendations provided in this section.

There are many factors to consider when creating pairs and groups in a lesson, and the advice I give new teachers is not to leave it to chance. Ability level may seem like the most obvious factor, but there are others as well, including gender, family relationships, learner expectations, and the purpose of the pair/group activity.

Ability level: There are benefits to both like-ability and cross-ability pairs and groups, but a teacher needs to make choices about activities and learner roles to make the most of these different groupings. From my experience and observations of ESL classes, learners seem to prefer like-ability groupings. In the case of beginning-level learners, it can be intimidating to work with someone who is more advanced. I have observed beginning-level students participating more openly with students at a similar level. Sometimes the advanced-level students complain about working with beginners, stating that they (the advanced students) 'do all the work.' They appear to be more challenged if working with others at an advanced level as well.

There are some advantages to cross-ability groupings. Stronger students provide beginning-level students with valuable language input. Helping others and acting as a peer tutor has value as well, but it is important that the learners perceive that there is a benefit to taking on this leadership role. Remind students that one of the best ways to learn is to teach others. Here are just few examples of roles and activities for cross-ability groups:

- Have more advanced learners ask the questions in an interview activity.
- Have more literate students transcribe stories of emergent reader/writers.
- Have more advanced students give verbal instructions to beginning-level students, who arrange pictures, complete an information gap, etc. The input is likely to be comprehensible to the beginner.
- In jigsaw activities, give the higher-level learners more demanding questions to answer.

(These ideas are adapted from Bell 1991.)

Gender: In a class I recently observed, a Muslim woman from Turkey was assigned a male partner for a pair activity. She worked with her male partner on the task, but she turned her chair so as not to face him. I had to ask myself how she felt, and wondered whether the teacher had given any thought to the groupings she chose. In fact, the teacher had not; she simply asked students to work with the person sitting next to them. In this case, it was clear that the learner would have been much more comfortable with a female partner. Learners from many cultures may be more comfortable with same-gender partners, at least until they get to know their classmates well.

Family relationship: In a class I observed over a 10-week period, a couple from Vietnam came to class together, sat together, and moved into groups together. Once in their groups, the husband dominated, interrupting his wife whenever she tried to participate. In conversations with her before and after class, it was clear to me that she was actually more advanced than her husband. The teachers I was observing were uncomfortable separating them—they thought it could be disrespectful and also very conspicuous if they asked Tran to move to another group. The teachers hadn't thought to employ less obvious ways to separate them, for example, having learners number off 1,2,3 and having all the ones together, the twos together, and the threes together (other grouping strategies are below). Once they tried this, the couple worked separately with no complaints at all.

Learner expectation: If it is clear that learners are unaccustomed to doing pair and group work, it is the teacher's job to explain the benefits of student-student interactions with the learners. As adults, students appreciate knowing why their teachers are using particular techniques, and are often open to trying new things if they know what the benefits to them are. Relating what you do in the classroom to what the learners need to do in the real world is one way to present pair and group work. If you ask the students to observe how and when they need to use English outside of the classroom, it will quickly become apparent that interactions outside of the classroom are not between them and a teacher figure. It is also important to reassure learners that you are listening and monitoring their English during pair and group activities. Take notes as you listen and give learners feedback, either individually or as a whole group wrap-up.

Purpose of task: Teachers who embrace a learner-centered, communicative approach to teaching often assume that pair and group work is always better than individual or whole group work. When a teacher gives learners a matching activity, or a fill-in-the blank activity, telling students to work with a partner, more often than not, there will be silence in the classroom. Why is that? The purpose of the activity does not lend itself to pair work; it is easier, and, from the learners' standpoint, more efficient to complete the activity on their own. Suppose the teacher gave one student a detailed photograph of a room and the other a list questions, and then models the following interaction:

Is there a lamp on the table?

How many chairs are in the room?

The activity promotes a genuine reason to communicate with a partner. In planning pair and group work, ask yourself: *Would this activity best be done alone or with a partner?* There are times when copying sentences, filling in sentences, and writing stories are useful and best done individually.

Strategies for Creating Pairs and Groups

From the discussion above, it is clear that it is often necessary to plan grouping arrangements in order for learners to have success with an activity. There are times, however, when pairs and groups can be created randomly. In fact, in classes where multiple pair or group activities are done each day, it will be important to vary the groupings. Creating groups can become a communicative activity of its own by having students gather together based on certain criteria, perhaps reviewing vocabulary or language from a recent lesson:

1 Favorite color

2 Month they were born

3 Number of people in their immediate family

Think of four more possibilities:

____

____

____

____

Learners need to communicate with one another in order to form groups. Once those groups are established, the teacher then proceeds with the lesson. It is important not to overuse this technique; regrouping many times in a lesson with different criteria would be confusing.

As an alternative to having students count off (as suggested previously), the teacher can review the alphabet, colors, names of seasons, or any vocabulary, by assigning a letter or word to each student and have students form like-word groups:

> Teacher (walking around the room): *spring, summer, fall, winter, spring, summer, fall, winter,* around the room until all students have a season. (The teacher can start the sequence and have the students continue it around the room).
>
> Teacher: *The spring group will work over here* (pointing to one part of the room), *the summer group here,* and so on.

Students benefit from repetition of words and phrases that they are learning. For short, controlled practice activities, line activities or concentric circles can be used to provide maximize practice, while maintaining interest through interactions with several class members.

> **Line activities:** One line of students stands in the same spot for the activity; a second line of students faces the first. The pairs complete the assigned activity (e.g., a set question: *What do you do on the weekend?*; *Tell me about your job.*) After a few minutes, one row moves down one student so that a new pair is formed. This is repeated until all students have spoken to all members of the other line (Shank and Terrill 1997).
>
> **Concentric circles:** Similar to line activities, form two concentric circles with equal numbers of students (if there is an odd number of students, the teacher can join one circle). The students interact with the person facing them, then the outer circle rotates one student to form new partners.

7.1.10 Establishing Appropriate Boundaries

ESL teachers are often students' only liaison to the mainstream and they may rely on teachers for assistance in areas that go beyond learning English. I think many ESL teachers appreciate the advocacy roles that they take on, and are willing to provide far more than language support for their students. But when does it go too far? When does a teacher's involvement become either excessive or inappropriate?

A supervisor in a large ESL consortium in Minneapolis shared concerns about the issue of establishing appropriate boundaries with students. She and the staff have had questions and concerns about the following issues:

1. Invitations
   - Entire class to teacher's home for party during class time
   - Entire class to teacher's home for party outside of class time
   - Entire class to park/restaurant or other neutral location for party during or outside of class time
   - Invitation from student to go for coffee, dinner at student's home (one teacher), or dinner at student's home (more than one teacher)
2. Gifts
3. Hiring of students
4. Transportation of students (appointments, shopping, job interviews)
5. Advocacy
   - Making nonemergency phone calls for housing/medical/police
   - Teaching students to drive
   - Writing letters for students (other than for verification of attendance)
   - Helping students find jobs

Most districts have a harassment policy; however, there are rarely written guidelines about student/teacher interactions such as the ones above. This program has developed a list of questions teachers can ask themselves to determine the appropriateness or potential for misunderstanding, legal repercussions, or problems of a given situation. There are so many variables that are unique to any situation, so a yes answer to these questions does not necessarily mean that your interactions are inappropriate. Answering yes to many of the questions, however, should signal the potential for problems.

TABLE 7.3

Establishing boundaries: Questions to consider

1 Have I considered safety and liability issues for staff and for students?	You need to consider what the liability issue would be if you had a car accident with your student during class time.
2 Will this activity put the ability of the student to participate in class and meet their goals at risk?	If the situation doesn't go well, the student may feel uncomfortable about returning to class.
3 Is there any sense of obligation for either the student or the teacher?	A student may feel they need to return a favor to a teacher, which may affect their participation in the program.
4 Is this activity something that you would consider doing with any or all of the students in the class (i.e., nonexclusive)?	Anything you do that appears to give only some students preferential treatment (hiring them to do work, driving them to appointments) could make others feel excluded.

5 Would I be able to read about this in the paper?	If there's the risk that your interaction with a student could appear the slightest bit inappropriate, you probably shouldn't take part in it.
6 Have I made appropriate referrals as needed?	Students often come to us for legal advice, concerns about landlords, etc. If you are not an expert, your assistance may do more damage than good. Refer the student to the appropriate assistance agency.

(Questions from Julie Pierce, personal communication)

Task 7. 4

Let's look at a scenario one of the teachers in this district encountered. Read the situation and ask yourself the questions in Table 7.3. Should Barbara have accepted her student's offer? Why or why not?

> *Barbara has an ESL student who was an auto mechanic in his country. He has started repairing cars at his home and has offered to do a minor repair for Barbara. Thinking it would be helpful to give him the business, she decides to have him do the work. A couple of weeks later, she realizes the problem hasn't been solved, and in fact is a bit worse. She takes her car into the garage she normally uses and has the repairs completed. The student didn't do any damage to her car, and she was in no danger driving it, but she feels funny about telling him the problem wasn't corrected.*

Follow-up The key questions in this situation revolve around liability and jeopardizing the student's ability to continue in the program. What if Barbara had an accident after the repair was made? Even if the student's work had absolutely no influence on the accident, how might it appear to the student? Does the student have a license to do the kind of work he did? Could he get in legal trouble?

CONCLUSION In this section, we have looked at the impact different learner and classroom variables have on learning. Given that most adult ESL classes can be characterized as multilevel, ESL teachers have no choice but to accommodate an array of learner strengths and needs as well as learning styles in every class they teach. Teachers need to make careful decisions about group assignments, learner roles, the classroom environment, appropriate boundaries, and more. The overarching goal should be to provide a context for learning that is as welcoming and as accessible as possible to a wide range of learners.

Part II ◆ Learners with Particular Needs

7.2.1 LEARNERS WITH LEARNING DISABILITIES

One of the most difficult assessments to make in working with ESL learners, children or adults, is whether or not a student has a **learning disability.** According to the National Joint Commission on Learning Disabilities (1994), "learning disabilities is a general term that refers to a heterogeneous group of disorders manifested by significant difficulties in the acquisition and use of listening, speaking, reading, writing, reasoning, or mathematical abilities. The disorders are intrinsic to the individual, presumed to be due to central nervous system dysfunction, and may occur across the life span." June Crawford's reflections about her learners highlight the responsibilities ESL professionals have with regard to adult ESL learners and learning disabilities:

> My teaching and training efforts are planned to meet the various learning needs of the students or professionals who are in my classes, but if I suspect that a learning need appears to be unmet through good teaching practices, I consider it my professional responsibility to recognize this. Once recognized, I need to be able to understand what the next logical steps should be for the learner and myself, and I need to be able to explain these steps to the learner. I also need to understand how a legal diagnosis is made and what the implications are for the learner and the educational system of which she or he is a part (June Crawford 1999).

Recognizing that learning needs are not being met can be problematic for those of us working with students with limited English. Many of the classic signs that experts look for in native-English speaking learners do not necessarily signal a problem with non-native English speakers. Learning difficulties can often be attributed to differences in educational experiences, lack of literacy in the first language, or any one of the other factors discussed in Chapter 1 (Table 1.1). Of course there are adult ESL learners with learning disabilities; the question is *How do I know if there is a problem?* Simons (1999) suggests that the following problems may be present for a student with learning disabilities. Many of the characteristics are present with beginning-level ESL learners, and all learners may exhibit some of these problems. If a learner has many of the problems in Table 7.4 on an on-going basis, there could be cause for concern.

Table 7.4

Area of difficulty	Signs to look for
Difficulties reading	Problems with word decoding, reading comprehension, rate, fluency, vocabulary.
Difficulties writing	Problems organizing thoughts, writing stories, spelling, handwriting.
Difficulties with oral language	Problems with listening, speaking, vocabulary, word finding.
Irregular social behavior	Problems with family or social relationships, social perception, humor, emotional behavior.
Problems with attention or concentration	Overactive, impulsive, or distractible behaviors; has difficulty staying on-task.
Problems with organization	Difficulty in breaking tasks down; planning, managing time, day-to-day organization.
Auditory processing problems	Unable to distinguish similar-sounding words and letters, difficulty in remembering what was said, difficulty in following more than one instruction at a time, mispronounces common words or sayings.
Visual processing problems	Reverses letters, unable to follow a line on the page, poor visual memory.

Few of us are experts in the field of learning disabilities, so ESL professionals need to learn how and where to access appropriate referrals within the school system and the community at large, and assist learners to make the contacts they need. Learners have the right to a formal diagnosis if it is merited. A diagnosis of a learning disability gives a learner access to certain **accommodations** that remove any barriers to completing a task in school or in the workplace, for example, allowing additional time for test taking or reading aloud to learners who have difficulty decoding print (Byrnes 2000).

Formal diagnoses of adult second language learners can be difficult to obtain. Tests used in the public schools have been designed for the K–12 audience, and most have not been tested with non-native English speakers. With or without a formal diagnosis, Lowry (1990), Baca and Cervantes (1991), and the University of Kansas Center for Research on Learning (1998) recommend many accommodations, techniques, and strategies for working with adults with learning disabilities, many of which benefit all learners. Many of these techniques are intended to provide additional structure and predictability to instruction.

Table 7.5

Helping Learners with Learning Disabilities
• Determine learners' strengths and build on those strengths.
• Structure lessons and activities; break them down into small steps. Provide time frames for completing activities.
• Provide checklists of tasks completed.
• Reinforce learning using visual and other sensory aids; have learners handle materials; use color-coding when possible.
• Use demonstration more than explanation.
• Give frequent positive feedback and help learners recognize success.
• Teach ideas concretely; make directions specific, concrete, and understandable.
Accommodations
• Allow extra time on tasks.
• Provide tutors to read material aloud or assign a peer coach.
• Have shorter work periods and frequent breaks.
• Allow adequate time for transitions.

(For an extensive list of accommodations, see *Accommodating Adults with Disabilities in Adult Education Programs*. University of Kansas Center for Research on Learning 1998.)

The area of learning disabilities and adult ESL merits far more attention than can be provided in this section. Two online resources that provide comprehensive information, resources, and further links are included here for easy reference:

LD and the English Language Learning is part of a NIFL Special Collection on Learning Disabilities. Robin Swartz provides an excellent overview of research and practice in the area of LD and adult ESL learners. Some of the questions addressed include: How do learning disabilities affect language learning? How do you diagnose LDs with second language learners? What are LD issues versus language acquisition issues? How can you support ESL learners with learning disabilities in your programs? This special report can be viewed online at: http://ldlink.coe.utk.edu/esl_ld.html

Bridges to Practice has been developed through a grant from the National Institute for Literacy (NIFL). The program consists of a series of guidebooks designed for teachers, social workers, employment counselors, job coaches, and others to help them recognize learning disabilities, learn how to screen for them, and learn what to do when an adult has been diagnosed with a disability. While the materials were not developed for ESL professionals, anyone concerned about learning disabilities and adult learners will find this site very helpful. The series can be viewed online at: http://www.nifl.gov/nifl/ld/bridges/materials/bridges_docs.html

7.2.2 Physical Handicaps

Five years ago, I walked into the first evening of an adult ESL class that was to be taught by student teachers in the certificate program I coordinate. I always teach the first class while the student teachers observe, and on this evening, we were expecting a group of 12 high-beginning Russian students. I had prepared a lesson on making introductions, talking about jobs held before coming to the U.S., personal interests, and wants and needs for the English class they were starting. I included practice with basic *wh-* questions for interviewing one another about their personal histories, wants, and needs. I relied heavily on visual aids to depict professions; I planned to use the flip chart and overhead transparencies for model sentences and prompts for practice for this literate Russian audience. Imagine my surprise when two young blind men from Poland joined the group.

These two students had heard about the class from a community agency and took a 50-minute bus ride to get there. I had to make some major adjustments to my lesson plan, many of which I believe enhanced learner participation by all of the students as the sighted students described pictures, activities, and read instructions to the blind students. The learners expressed enthusiasm about the opportunity to return every Tuesday and Thursday evening in the dead of winter. My concern was whether or not the student teachers in the program had been given adequate tools and strategies for dealing with the new makeup of the class. So much of what they had read and learned about the months before the practicum relied on visual representations (pictures, written models, labels around the rooms) and written texts and activities.

My story illustrates the unpredictability of every teaching situation and the need for teachers to be resourceful and flexible. For teachers in a large district, the first step is to inquire about and locate appropriate resources available through their school or community. Does their school disabilities service provide tutoring support? Are special materials available, for example, large print readers? To my delight, the four student teachers in our program immediately started brainstorming adjustments they would need to make in upcoming lessons. They proved to be extremely resourceful teachers and highly sensitive to their students' strengths and limitations. Here are just two examples of how they incorporated a variety of instructional means and learning modes into lessons that followed that term.

Tor was doing a lesson on getting around the neighborhood, asking for and giving directions, and names of common services (restaurant, bank, grocery store, etc.). To give learners practice, he prepared a tactile information-gap using specially designed maps. Masking tape marked the roads, a coffee bean represented the coffee shop, a penny represented the bank, and a piece of fabric represented the laundromat. Students worked in pairs and, each one with a different map, gave directions to their partner on how to get around their assigned neighborhood.

Sarah was doing a vocabulary lesson on clothing and colors in the assigned textbook. The color swatches and pictures in the book were going to be of little help in making the language meaningful to the blind students, so she added the dimension of fabric types and texture to the lesson. For one of the practice activities, learners stood in a circle and were given an article of clothing. Sarah put on music and had the students pass the articles to the left until the music stopped, at which point the learners described what they had in their hands in terms of fabric type and texture. This continued until everyone had a chance to describe several items. The activity elicited words such as these: *corduroy, wool, fur, soft, rough, furry, bumpy, smooth.*

If you have learners with physical handicaps or limitations, you need to plan lessons accordingly, asking yourself these questions:

- *Do the instructional techniques accommodate all the learners?*

The teacher who uses mingles and multiple groupings in most lessons needs to think of ways to accommodate a learner with mobility problems, making the lesson equally rich for all learners. Tor's tactile information gap accommodated the needs of the blind students.

- *Are multiple modes of learning encouraged (visual, oral/aural, kinesthetic, tactile)?*

Both Sarah and Tor incorporated hands-on, physical activity that helped to make language practice equally effective for the blind and sighted students. A learner with hearing problems would benefit from visual reinforcement, both pictorial representations and words written on the board.

- *Do classroom aids enhance learning (visual aids, audio/video tapes)?*

Sarah's choice of clothing with varied and interesting textures made the lesson much more relevant to her students, i.e., that is how they would probably describe a piece of clothing. Older students with impaired vision struggle with small visuals or small print on overhead transparencies, so it is important to use large, vivid photographs, drawings, and print. While authentic-sounding listening passages are beneficial to ESL learners, poor quality recordings can frustrate learners with hearing problems.

Few students will volunteer that they have a problem, so it is up to the teacher to be observant and to ask himself or herself the questions above, regardless of whether or not you are aware of students with physical handicaps or limitations.

7.2.3 Victims of Torture or Abuse

A potential obstacle to learning is past experiences with torture, or past or present experiences of domestic abuse or other forms of trauma. In 1948, the United Nations defined torture as:

> . . . a systematically performed physical and mental violence directed against persons confined in prison or in another way deprived of their freedom. Torture aims at breaking down the victim's personality and identity and getting information. But it is also an instrument of massive political oppression (cited on the Canadian Centre for Victims of Torture [CCVT] Website).

The consequences of torture are long lasting, and students in your classes may be living with the effects for years, if not for a lifetime. Those effects include an inability to concentrate, feelings of disorientation, disrupted sleep patterns, post-traumatic stress, depression, or side effects of prescribed medication. As ESL professionals, our primary responsibility is to provide language instruction. Trying to counsel learners in any way will cause more harm than good, so referring learners to appropriate counseling services is key. However, there are means of making students who have experienced torture or trauma more comfortable while they are in our classrooms. The Canadian Centre for Victims of Torture offers these suggestions for teachers working with victims of torture:

For learners who exhibit difficulties with concentration:

- Keep lessons short and provide frequent breaks.
- Give brief instructions followed by demonstrations.
- Include physical activity when feasible for the students; hands-on tasks are easier to complete than those that require sitting passively listening.

To minimize the possibility of activating painful memories:

- Avoid discussions that deal with politics and religion in a controversial way i.e., the merits of one leader or form of government over others.
- Avoid using pictures and situations that are violent in nature, for example, those involving robberies, imprisonment, fires, and arrests. Photos depicting doctors and doctors' offices can be troubling because of the involvement physicians may have had in the torture they experienced.
- Discuss the content of presentations with guest speakers before they come into your class.

- Be aware of teaching practices that involve too much stimuli. Survivors have increased sensitivity to external stimuli and too much frantic movement, for example, TPR activities, could be a reminder of when the military entered a village and attacked the inhabitants.

Finally, the CCVT recommends that doors, blinds, and curtains be kept open as much as possible and, if the weather permits, at least one window. Assure learners that if they need a break at any time during the lesson, they are free to step outside for a few moments. Have the learners organize the room the way they would like it to look.

Immigrants who are experiencing the trauma of abusive relationships within a new culture, living with the effects of surviving political persecution, or witnessing violence in their homelands, may be hesitant to seek help, or may not even know where to go or whom they can trust. Cultural norms and support systems may be very different from what they knew in their own country. A social worker working with undocumented migrant workers shared with me the fear of deportation many victims face. Even legal immigrants and U.S. citizens are often wary of government involvement in their lives. Again, locating local counseling services that specialize in the area of trauma and abuse is the first step to take. Janet Isserlis (2000) makes the following recommendations for working with students who are or have been victims of abuse. These recommendations are equally applicable to students who are victims of torture:

- Find out about community resources. Find out what happens when one calls an emergency victims of violence hotline so that learners will know exactly what to expect when they call: What information will be asked for? What language assistance is available? What assurances of confidentiality exist? Consider providing instruction in the language they'll need to make these calls. Victims of violence hotlines are available to men and women; avoid framing issues of violence against women, per se, especially if so doing might call unwanted attention to any one learner's situation. The overarching rationale is to make learning safer for *all* students in the group.
- Listen to learners and allow their concerns about violence to surface in one form or another through, for example, conversation circles, readings, dialogue journals.
- Allow learners to share as much or as little information about themselves as they want, particularly when they are just beginning to study together. Let learners know that while they are invited to share information about their lives, they are not obliged to do so (Isserlis 1996a). Allow learners to choose their own level of participation in classroom activities.
- Validate learners' strengths. This is crucial for adults who have received negative messages about themselves or their learning abilities.
- Use learners' native languages for content learning, activities, and discussion to build trust and community (Florez 2000; Rivera 1999).

CONCLUSION Most ESL teachers are not experts in working with students who have particular needs, so they must be aware of their own limitations in regards to helping students who may have learning disabilities, physical or mental handicaps, or post-traumatic stress disorders. ESL professionals need to learn how and where to access appropriate referrals within the school system and the community at large, and assist learners to make the contacts they need. Teachers need to be active listeners and observers at all times and challenge themselves to create lessons that are inclusive and responsive to their students.

KEY TERMS

CHECKLIST OF KEY TERMS	On your own, or with a partner, provide an example or brief definition for each concept.
semiscripted dialogue	
discourse chain	
think-pair-share	
open enrollment	
managed enrollment	
line activities	
concentric circles	
learning disability	
accommodations	

Applying What You Learned

1 Adapting Activities for Multilevel Classes

If you are already teaching. . . choose an activity that you commonly use, but that has been difficult for some learners to complete (perhaps those who are less literate, quiet students, students unaccustomed to working in groups). Develop two variations for the activity that would make it more accessible to different ability-level learners.

If you are not teaching. . . select an activity in an ESL textbook. What problems would learners with minimal literacy skills have doing the activity? Develop an alternative task that meets the same language objectives, yet is more accessible to learners with limited literacy. Choose a listening or reading passage in an ESL textbook and create multiple options (e.g., assigning different roles, creating different comprehension questions, designing different follow-up activities) for working with the passage.

2 Learning from Others

One of the best ways to develop a repertoire for managing ESL classes is to talk to other teachers about what has worked best for them.

If you are already teaching. . . make note of something you've tried and ask at least two other teachers at your school for suggestions of ways to respond to the areas listed in the chart below.

If you are not teaching. . . visit a school and interview teachers and/or observe classes and gather ideas that you may be able to use in the future.

Ways of Managing Adult ESL Classes	
Adapting an activity for multilevels in class	
Handling open enrollment	
Working with learners with disabilities or physical handicaps	
Managing large classes	
Setting up the classroom	
Managing pair and group work	

Recommended Reading

Multilevel Activities

Bell, J. 1991. *Teaching multilevel classes in ESL.* Carlsbad, CA: Dominie Press (new edition 2003 from Pippin Publishing).

This is the definitive text on the challenges and suggested practices for managing multilevel classes.

Hess, N. 2001. *Teaching large multilevel classes.* Cambridge: Cambridge University Press.

This text is rich with ideas for managing large, multilevel classes, including ideas for motivating students and establishing class routines.

McKay, H. and **A. Tom.** 1999. *Teaching adult second language learners.* Cambridge: Cambridge University Press.

This book includes a wide array of interactive language tasks that can be used in a variety of adult ESL settings. Many of the suggested activities are open-ended and flexible, making them ideal for multilevel class.

The following articles address issues of working with learners with particular needs.

Adkins, M.A., B. Sample, and **D. Birman.** 1999. Mental health and the adult refugee: The role of the ESL teacher. *ERIC Digest.* Washington, DC: National Center for ESL Literacy Education (EDO-LE-99-06). http://www.cal.org/ncle/digests/Mental.htm

Almanza, D., K. Singleton, and **L. Terrill.** 1995/96. Learning disabilities in adult ESL: Case studies and directions. *The Year in Review,* 5, 1-6. http://www.cal.org/ncle/LDcase.htm

T. Holcomb, and **J. Peyton.** 1992. ESL literacy for a linguistic minority: The deaf experience. *ERIC Digest.* Washington, DC: National Center for ESL Literacy Education (EDO-LE-92-03). http://www.cal.org/ncle/digests/ESL_Literacy.html

Isserlis, J. 2000. Trauma and the adult English language learner. *ERIC Digest.* Washington, DC: National Center for ESL Literacy Education (EDO-LE-00-02). http://www.cal.org/ncle/digests/trauma2.htm

R. Schwarz, and **L. Terrill.** 2000. ESL instruction and adults with learning disabilities. *ERIC Digest.* Washington, DC: National Center for ESL Literacy Education. (EDO-LE-00-01) http://www.cal.org/ncle/digests/LD2.htm

Useful Websites

Literacy Resources Rhode Island maintains an extensive and up-to-date listing of resources for working with learners with disabilities. http://www.brown.edu/lrri/ld.html

LD and the English Language Learning **is part of a NIFL Special Collection on Learning Disabilities.** Robin Swartz provides an excellent overview of research and practice in the area of LD and adult ESL learners. http://ldlink.coe.utk.edu/esl_ld.html

Bridges to Practice A series of National Institute for Literacy guidebooks to help professionals who serve adults with learning disabilities. http://www.nifl.gov/nifl/ld/bridges/materials/bridges_docs.html

8 Selecting Instructional Materials and Resources

Part I ◆ Evaluate, Select, and Supplement Textbooks

8.1.1 Introduction

Among the many decisions teachers need to make is the selection of appropriate instructional materials. With myriad textbooks, computer software, videos, and classroom aids available, how can an ESL teacher make the right decisions? In Part I of this chapter, criteria for evaluating and selecting textbooks are considered as well as ways to supplement and adapt materials in order to meet the needs of a particular group of students. In Part II we consider the importance of taking learning outside of the classroom through activities such as field trips, scavenger hunts, interviews, or surveys. Part III focuses on ways to integrate technology in teaching, including computer-assisted language learning (CALL), which includes the use of commercial software, Internet activities, student-produced Web pages, and e-mail. Uses of video are explored in this section as well.

CHECKLIST

After reading this chapter and completing the activities, you should be able to

- describe different types of textbooks and explain the benefits using textbooks.
- evaluate the suitability of textbooks for your learners and within your programs.
- explain a variety of ways to supplement and adapt existing materials.
- articulate the benefits of integrating computer-assisted language learning in instruction.
- develop activities that take learners outside of the classroom.

Getting Started

Task 8.1

Lyle coordinates the daytime ESL program of an Adult Basic Education center in St. Paul, Minnesota. There are around 400 learners enrolled at any time. How do Lyle and his colleagues handle each of the following in their program? Read the description on the next page and complete this table with the different ways in which he and his colleagues select and make use of textbooks and other resources.

Lyle and the teachers in his program have many decisions to make about textbooks and materials. Lyle compiles lists of suggested texts for each level, and teachers design class syllabi, identifying the texts they will use along with performance outcomes. The program purchases class sets of textbooks for classroom use only, and these sets are used with different classes from one term to the next; the books are not given to the students to keep. The textbooks are also available for purchase at the school bookstore for those who want their own copies. A limited number of texts are also available through the school library. In addition to textbooks are teacher-developed units around core themes in their curriculum (health, education, family, culture). These units include suggested activities from texts, teacher-made activities, activities for the computer lab, authentic materials, and classroom aids. Learners also complete supplementary activities with commercial software and Internet resources in the computer lab. Lyle wants to be sure teachers have adequate resources to support teaching and learning.

Text selection	
Textbooks for learners	
Development of thematic units	
Technology	

Follow-up Every program is unique and learner variables, program expectations, fiscal restraints, and technological resources, among other things, will have an enormous impact on the decisions that are made about textbooks, software, and other materials. In the case of Lyle's program, for example, providing a textbook for every student to keep is not feasible; neither the program nor many of the learners have the resources necessary to do so. Purchasing class sets that are reused by different classes, however, is feasible and allows learners access to materials. The on-site bookstore gives those learners who can purchase materials the option of doing so. This large urban adult education center has computer labs and a budget to purchase software. A small community-based program may have only one computer in each classroom and only limited funds for software. The process of selecting textbooks varies as well. The large evening program at Lyle's site has a selection committee, while teachers in the day program make their choices from a list of recommended texts.

This chapter focuses on the following decisions that classroom teachers need to make:

- When given different books to choose from, how will I know which is best for my students?
- How can I adapt and supplement the text I'm using?

- What other resources can I draw on, both inside and outside of the classroom?
- How can I integrate technology to enhance learning?

We begin with a process for selecting and evaluating textbooks.

8.1.2 Types of Textbooks

In a discussion of textbooks, it is important to make distinctions among the types of materials available to teachers. There are many different types of textbooks to choose from, and while not every one fits cleanly into a category, there are some key categories worth noting (examples of each are provided in the Recommended Reading section at the end of the chapter).

a **Core series,** or **basal series,** consist of a sequence of books for beginning through high-intermediate or advanced-level learners. All skill areas are integrated, although many series put a stronger emphasis on listening and speaking skills development and have a life-skills focus. Grammar points and functions of language are presented in each unit, along with competencies and vocabulary. Most core series written with an adult ESL audience in mind have correlations to CASAS, BEST, SCANS, EFF, and state standards (e.g., California model standards). Core series normally consist of a multimedia package, including audio/video tapes, CD-ROMs, pre- and postassessments, and teacher texts with suggestions for lesson planning and implementation. Some series provide an accompanying Website with Web-based activities.

b Like core series, **integrated-skills texts** provide practice in all skills areas, but are not part of a multilevel, multimedia series. They function as stand-alone resources to which teachers may add other elements.

c **Grammar texts** come in many forms. There are core grammar series, ranging from beginning to advanced, that include grammar presentations and practice, both written and oral. They may be accompanied by audiocassettes, CD-ROMs, and Websites for learners and teachers. **Reference grammars** are those texts that list the rules of form and usage of grammar structures. They do not contain activities for learners and would not normally be used as the textbook for an ESL class. Many teachers keep a reference grammar in the classroom for learners to check or clarify a grammar point, or for the teacher's own reference as questions arise.

d **Skill-specific texts** provide learners with a focus on the development of a particular skill area (reading, writing, listening, speaking). A good text will provide learners with practice in all skill areas, however, the emphasis is on development of strategies to become, for example, a more effective reader (e.g., predict, read for gist, find meaning of new words in context), writer (e.g., prewrite, organize ideas), listener (listen for specific information), or speaker (e.g., ask for clarification, speak with intelligible pronunciation).

e **Literacy texts** are intended for learners with limited literacy skills. The texts often include passages written by ESL learners, and include practice in both top-down skills such as predicting, reading for gist, as well as bottom-up skills such as copying, filling in letters, recognizing sound/spelling correspondences.

f There are **content-based texts** for particular subject areas (citizenship) and **vocational English as a second language (VESL)** texts for learners preparing for specific jobs and industries (food service, retail, manufacturing). Texts for GED or GED preparation focus on subject areas such a math or social studies.

g Also worth considering in this section are the multitude of **teacher resource books** that provide teaching suggestions and activities for skills area, grammar, functions, competencies, and vocabulary. These books can provide teachers with a wealth of information for supplementing and adapting core texts.

8.1.3 Evaluating and Selecting Textbooks

No textbook can provide everything needed in a class; it is just one of many resources from which teachers develop their curriculum. The process of choosing materials starts by asking these questions:

- Will I use an assigned text and follow it throughout the class?
- Will I use an assigned text and supplement it with other activities as well as authentic materials?
- Will I adapt a text?
- Will I create all of the materials myself?
- Will I work with colleagues to create units that we can share?

Unless you have unlimited time on your hands and you are also an expert materials writer, the last two options are probably not very realistic or even desirable. Writers and publishers spend a lot of time and energy assessing the needs of programs and are constantly producing new materials (some better than others) from which teachers can choose. For those teaching 20 or more hours a week with little or no paid preparation time, having a textbook as a backbone to a curriculum is essential and can have many advantages. There are also a few potential pitfalls of which teachers, particularly those new to the profession, need to be aware. Table 8.1 outlines both the benefits of using a textbook as well as some cautionary notes that need to be considered.

In weighing in on the benefits and drawbacks to using assigned textbooks, the most promising practice is to select a text that corresponds as closely as possible to the needs of your learners, the program, and the teacher, and supplement it with activities from teacher resource books, authentic materials, or learner-generated texts as needed. Selecting the text that has the best fit for learners becomes essential, which means that selection committees and teachers need to take the selection process seriously, taking into consideration a number of variables.

TABLE 8.1

Benefits of using a textbook	Potential drawbacks of using a textbook
• It assures a measure of structure, consistency, and logical progression in a class. Textbook writers have taken a considerable amount of time and effort to produce material that is logically sequenced and is as comprehensive as possible.	• Not all of the content corresponds to the needs of learners and it may require a substantial amount of supplementation and adaptation.
• It minimizes preparation time for teachers with heavy teaching loads and little time to prepare.	• It may not allow for the degree of learner input desired by both the class and teacher.
• It allows learners to review the material and preview other lessons.	• Inexperienced teachers may rely too heavily on a textbook, following it in lockstep sequence regardless of learner strengths, wants, and needs.
• It meets a learner need/expectation of having something concrete to work from and take home for further study.	
• It provides those new to teaching with guidance in course and activity design as well as grammar and other aspects of English (Ur 1996).	
• It may provide multiple resources: tapes and videos, pre- and postassessments, CD-ROMs for practice in a computer lab, and self-study to meet different learning modalities.	

Task 8.2

What do you look for in a textbook? Brainstorm all of the considerations you make and then identify the five criteria that are the most important to you. For those of you already teaching, draw on experiences from your program. Those of you new to teaching can draw on the skills and knowledge you have gained though your training and this text.

Considerations in selecting a textbook

Five most important criteria:
1 __________
2 __________
3 __________
4 __________
5 __________

Follow-up If you are working in class, compare your list with five other people. What seem to be the most important considerations in this group?

I asked several practicing teachers what they look for in a textbook. Here are the responses from two veteran ESL teachers, both program coordinators. Do you see any similarities between their responses and your own? Read what Beth and Lyle have to say and identify factors that you and your classmates or colleagues had not considered, and then add them to the box in Task 8.2.

Beth[1] I look for textbooks that are. . .

Relevant to the students' lives and/or within the realm of their experience.

Straightforward layout that is easy to follow, without excessive clutter. (Many ESL texts designed for the pre-academic and/or overseas market are too flashy and busy for adult ESL students.) Print size is large enough for older students. Directions are clear and simple.

The language is natural; examples of realia in survival/literacy texts (classified ads, checks, application forms, etc.) are authentic.

The book follows sound pedagogical principles for the skill that you want to teach. There are a variety of exercises for different learning styles.

There are nonverbal or nonlinguistic elements such as pictures, humor, and character development that will help students to retain what they've learned.

Beth adds considerations such as the quality of artwork, usefulness of the teacher's manual and notes, whether or not there are masters that can be photocopied for some activities, as well as a publisher's reputation and willingness to provide examination copies.

Lyle I look for a learner-friendly format—which is not cluttered, has good visuals, and is generally pleasant and inviting. The material and exercises need to be relevant and engaging, but not overwhelming or intimidating. I look for materials which learners could comfortably use independently as well.

I look for a variety of relevant, timely topics addressed in fairly concise units which are more broadly appealing and considered generally important to ESL adults. I also look for a balanced approach to both functional skills and academic development.

I look for texts or curriculum programs that integrate all the communication skills and offer a wide variety of ideas and support related to

[1] Beth Easter is in charge of Distance Learning at the Lehmann Center, ABE, Minneapolis Public Schools. Lyle Heikes is Coordinator of the adult ESL day program at the M. Hubbs Center for Lifelong Learning, ABE, St. Paul Public Schools.

teaching and learning these skills. A very important part of this is the critical thinking component. I look for material which fosters further development of higher-order thinking skills.

I look for material that is multicultural in nature—takes into account the lifestyles, approaches, perspectives, and experiences of people living in other cultures as well as of those who are adjusting to life in the United States. I think it's crucial to use sound educational materials to not only facilitate the development of literacy skills, but also to assist in the successful transition into a new culture and society. I also like materials that have a problem-solving component in order to help learners feel/become more empowered in their lives.

Central to both Beth and Lyle's considerations is a focus on the fit between the text and the learner, which is in keeping with the principles of learner-centered teaching. In assessing the extent to which a text would be responsive to learners, a teacher needs to consider the questions in Table 8.2.

TABLE 8.2 Textbooks and principles of learner-centered teaching

Learners' knowledge and experiences are validated	Does the text include activities that activate learners' prior knowledge about the context or theme of the unit? Are there warm-up and previewing tasks?
Learners have active roles in the classroom	Does the text provide a variety of interactions and sufficient pair and group work?
Learners control the direction of activities	Do the activities allow learners to take direction of activities, or is everything written with a teacher-led mode of learning in mind?
The content of instruction is relevant to the students' needs and interests and draws on their experiences and knowledge	Are the contexts and themes in the chapter relevant to learners' lives? Who are the people represented in the text? In what ways are they represented? Are they depicted in roles to which learners could relate and that are respectful to adult learners?
Classroom interactions and tasks are authentic	Does the language produced through the activities in the text represent authentic use of language?
Learners acquire strategies that help them learn inside and outside of the classroom without the help of a teacher	Are learners presented with and given practice learning strategies that they can use outside of class (e.g., predicting, guessing)?

Byrd (2001) suggests that the fit between the text and the program as well as the fit between the text and teacher need to be considered. Does the text adequately address the core program outcomes? Does the text correspond to standardized tests (e.g., CASAS, BEST) and standards (e.g., state, EFF, SCANS) that are used to assess students? Are there means of assessing learning within the text? Are the supporting materials going to help me in my day-to-day planning? All of these considerations can come together to create a checklist for evaluating textbooks. Table 8.3 incorporates questions about the learner, the program, and the teacher.

TABLE 8.3 A Textbook Evaluation Checklist

1 The textbook and the learner	1 Disagree	2 Agree	3 Strongly agree	Strengths and weaknesses
a Learner knowledge and experience are connected to learning through schema-building activities.				
b Contexts for presentation and practice relate to learners' life circumstances.				
c People in the book are depicted in nonstereotypical roles, and roles to which learners can relate.				
d The material challenges students and promotes higher-order thinking skills.				
e Language practice represents real-life use of language. Examples of realia (classified ads, checks, application forms, etc.) are authentic.				
f The text provides learners with a wide variety of activities and modalities for learning. It appeals to a variety of learning styles.				
2 The textbook and the curriculum	**1**	**2**	**3**	**Strengths and weaknesses**
a The text adequately responds to the outcomes of the program.				
b The book contains assessment tools that can be used to measure progress in our program.				
c The language and content corresponds to the core standards (e.g., California Model Standards, CASAS, EFF, SCANS) and assessments (e.g., CASAS, BEST) used by the program/state.				
3 The textbook and the teacher	**1**	**2**	**3**	**Strengths and weaknesses**
a The approach used in the text corresponds to my beliefs about teaching and learning and represents current knowledge about teaching and learning.				
b The supplements, resources, and teacher aids are adequate. The teacher's edition provides helpful suggestions and guidelines, especially for new teachers.				

8.1.4 Choosing Literacy-Level Materials

Publishers of adult ESL materials provide a range of options, including textbooks that are intended for emergent readers (see Table 5.1 for descriptions of preliterate, nonliterate, or semiliterate learners), often referred to as literacy-level learners. Teachers new to ESL often have difficulty recognizing the elements that make materials appropriate for literacy-level learners. Sometimes books are selected for a program without having a clear idea of the true language competency of students, and then a teacher finds himself or herself with a textbook that has far too much print and not enough visual support. In fact, one of the most common complaints I hear from teachers of beginning-level learners is that the text selected for the class is really too difficult for the students. The literacy-level learner and a beginning-level learner who has basic literacy skills have very different needs, so in evaluating textbooks for literacy-level learners, the teacher needs to add some key questions to his or her textbook evaluation checklist.

- Does the material build on learners' knowledge of spoken language and build literacy from there?
- Does the material provide practice in basic literacy development (copying letters and words, phonemic awareness, spelling) while at the same time presenting and practicing vocabulary and competencies?
- Is the vocabulary supported with clear, unambiguous visual support?

Task 8.3

Compare excerpts from two units on the topic of family. The first one is from *First Words in English* (Mrowicki 1990) and the second one is from a beginning-level core text from the *Contemporary English* series (Simons and Weddel 1999). Each has been designed with a different learner audience in mind, but can you identify what makes them different? Review the two units and answer these questions:

1 Which unit is designed for the literacy-level learner? How can you tell?

2 Does the material build on learners' knowledge of spoken language and build literacy from there?

3 Which activities in the units provide practice in basic literacy development (copying letters and words, phonemic awareness, spelling)?

4 Is the vocabulary supported with clear, unambiguous visual support?

Excerpt 1 *First Words in English*

LETTER AND SOUND PRACTICE.

Write the words with S.

s __ __

s __ __ __ __ __

Write the words with ER.

__ __ __ __ er

__ __ __ __ __ er

__ __ __ er

__ __ __ __ er

READING PRACTICE.
Read.

mother	father	husband	wife
sister	daughter	brother	son

Write the words under the pictures.

A and B: ____________

A and C: ____________

B and C: ____________

A and B: ____________

A and C: ____________

B and C: ____________

13

Write the correct words.

A and D: ____________ C and D: ____________

B and C: ____________ A and C: ____________

A and B: ____________ B and D: ____________

Read. Write. Remember.

Write the first names of your family.	Write the relationship.

14

(Mrowicki, First Words in English, *Linmore Publishing, 1990)*

Excerpt 2 *Contemporary English*

CULTURE CORNER

Read about Chan Luong's family tree.

Chan Luong is from Vietnam.
He lives in San Diego now.
His wife, Kim, is American.
Chan's parents live with them.
Kim's parents are in New York.

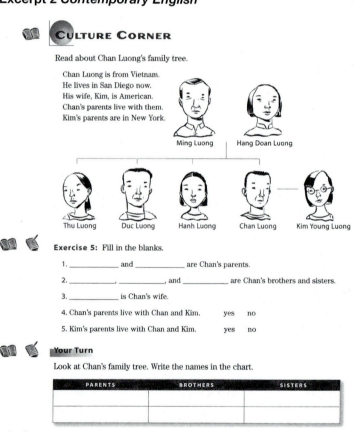

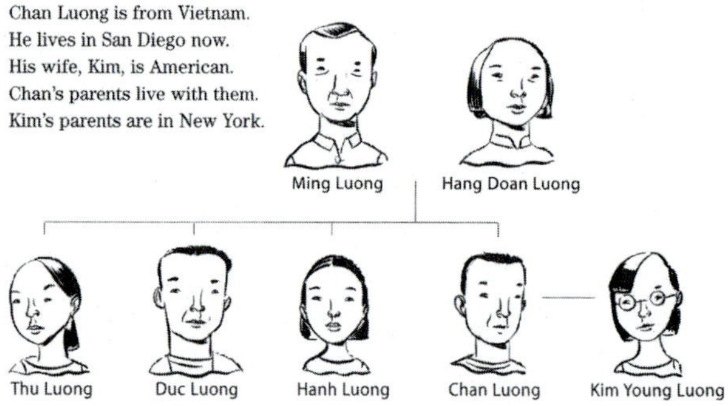

Exercise 5: Fill in the blanks.

1. ____________ and ____________ are Chan's parents.
2. ____________, ____________, and ____________ are Chan's brothers and sisters.
3. ____________ is Chan's wife.
4. Chan's parents live with Chan and Kim. yes no
5. Kim's parents live with Chan and Kim. yes no

Your Turn

Look at Chan's family tree. Write the names in the chart.

PARENTS	BROTHERS	SISTERS

In Your Experience

Talk to a partner. Do parents live with adult children in your country?
Make your family tree on a piece of paper. Write the names.
Then talk about your family tree. Use *am*, *is*, and *are*.

(Simons and Weddel, Contemporary English, Book 1, *McGraw-Hill Contemporary)*

Follow-up Compare **Read Write Remember** from *First Words in English* and **In your Experience** from *Contemporary English.* In both cases, learners with sufficient oral proficiency could engage in a discussion about their own family. However, the example from *First Words in English* does not require that the students have very developed literacy skills to complete the task. Activities in *Contemporary English*, like most Level 1 texts, presume a level of literacy adequate to read discussion questions, fill in longer sentences, and read short passages like the one about Chan Luong's family tree.

8.1.5 ADAPTING AND SUPPLEMENTING TEXTBOOKS

Even after careful selection of a textbook, a teacher often needs to adapt and supplement the book to make material more relevant or accessible to learners, to challenge them, to provide additional practice, or to appeal to a greater range of learning styles and intelligences. It is important to maintain the overall theme, sequence, and flow of a curriculum when making modifications. Here are just a few recommendations.

1 Adapting units and activities to meet broader needs

a Before working with a dialogue in the book, co-construct a similar dialogue with the class. This allows for learner input and assures that the language used in the dialogue is within the learners' reach. Learner-generated dialogues have a stronger connection to the learners' lives as they use their own names and places in their community. The students can compare their dialogue to the one in the text, providing them with more than one way to express themselves and communicate with others.

b Evaluate a chapter ahead of time in terms of relevance to learners' lives and interests, and prepare visuals and realia that will make the material more meaningful to your students.

c Evaluate the lesson ahead of time in terms of difficulty. Could the vocabulary, grammar, or functional language be more challenging? If so, brainstorm other words, forms, or phrases around the same theme that you want to present and practice. Are there many words that you anticipate will be particularly difficult in this lesson? If so, be prepared to demonstrate those words through multiple means, both visual and aural/oral.

d Some texts may favor a particular learning style. Think of ways to enhance the lesson to appeal to many learning style preferences. In a lesson on foods, I bring in spices that learners smell, and foods that they can taste. For learners who have difficulty understanding written or verbal explanations of verb tenses, use simple time lines to illustrate the meaning of the grammar (see Azar's *Chartbook*). Tactile learners may learn best by using manipulatives—realia, flashcards, or pictures.

e It is also important to respond to multiple intelligences. A common activity in ESL books is to place information in a sequence, either a dialogue, or information from a listening or reading passage. For someone who has a strong spatial intelligence, this task can be made easier by copying the sentences from the book, cutting them into strips, and having learners sequence information on a table. I have seen learners who have difficulty doing this task in the book exhibit tremendous success with the adapted version.

2 *Activities and materials for supplementing a textbook*

a Incorporate a video clip related to the theme of the unit. In a grammar lesson on the simple future and making predictions, videotape the morning weather forecast. Give learners a simple listening task to complete:

Monday	Tuesday	Wednesday	Thursday
High ______	High ______	High ______	High ______
Low ______	Low ______	Low ______	Low ______

In reporting their findings, students use the simple future tense: *The high will be 70° on Tuesday.* This allows learners to see how the grammar is used in real-world contexts. The same can be done by sending the learners to a weather website (see more ideas on supplementing with Web-based activities in 8.3.2/8.3.3).

b Supplement the lesson with short, authentic reading texts related to the theme of the unit. For students who enjoy watching television, bring in the TV schedule when working on times and making plans. Learners interview each other using simple questions:

What do you like to watch on TV?

When are you free this evening?

What stations do you have at home?

Learners check the schedule and make suggestions for their partner based on the information they collected in the interview.

c Bring in circulars from stores your students frequent when conducting lessons on shopping for food, clothing, or household items. Create simple selective reading tasks, e.g., What soap is on special this week? How much is chicken per pound?

d Supplement activities in the book with easy-to-prepare information-gap or grid activities like the following:

In working on the simple present and routines, have learners copy a grid like this from the board:

Name	When you get up	On weekends	In the evening

Learners mingle and gather information about their classmates by asking:

What do you usually do when you get up/on weekends?

Then report their findings.

e Select additional practice activities from any of the multitude of teacher resource books available, for example, *Teaching Adult Second Language Learners* (McKay and Tom 1999) or *Grammar Practice Activities* (Ur 1988) (see Recommended Reading at the end of this chapter). Most of these books contain a listing of activities by grammar point or language function, making them easy to cross-reference with more theme-based textbooks.

8.1.6 Making Use of Teacher Editions

Whenever I conduct workshops or teach classes on textbook selection with teachers new to ESL, I get the same reaction to beginning-level and literacy-level ESL textbooks: *How could I possibly spend more than five minutes on this activity?; How could this unit take up an entire class period?* Good beginning-level ESL texts are those that make use of large, clear visuals, minimal clutter, and simple instructions.

Task 8.4

How would you exploit the following page with a group of literacy-level ESL students? Take a few minutes to brainstorm ideas with a partner or write ideas if you are on your own.

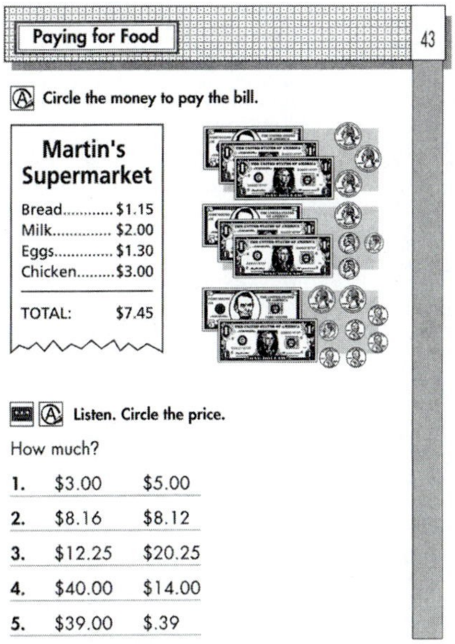

Paying for Food 43

A Circle the money to pay the bill.

Martin's Supermarket

Bread	$1.15
Milk	$2.00
Eggs	$1.30
Chicken	$3.00
TOTAL:	$7.45

A Listen. Circle the price.

How much?

1.	$3.00	$5.00
2.	$8.16	$8.12
3.	$12.25	$20.25
4.	$40.00	$14.00
5.	$39.00	$.39

(From LifePrints, *Florez 2002)*

Follow-up What makes a text complete for the teacher is a clear, comprehensive teacher's edition that provides guidelines on materials, previewing tasks, implementation activities, and extension activities. Now look at the same lesson from the teacher's edition of *LifePrints*. It includes a complete list of recommended realia (bills, coins, grocery store receipts, etc.) for presenting the concepts in this portion of the chapter as well as clear recommendations for implementing the lesson. Those who are more experienced will not necessarily follow these recommendations to the letter but, for the new teacher, this teacher support is invaluable. Compare these recommendations to the ideas you brainstormed.

Paying for Food

Purpose: To give practice in identifying amounts of money

Teacher Preparation and Materials

1. Copies of a simple receipt from a supermarket or drugstore
2. Sets of money (bills and coins) from Handout 14, Money
3. Audiotape for Literacy Level
4. Multiple copies of circulars from several local supermarkets *(Expansion/Extension)*

Warm-up

1. Say five prices, and have learners write the prices they hear. Have volunteers write each price on the board, and have learners check their answers.
2. Give learners copies of a simple receipt from a local supermarket or drugstore. Hold up a copy or the original receipt, and say *receipt.* Have learners repeat. Ask learners where they get a receipt. Have volunteers read the price of each item on the receipt. Write the prices on the board as they say them. Ask *What is the total?* Write *total* on the board. Have learners find the word on the bill. Ask *What does* total *mean?* and elicit an explanation. Ask learners for the amount of the total. Draw a line under the prices on the board and write the total beneath it. Give the learners each a set of the money from Handout 14. Have them combine bills and coins to pay the amount on the receipt. Circulate and check that they are correct.

Presentation

1. Have learners turn to page 43 and look at the first exercise. Ask them what they see (a receipt). Have volunteers read the items and their prices on the receipt. Ask for the total. Have learners circle the set of money in the pictures to the right that matches the total.
2. Have learners use the money from Handout 14 to create other combinations of bills and coins to pay the amount.
3. Play the audiotape, and have learners complete the exercise at the bottom of the page. Review the answers as a class. Practice saying and listening for any numbers that learners identify as difficult to distinguish, such as $14.00 and $40.00 or $39.00 and $.39. Practice distinguishing other similar numbers (FOR EXAMPLE: 13 and 30).

Paying for Food 43

(A) Circle the money to pay the bill.

Martin's Supermarket

Bread............ $1.15
Milk.............. $2.00
Eggs.............. $1.30
Chicken.......... $3.00

TOTAL: $7.45

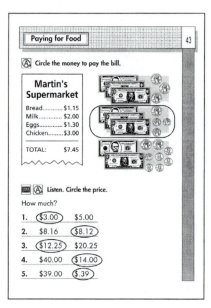

(A) Listen. Circle the price.

How much?

1. ($3.00) $5.00
2. $8.16 ($8.12)
3. ($12.25) $20.25
4. $40.00 ($14.00)
5. $39.00 ($.39)

Expansion/Extension

- Bring in circulars from competing supermarkets in the area. Pair learners. Have them find the same food items in the different circulars and compare the prices. Have each pair record at least three items and their prices and report back to the class where the best price can be found.
- Have learners prepare a simple shopping list. Then have them choose one of the supermarkets and use its circular to find prices for as many of the items on their lists as possible.

(From LifePrints, *Florez 2002)*

CONCLUSION Textbook selection depends on learner variables, program, and teacher needs as well as available resources, and making sound decisions can make all the difference for everyone involved. Adapting and supplementing the texts we choose can bridge the gaps that exist between a textbook and learner needs. This can be achieved by adding visuals, realia, and authentic materials, by adjusting activities to promote more interaction, or by implementing activities in ways that appeal to multiple intelligences and learning styles.

8.2 Community Activities

Given the limited amount of time learners actually spend in ESL classes, it is crucial that teachers provide opportunities to take learning beyond the four walls of the classroom. We know that a feature of effective ESL teaching and learning is authenticity of content and tasks. We do the best we can in ESL classrooms to replicate authentic use of language; we use authentic materials for listening and reading practice; realia connects new concepts to the outside world. But taking learning outside of the classroom expands learners' opportunities to engage in meaningful and authentic exchanges with others in their community. The question is, what should students be asked to do? Are whole-group field trips, which require extra funds and transportation, practical or even possible? Are there tasks other than field trips that can provide an extension to learning?

Task 8.5

Before we go on, brainstorm activities learners could do outside of the classroom. You can include ideas for class field trips, but also think of individual tasks that learners can complete in the community, on the job, or at home.

Taking Learning Outside of the Classroom

Follow-up Activities that take learning outside of the classroom may fall into one the following categories. See if your answers in Task 8.5 fit any of these categories.

a Field trips: group or independent

b Scavenger hunts

c Surveys/Interviews

d Community events and resources

e Project-based learning

Regardless of the tasks you choose to assign, the key to successful completion of the task is preparation done beforehand in class. Let's look at examples of tasks for each category along with suggestions for preparing learners in class before they go out on their own.

A. Getting Ready for Field Trips (Group and Independent)

Programs that have transportation (a van, bus, easy access to public transportation) may take students to libraries, schools, museums, performances, or community services in order to complement and enhance their curricula. A VESL class might visit a company that employs individuals in the area the students are learning about (e.g., health care, auto mechanic) so that they can observe firsthand what a job in that field entails. In a citizenship class, a speaker from the INS may be invited in, followed by a class visit to an INS office.

What do learners do when they get to their destination? How do they know what to expect? Preparing for a field trip is much like conducting prelistening or prereading activities; you want to activate the learners' prior knowledge and expectations about what they are going to experience when they get someplace. The teacher also needs to preview vocabulary and preteach key questions they may need to ask once they get there. Finally, students need to go on the field trip with a specific task to complete, in pairs or individually.

For those programs with limited funding and no access to transportation, **independent field trips** with a purpose can be assigned. Rather than taking the entire class somewhere, students explore a location in their neighborhood. Everyone can visit the bank near his or her home to gather information about opening an account. Afterward, the class can compare which bank has the lowest fees. The class can generate a list of foods they commonly buy and then visit their local market to record prices. Again, the whole group can then compare prices at different stores and in different neighborhoods. For group or individual field trips, have students gather information using grids like the ones below (Parrish and Pecoraro 2002). In Sample 1, each class member gathers different information at the chosen destination, be it a store or service. Upon returning to class the next day, the students mingle using Sample 2 to collect information from everyone's experiences.

Sample 1 Preview these questions with the class and ask the students to gather the information when they complete their visit to a location in their community.

Answer these questions when you go on your field trip.	
1 What did you see? Did you talk to anyone there? Who?	
2 What was one new thing you saw or did?	
3 What did you bring home from your trip? Examples: library book, food, clothes, information, schedule	
4 How did the field trip help you?	

5 Was speaking English easy or difficult? Why? Did you have any trouble saying what you wanted to say in English? When did this happen?	

Sample 2 The day after the students have completed their independent field trip with purpose, have them gather information from all of their classmates about what they learned from their experiences:

Name	**What they visited**	**Report from their trip**
Petra	Garden store	Bought some seeds Learned when to plant tomatoes Enjoyed looking at all the flowers

(Parrish and Pecoraro 2002)

For intermediate to advanced-level classes, let students create their own grids for either whole-group or independent field trips.

Sample 3 Class-generated task

What do you want to find out on your field trip?	
Question 1	
Question 2	
Question 3	
Question 4	

(Parrish and Pecoraro 2002)

B. Scavenger Hunts

Scavenger hunts can be conducted for a variety of purposes. Learners can gather information from stores and services in their neighborhoods, their children's school, from work, or from the Internet (and as a follow-up activity, check to see if the Internet gave accurate information). At the beginning level, they may complete the scavenger hunt through observation, as in Sample 1. Higher-level learners might read manuals and talk to others to find the information they need as illustrated in Sample 2.

Sample 1

Find stores and services in your neighborhood. Write the names of the places you find. . .		
For buying groceries	**For washing clothing**	**For buying gasoline**
____________	____________	Dave's Amoco
____________	____________	____________
____________	____________	____________
For buying clothing	**For buying medicine**	**For opening a bank account**
The Clothes Horse	Walgreens	____________
____________	____________	____________
____________	____________	____________

This next example is designed for learners who are already working and can be used in conjunction with a unit on safety and work.

Sample 2

Look for the following information at your job. You may look at signs or manuals at your job, or you can talk to your co-workers.
1 Do you know how to report an accident? Find out how to report an accident.
2 Where can you find first aid at your work station?
3 What hazardous materials are at your workplace?
4 What safety precautions do you need to follow?
5 How many breaks can you take?
6 What should you do if you feel sick at work?
Write three more things you want to find at your workplace: ________________________ ________________________ ________________________

C. Surveys/Interviews

As with field trips, surveys and interviews should be conducted for a concrete and meaningful purpose. It is up to the learners and the teachers in a class to develop questions that are appropriate and connected to the curriculum. Here are just a few examples of the types of tasks adult ESL learners might complete. For all of these, the class can brainstorm the questions they want to ask:

- Interview someone whose first language is not English and who speaks English at work. What helps them communicate with others on the job?
- Interview someone who has become a citizen. How did they prepare for the test? What suggestions can they give you to practice for the citizenship test?
- Interview a teacher or other parent at your child's school. What are some suggested homework routines (when and where should children study)? What are some good resources for homework (teacher phone lines, Websites)?

D. Community Events and Resources

For those students living in large urban areas, there may be free or low-cost concerts or other performances, community education classes, health services, or legal services from which they can benefit. Learners may be more inclined to take advantage of them if the teacher uses materials about these resources in class. One teacher shared student outcomes that resulted from a lesson she conducted with her class on community education: one class member enrolled in a basic computer class, another took advantage of an exercise class, and another ended up teaching a class about her language and culture (Celeste Mazur, personal communication).

E. Project-based Learning

Implementing projects is yet another way to get students into the community (project-based learning is described in detail in section 2.1.10). Doing so informs learners about resources, both material and human, available to them in their communities. Bronz and Dorwaldt (2001) report on a project developed as a class by a group of single mothers facing time limits on welfare benefits. The class chose the topic of welfare reform and incorporated activities such as the following:

- Invited legislators to class.
- Studied policies of welfare and welfare reform.
- Discussed and debated issues of public assistance, jobs, and education.
- Researched different forms of welfare.
- Presented information to lawmakers on the Joint Committee on Health and Welfare.

Civic Participation and Community Action Sourcebook (Nash 2001) includes reports on several other projects initiated by ESL classes, including projects on AIDS awareness, domestic violence, bringing transportation to a rural community, and peace and tolerance.

8.3.1 Using Computer-assisted Language Learning and Internet Resources

In this day and age in which computer literacy is as commonplace as print literacy, computer-assisted language learning **(CALL)** can be as much a part of ESL instruction as the textbooks, classrooms aids, realia, and activities teachers use.

> I think teachers need to realize that technology is an important tool for our students. It is a part of almost every job in this country; their children are using technology in schools; and it levels the playing field because our students have free access to information. Also email is a very important way for our students to communicate with friends and family in their native country.
>
> *Sylvia Ramirez*

> Teachers really need to buy into the idea that we can't wait until students are in the higher levels to teach computer skills. We need to integrate language instruction with computer skills at the very basic level of ESL because of the economy and the access to community resources students need to know about on the Internet.
>
> *Donna Price-Machado*

(Responses to survey completed 1/03[2])

While some programs are farther along than others in integrating this technology, both Donna and Sylvia point out that CALL is not something to save for intermediate to advanced-level students. Teaching students basic computer skills, even something as basic as using a mouse, or point and click, provides them with skills they can develop, strengthen, and/or use at the workplace, in their communities, with their children and beyond. In some programs, lab time is conducted as a stand alone or supplemental activity with a different instructor. Learners might complete grammar review activities or practice word processing in ways that are unrelated to the themes or content of the ESL class. It is important that in cases where the computer time is offered as a self-access option or stand-alone class, ESL teachers collaborate with computer teachers to find ways to align CALL with the core ESL outcomes.

---

[2] Thanks to Sylvia Ramirez and Donna Price-Machado for sharing their expertise and experience with using computer-assisted language learning in their programs at MiraCosta Community College and San Diego Community College Adult School, respectively. References to Sylvia and Donna in this chapter are from the survey responses.

8.3.2 Developing Computer Skills from the Very Beginning and Beyond

When ESL teachers choose not to integrate computer-based instruction in their classes, it is often a reflection of their own fear of technology.

> I have a theory that computers are not as confusing to ESL students as they may be for other students. ESL students are used to being confused. They are constantly struggling to make themselves understood. So, for many of my students, technology is just another form of communication—and it is no more difficult than the other tasks they try to do in English. Technology doesn't replace a teacher or interfere with good ESL instruction—it is a tool to help students learn. It is often the students who are more comfortable with computers than teachers. Teachers need to learn about this tool and not be afraid of it!
>
> *Sylvia Ramirez*

Avoiding the computer because of our own fears is limiting learner access to an invaluable tool. I have spoken to teachers of literacy-level learners who suggest that developing computer skills is simply not an option for students who have not been exposed to literacy of any kind, let alone computer literacy. What if that student has a job in a factory where the instructions are provided primarily with visuals on a computer screen? What if she or he needs to check out of work on a computer with a simple point and click procedure? How about the beginning-level student who needs to pass a computer-based driver's test? All of these skills require computer literacy, even for those tasks that require minimal print literacy.

So where can a teacher begin? The answer to that question constitutes an entire book on the ways of integrating computers and the Internet in instruction. In this section, activities are suggested that are representative of the types of tasks learners can complete in ESL programs. In programs that do not have a computer lab, but have only one or two computers in the classroom, the teacher can provide a system of computer-work time to complete tasks independently or in small groups. All of the activities could be completed outside of class for those learners who have access to computers. They include basic word processing, Web-based activities, and the use of software. What is common to all of them is that learners engage in a purposeful task. Let's start by looking at some sample activities for literacy-level to beginning-level learners:

- After learning to say and write their name and address, learners type the information and print a label for their binders (Price-Machado 2003).
- After writing a class-generated language experience story, learners can first copy the story by hand, and then type and print their story during computer lab time or during independent work time in class.
- Students work in small groups to create descriptive lists of items in the classroom (or around other themes) while at the same time learning how to create tables on the computer (or, as Bakin suggests, a publisher tool).

The learner-generated lists can then be used for conversation practice (Bakin 2003). Susan Gaer suggests a similar approach for working on foods and pricing, starting with students visiting their local supermarket to collect prices for a list of foods the class generated. The data gathered is then used to create a price comparison chart (Gaer 1998b).

Name of item	Quantity	Color	Description
Tables	6	white	3 rectangular 3 round
Chairs	30	brown	Plastic and cloth
Computers	3	white	Desktop

(Bakin 2003)

- In a lesson on the climate and weather, learners can go to a Website such as CNN and gather information about the weather where they live in North America, or the weather conditions in their own country (Salehi 2000). These sites use minimal print, vivid visual presentations with maps and weather symbols, making them ideal for those learners who have limited literacy.
- Paired dictations or other activities in which one learner transcribes the language of another student can be completed in pairs at one computer.
- Student-produced Web projects can take many forms. A Website of home remedies provides a forum for learners to share their culture and expertise (Gaer 2003).

Learners can read about remedies from around the globe, and submit home remedies of their own, allowing them to develop their reading and writing skills as well as vocabulary related to the theme of health and wellness.

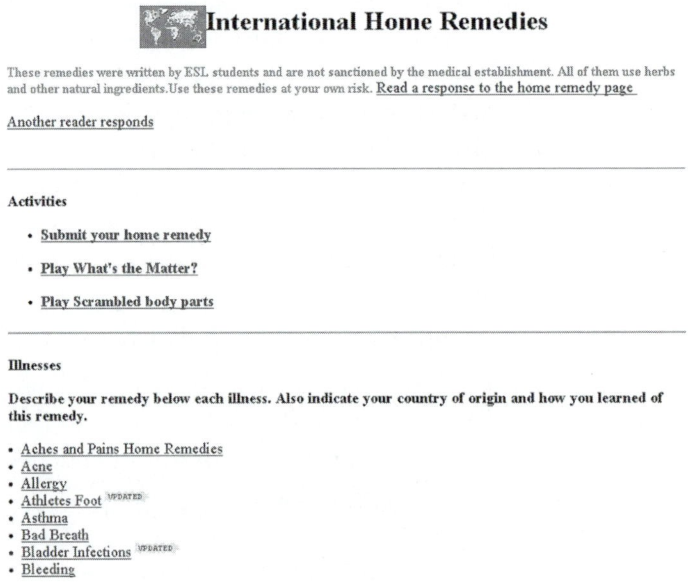
International Home Remedies

These remedies were written by ESL students and are not sanctioned by the medical establishment. All of them use herbs and other natural ingredients.Use these remedies at your own risk. Read a response to the home remedy page

Another reader responds

Activities

- **Submit your home remedy**
- **Play What's the Matter?**
- **Play Scrambled body parts**

Illnesses

Describe your remedy below each illness. Also indicate your country of origin and how you learned of this remedy.

- Aches and Pains Home Remedies
- Acne
- Allergy
- Athletes Foot UPDATED
- Asthma
- Bad Breath
- Bladder Infections UPDATED
- Bleeding

- To reinforce vocabulary or grammar covered in class, learners can use commercial software particularly well suited to the beginning-level (even literacy-level) learner (see resource section for suggestions). Using a program such as *Rosetta Stone*, learners practice using a mouse, pointing and clicking, basic keyboarding, and at the same time practice listening, speaking, reading, and writing. In Sample 1 below, learners review and practice the present continuous with basic vocabulary. They see the written prompt and hear the statement spoken, making it accessible to nonliterate learners. Then the student clicks on the corresponding photo. In Sample 2, Dictation, the learner hears a sentence and sees the corresponding photo highlighted, then types the sentence in the box. In using software like this to support and enhance classroom learning, a teacher needs to preview the material thoroughly to make sure the vocabulary is familiar and relevant to the students.

Sample 1 Reading and listening

Sample 2 Dictation

- Make use of learner Websites that have literacy or beginning-level activities. *The Learning Edge* is an interactive, adult literacy newspaper with tasks appropriate for independent literacy learning on topics such as missing work, reading utility bills, and finding an apartment. As learners hear the text read aloud, the portion they are hearing is highlighted. Each passage is followed by a quiz to check comprehension.

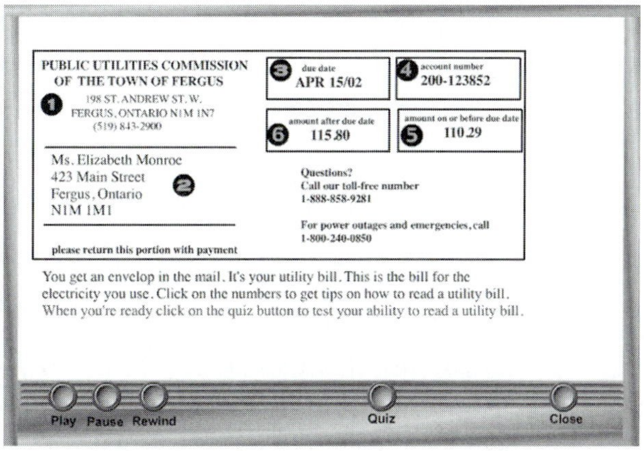

http://www.thewclc.ca/edge/

INTERMEDIATE LEVELS AND BEYOND

Potentially, any learner could access and make use of information on the Internet. Most Websites, however, have been designed for a native-English speaking audience. As with any form of authentic text, a teacher needs to create activities that facilitate the learners' ability to make educated guesses about where to find information and to read selectively to find what they need at the site. Some Websites are particularly dense, have biased or dated information, or are serving to advertise products or points of view, all of which can be problematic for learners (Hacker and Capehart 1999). A good Web-based lesson begins with careful selection of Websites.

8.3.3 SELECTING WEBSITES

Task 8.6

What do you think makes a good Website? What would you consider when selecting Websites for class use? Compare your responses to the recommendations that follow.

Hacker and Capehart suggest that teachers consider authorship, content, and currency, as well as design and navigation, when evaluating Websites for use with ESL students. Some key questions to consider are (Hacker and Capehart 1999):

- Is the author/creator of the Website clearly identified and are his or her institutional affiliation and credentials clearly identified?
- Is the information provided reliable; is it possible to verify the author's or organization's credentials?
- Is it written at a level and in a style accessible to your students? Will the content help you achieve the objectives of your lesson plan?
- Is the site free of bias and stereotypes?
- Can you easily locate the date when the site was last updated? Has it been updated recently?
- Does the site download quickly? (A page should be completely viewable in under 30 seconds.)
- Do the navigational buttons or links give you a clear sense of where they will take you?
- Is the overall design appealing or distracting?
- Is the site accessible to low-end technology users or does it require high-speed hardware with the latest versions of browsers and plug-ins loaded?

8.3.4 PREPARING FOR WEB-BASED ACTIVITIES

Sending learners to a Website with no preparation or specific task to complete would be like handing them an article from *The New York Times* and saying, "Read this." As with a reading lesson, a trip to the Internet needs to be preceded with schema-building activities. What do learners already know about the topic? What do they expect to find at the Website? Once at the site, learners need a specific task to complete. The example below includes a selective reading activity, followed by an information-gap activity where pairs of students share the information they gathered from the local Department of Motor Vehicles Website on getting a driver's license.

Student A	**Student B**
You are at the California Department of Motor Vehicles Website. You need to find the following information for yourself and your classmates.	**You are at the California Department of Motor Vehicles Website. You need to find the following information for yourself and your classmates.**
1 The Website gives nine steps to follow to get an original driver's license. What are the first five steps?	**1** The Website gives nine steps to follow to get an original driver's license. What are the last four steps?
2 Click on DMV office. Find the office closest to your home.	**2** Click on DMV office. Find the office closest to your home.
3 Click on make an appointment. What number do you call to make an appointment?	**3** When are DMV offices closed?
4 Click on social security number. What can you use to show your SSN?	**4** Click on birth date and legal presence. Give three examples of documents you can use as proof of birth date and legal presence.
5 Click on vision exam. How good does your vision need to be? What happens if you don't pass the vision test?	**5** What is a passing score? How many times can you take the test?
Now ask your partner what he or she found at the Website and record that information. Share what you learned as well.	Now ask your partner what he or she found at the Website and record that information. Share what you learned as well.

This is what learners see at the Website:

How to apply for a driver license if you are over 18

If you are a visitor in California over 18 and have a valid driver license from your home state or country, you may drive in this state without getting a California driver license as long as your home state license remains valid.

If you take a job here or become a resident, you must get a California driver license within 10 days. Residency is established by voting in a California election, paying resident tuition, filing for homeowner's property tax exemption, or any other privilege or benefit not ordinarily extended to nonresidents.

To apply for an original driver license if you are over 18, you will need to do the following:

- Visit a DMV office. (Make an appointment for faster service.)
- Complete application form DL 44. (An original DL 44 form must be submitted. Copies obtained by xeroxing, faxing or other methods will not be accepted.)
- Give a thumb print.
- Have your picture taken.
- Provide your social security number.
- Verify your birth date and legal presence.

- Pay the $12 application fee. (The application fee for a commercial driver license is $57.)
- Pass a vision exam.
- Pass a traffic laws and sign test. There are 36 questions on the test. A passing score is at least 31 correct answers. You have three chances to pass. (Sample Test)

You will then be issued a permit if you have never been licensed before. You may use the permit to practice driving with an accompanying adult who is 25 years of age or older, with a valid California license and close enough to take control of the vehicle if necessary. It is illegal for you to drive alone.

If you have a license from another country, you will be required to take a drive test. If you have a license from another state, the drive test can be waived.

To take your drive test, you will need to:

- Call a DMV office to set up an appointment. (Drive tests are not given without an appointment.)
- Provide proof of financial responsibility.

After you pass your drive test you will be issued an interim license valid for 60 days until you receive your new photo license in the mail. Double-check your address before you leave DMV and tell the DMV representative if you have moved or if your address is incorrect. If you have not received your license after 60 days, call (916) 657-7790 and they can check on the status for you. Have your interim license with you to provide information when requested.

You have three chances to pass the drive test. If you fail, you may practice for a while, then call DMV to set up another appointment. There is no waiting period, but you must make an appointment.

Other possibilities include sending learners on a **virtual field trip** or scavenger hunt, having learners conduct research online when taking part in project-based learning, or using one of the many Websites to help language learners practice specific grammar points (suggested sites for each of these are included in the Recommended Reading section).

E-mail, chat rooms, and electronic bulletin boards are Internet tools that can promote interaction at a distance between teachers and learners, among learners, and with individuals all over the world. In writing classes, email is a vehicle for sharing drafts and receiving feedback outside of class time. Chat rooms or bulletin boards provide a forum for discussion and questions. These tools are particularly well suited to advanced-level adult ESL or transition classes that are preparing students for academic programs where faculty expect a high level of computer and Internet literacy and knowledge. Using these tools takes a degree of skill and training, which should be integrated into instruction.

8.3.5 Integrating Software in ESL Instruction

A use of computer assisted language learning cited by all teachers I surveyed, even those new to teaching ESL, was the use of commercial software. Many of the new teachers expressed uncertainty about how best to select software and make use of learners' time in the computer lab. The selection and evaluation of software must be taken as seriously as any other choice made by ESL teachers. CALL experts have provided guidelines that can assist new teachers in making the best choices possible for their learners (Gaer 1998a, Healey and Johnson 2002).

- Does the language and content of the software reinforce my curriculum?
- Does the software meet the goals of the learners?
- Is the language and content familiar and relevant to my students?
- Is the software easy for my students to use?
- Does the software allow for pair activities in cases where I have few computers?
- Can learners use the software independently in cases where no teacher is available during self-access time?

Other challenges arise in the selection and implementation of software in ESL curricula. In programs with open enrollment, software needs to be simple enough to use so that learners can be trained to use it quickly as they enter the program. Assigning veteran students as trainers is one way to overcome this obstacle (Gaer 1998b). Yet another consideration is the cost of software, which can be prohibitive for small community-based programs. Most large programs have someone on staff who can handle questions about costs and licensing agreements.

There are other considerations with any of the computer-based activities presented in this section. In cases where a different teacher is in charge of the computer lab, there can be a disconnect between the computer-based instruction and in-class instruction. Learners should engage in follow-up activities after lab time in order to process and report on what they learned (Gaer 1998a). A student new to computers may lose work if she or he is unfamiliar with the process of saving documents, so make sure that you or a more experienced learner frequently saves learner work (Bakin 2003).

8.3.6 Using Video in the Classroom

Before computers, there was video. Many textbook series are accompanied by videotapes; there are video-based curricula such as *Crossroads Café* (1996) or *On Common Ground* (1999) that provide the core medium for instruction. Teachers may videotape news clips, scenes from television programs, or advertisements to supplement their lessons, or they may use feature films as the basis for instruction. Video is used in distance-learning programs and for self-access learning in order to provide visual support and context for instruction (Burt 1999). Whatever the case, video viewing should be anything but a passive endeavor for the learners. A video is simply another form of text (like a listening or reading passage) that needs to be accessed through previewing/prelistening, viewing and listening activities, and follow-up activities.

Videos have an advantage over audiotapes in that learners can look for visual clues to aid in their understanding of what they hear. Videos highlight non-verbal behaviors such as facial expressions, gestures, and body language (Bello 1999). They provide learners with more vivid representations of language use in a variety of contexts, e.g., in the community, at home, or at work. The following examples demonstrate just a few of the many ways video can be used in ESL classes:

- View a segment with the sound off. Identify nonverbals and discuss how the people in the scene are feeling. Predict what they are talking about. Watch a scene and co-construct a dialogue with the class that corresponds to the scene. Listen and compare class dialogue to dialogue in scene.
- Stop a scene and have class predict what will happen next.
- Videotape headlines at beginning of the news broadcast.

  Prelistening: Elicit stories in the news (jot student ideas on the board) or show a list of story topics to lower-level students and have them guess which ones might be in the news.

  Listening to Check Predictions: Check off topics predicted on board if they are in the news. Check off story topics that are included from list above.

  Listening Task: Give a list of one-sentence summaries (each corresponding to a headline in the news). Students check them off as they hear them. Add summary sentences not included in the news for a greater challenge.

Working with news broadcasts helps learners to see the value of listening to authentic language, something they could do on their own as a good learning strategy. They could replicate many of these activities at home while listening to the news, weather, or favorite TV program in English.

- Videotape learners as they role-play interactions, give presentations, or enact a skit. This can provide learners with immediate and powerful feedback on their performance (Taggart 1996).
- Teachers can videotape authentic interactions around the community (with permission from participants), such as returns and exchanges at a store, checking out at the grocery store, or cashing a check at the bank, and use the video as a means of introducing a competency to the class.
- If programs have video cameras (small digital cameras are ideal for turning projects into webcasts), learners can produce stories, presentations, and projects.

CONCLUSION

ESL experts have made a compelling case for the integration of technology in ESL instruction from the very start. ESL programs have recognized the need to prepare learners to use technology through computer-based activities, the Internet, student-produced Websites and more. Doing so allows adult learners access to an abundance of information, including job announcements, news from every corner of the globe, or parenting information. The ESL teacher's job is to create purposeful and achievable activities, to choose Websites and software that align with instructional and learner goals, and to support learners in developing technological literacy in ways that are at their pace and within their means.

Key Terms

Checklist of Key Terms	On your own, or with a partner, provide an example or brief definition for each concept.
core series	
integrated-skills texts	
literacy-level texts	
independent field trips	
scavenger hunts	
CALL	
virtual field trips	

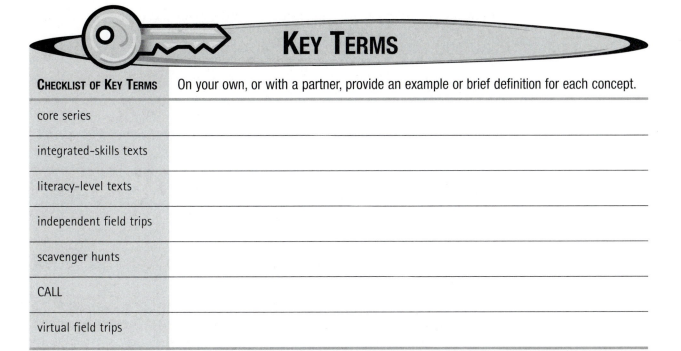

Applying What You Learned

1 Textbook Evaluation

If you are already teaching. . . evaluate texts that you could use for at least two of the groups you currently teach. Use the checklist on page 230, or adapt it if it does not address criteria that are particularly important to you. Evaluate one core text for each level, as well as one skill-specific text (reading, writing, listening, speaking, or grammar) for each level—four texts in all.

For those of you who are not yet teaching. . . evaluating a textbook using the textbook evaluation checklist has some limitations. You do not have a learner audience as a frame of reference for your evaluation. Therefore, create a description of a class based on an observation you have completed. Evaluate two core texts and one skill-specific text (reading, writing, listening, speaking, or grammar) for that level using the textbook evaluation checklist on page 230.

2 Adapting Textbooks

If you are already teaching. . . choose a unit in a book that you recently used that did not respond adequately to your learners' needs.

If you aren't teaching. . . choose a unit from an ESL textbook and identify ways in which you think it could be enhanced with visuals, realia, and authentic materials. Do the following:

- Make a list of realia and visual aids that would enhance the unit.
- Find an authentic text (short article, brochure, radio/video clip) that could be integrated into the lesson.
- Choose one of the activities and adapt it so that it would appeal to a greater range of learning styles.

3 Developing Web-based Activities

If you are teaching. . . choose an upcoming theme in your curriculum for which you would like to develop a Web-based task. Consider the questions on page 246 in making your selection. Develop a lesson that includes the following parts:

1. A preactivity that prepares learners for their visit to the Website.
2. A task that allows them to gather specific information at the site.
3. A follow-up task that allows learners to use the information they gathered for any number of purposes: as part of a project, to review and practice grammar or vocabulary, or as part of a competency-based lesson, such as the sample on getting a driver's license.

Recommended Reading

Core Series

Bernard-Johnson, J., D. Moss, L. Terrill, and **J. Huizenga.** 1996. *Collaborations: Beginner 1.* Boston, MA: Heinle and Heinle.

Florez, M. 2002. *LifePrints.* Syracuse, NY: New Readers Press.

Jenkins, R., and **S. Sabbagh.** 2002. *Stand out.* Boston, MA: Heinle and Heinle.

Molinsky, S., and **B. Bliss.** 2000. *Side by side.* White Plains, NY: Pearson.

Molinsky, S., B. Bliss, and **A. Kennnedy.** 1995. *Expressways.* White Plains, NY: Pearson.

Simons, A., and **K. Weddel.** 1999. *Contemporary English.* Lincolnwood, IL: Contemporary Books.

Steck-Vaughn. 1994. *Real-life English: A competency-based program for adults.* Austin, TX: Steck-Vaughn.

Literacy

Boyd, J. and **M. Boyd.** 1998. *Begin at the beginning.* Towanda, IL: Abaca Books.

Mrowicki, L. 1988. *Starting to read.* Palantine, IL: Linmore Publishing.

Mrowicki, L. 1990. *First words in English.* Palantine, IL: Linmore Publishing.

Listening/Speaking

Helgesen, M., and **S. Brown.** 1994. *Active listening: Building skills for understanding.* Cambridge: Cambridge University Press.

Mrowicki, L., and **J. Isserlis.** 1995. *Conversations in English.* Palantine, IL: Linmore Publishing.

Rooks, G. 1994. *Let's start talking.* Boston, MA: Heinle and Heinle.

Grammar

Azar, B. 1996. *Basic English grammar.* White Plains, NY: Pearson.

Elbaum, S. 2001. *Grammar in context.* Boston, MA: Heinle and Heinle.

Foley, B. and **E. Nesblett.** 1998. *The new grammar in action.* Boston, MA: Heinle and Heinle.

ESL Textbook Publishers

Cambridge University Press
http://www.cup.org

Delta Systems Co., Inc.
http://www.delta-systems.com

Dominie Press
http://www.dominie.com

Heinle/Thompson
http://www.heinle.com

Linmore Publishing
http://www.linmore.com

McGraw-Hill ESL/ELT
http://mhcontemporary.com

National Centre for English Language Teaching and Research
http://www.nceltr.mq.edu.au

New Readers Press
http://www.newreaderspress.com

Oxford University Press
http://www.oup-usa.org

Pearson Education ESL
http://www.pearsoned.com

Pro Lingua Associates
http://www.prolinguaassociates.com

University of Michigan Press
http://www.press.umich.edu/esl/

Commercial Video

Crossroads Café

INTELECOM

This television and print series for adult ESL instruction is appropriate for use in school-to-work, workplace literacy, family literacy, and citizenship programs. Twenty-six episodes center around six characters and a neighborhood cafe. Each episode has two video sidebars: **Culture Clips**, a documentary segment focusing on the story's cultural issues, and **Word Play**, an animated segment demonstrating appropriate language for communicating specific types of information.

Print materials are available through Heinle and Heinle.

Daily English Series

Open Learning Agency

In this 13-episode video course, learners are introduced to a series of scenarios presenting people in various day-to-day situations, using specific language and grammar. Each episode contains a pronunciation segment featuring two (phonetic) sounds, and a classroom section in which an instructor and student review the language and grammar covered in the episode.

A Day in the Life of the Gonzalez Family

Center for Applied Linguistics & Delta Publishing

This video and accompanying workbook for high-beginning to intermediate adult ESL students focuses on an immigrant family from Mexico. It portrays five family members and their experiences in looking for a job, furthering their education, and meeting the daily demands of working parents with three children. The workbook uses the video as a springboard for developing language, communication skills, and critical thinking.

On Common Ground

INTELECOM

Fifteen episodes address key civic and government concepts for U.S. studies and citizenship education.

Software

There is myriad software available for ESL learners. Visit the TESOL CALL Interest Section list, compiled by Deborah Healy and Norm Johnson, for a comprehensive, up-to-date listing of software.

http://128.193.24.180/softlist/slsearch.asp

Below is a sample of commonly used software:

Azar Interactive

Prentice Hall Regents

The exercises on this CD-ROM supplement the text. It includes over 50 topics with charts, exercises, and audio and video clips.

Better Accent Tutor

Better Accent

This software focuses on the development of intonation, stress, and rhythm.

Focus on Grammar

Exceller Software

This is a companion work to *Focus on grammar: An intermediate course for reference and practice* by Marjorie Fuchs and Miriam Westheimer with Margaret Bonner, Longman, 1994.

Grammar 3D: Contextualized Practice for Learners of English

Heinle and Heinle

This software can be used with any grammar text. Students control the sequence of activities and record keeping. It includes exercises for high-beginning to advanced EL learners.

Live Action English Interactive

SpeakWare

This is a TPR-based tool that gives learners practice in listening, speaking reading, and writing as they respond to people and objects on the screen. It is intended for beginning to intermediate-level learners.

New Oxford Picture Dictionary Interactive
Oxford University Press

This is the CD-ROM version of the classic picture dictionary for beginning-level ESL learners.

Pronunciation Power

English Computerized Learning

This contains a variety of exercises for pronunciation practice. Learners can listen, record, and review different sounds.

Reading in the Workplace

Educational Activities Software

Consists of reading activities for different careers, including food service, electronic, health care, and construction.

Rosetta Stone Language Library, English CD-ROM

Fairfield Educational Technologies
Harrisonberg, VA.

This is a comprehensive tutorial system that includes practice in all skills areas. It includes drills, listening tasks, dictation, and speech recognition features.

Teacher Professional Resources

Laubach Literacy Action 1996. *Teaching adults: An ESL resource book.* Syracuse, NY: New Readers Press.

A practical handbook for teachers new to ESL with numerous examples of practice activities for developing oral/aural skills as well as literacy.

Lewis, M. (ed.) 1997. *New ways in teaching adults.* Alexandria, VA: TESOL.

This text contains a collection of activities submitted by teachers of adult ESL learners from all over the world. Steps for implementing activities are explained in detail.

Teachers of English to Speakers of Other Languages (TESOL). *New Ways in Teaching* series. Alexandria, VA: TESOL.
http://www.tesol.org

CALL/Internet

Windeatt, S., D. Hardisty, and **D. Eastment.** 2000. *The Internet.* Oxford: Oxford University Press.

This book contains detailed examples of classroom activities that exploit the Internet in ESL classes, including searching on the Web, evaluating Web pages, creating language learning material, and communicating using the Internet.

Online Resources

Captured Wisdom on Adult Literacy: Integrating Technology Into Adult Literacy Instruction

http://www.ncrtec.org/pd/cw/adultlit.htm

Available online or on CD-ROM, Captured Wisdom demonstrates teachers integrating technology in their instruction. View sample classes and hear teachers talk about their practice. Viewers have the opportunity to chat with the practitioners as well.

Computers in Action: Integrating Technology into the ESOL Curriculum

Quann, S., and **D. Satin.** 2000.

An online teacher's guide to introducing students to computer use while teaching ESOL.
http://hub1.worlded.org/docs/cia/

E-Mail Projects Homepage

http://www.otan.dni.us/webfarm/emailproject/email.htm

This site, created and maintained by Susan Gaer, contains project-based learning activities that have been carried out by teachers and learners.

Surfing for Substance: A Professional Development Guide to Integrating the World Wide Web into Adult Literacy Instruction

Hacker, E., and **M. Capehart**
http://literacytech.worlded.org/docs/surfing/index.htm

9

Assessing Learning and Teaching

Part I ◆ Formal and Informal Assessment Processes

9.1.1 Introduction

Assessment occurs every day in ESL programs. ESL learners take standardized tests for placement and advancement; they complete entrance interviews and educational plans at intake. Assessment occurs as teachers observe students and provide feedback, and as learners provide feedback to one another. Teachers conduct in-class assessments to measure performance and achievement in relation to student goals and course outcomes; learners assess their progress as well. Assessment plays an important role in program evaluation and accountability. Finally, teachers undergo assessment; a supervisor may formally evaluate them; teachers may engage in self or peer assessment for professional development purposes. All of these processes are complex and require careful planning and implementation.

Up until now, this book has focused on what teachers do in the classroom. As we turn to the topics of assessment, accountability, and standards in this chapter and in Chapter 10, it is time to consider how everything ESL teachers do fits into the bigger picture:

> Teachers want to teach, but there are greater goals than theirs. Teachers come to programs with good training and good intentions, but may not know what drives the system. What funding, what standards, what accountability requirements, what national initiatives drive practice? So what I'd like teachers to know is who the funder is and what the funding requirements are for that program. Teachers need to know what data to collect for accountability purposes, and as they gain more time and experience in the program, more about broader national philosophical initiatives that drive policy (e.g., EFF, SCANS). And finally, they need to know how to reconcile learner goals with program goals that don't appear, at first glance, compatible.
>
> *Diane Pecoraro ◆ ABE/ ESL State Specialist*
> *Minnesota Department of Education*

Checklist

After reading this chapter and completing the activities, you should be able to

- describe the purposes for using standardized tests as well as the benefits and limitations of doing so.
- define alternative assessment and describe several alternative assessment techniques.
- develop an assessment tool that relates to learning outcomes of a lesson.
- explain accountability in adult ESL and describe a number of means of collecting data for accountability purposes.
- develop tasks that learners can use for self-assessment.
- describe means of developing as a teacher and integrate self-assessment and reflection into your teaching and learning.

As Diane points out, the perception of many ESL teachers is that their primary job is to teach. While this is absolutely true, she brings home the need for teachers to understand how they fit into the larger system of ESL, both locally and nationally. Teachers need to understand the importance of capturing learner achievement. Gone are the days when funding hinges on the number of hours learners spend in classrooms. Programs increasingly need to be accountable to funders in terms of gains in learner performance, and teachers need to have the tools to gather information in their classes that can provide evidence of learner progress and achievement of goals. Teachers and students may be doing an outstanding job, but how do teachers know that students are learning and how do students understand their own progress? This chapter focuses on assessment processes for day-to-day use and for broader accountability purposes. Chapter 10 turns to the issue of standards and how those relate to accountability systems at the state or federal level.

Getting Started

Task 9.1

Read the following assessment dilemmas. Identify the issues involved in each one and list the teachers' concerns in the box below:

Assessment Dilemmas

I have always used a participatory approach, developing a curriculum from my learners expressed needs. My program uses CASAS tests, which focus on many life skills that we don't necessarily work on in my class. I find that my students aren't promoted to the next level as quickly as before, but I don't want to teach to a test that doesn't represent what I do. Also, I'm feeling pressure from my supervisor to adjust my approach to teaching.

My learners are highly motivated and work very hard at improving their English. We use a standardized test to place learners, and a different version of that test at the end of each class level, but I don't know how to show them that they are making progress during the class. I teach level 1 students, many who have limited formal education from their countries. They have a lot of difficulty with test taking. Because of this, I don't know if the test really captures all that they've learned. I'm thinking I should do more on testing strategies in my class, but we have so little time together.

I find assessment to be the most difficult part of my job. We need to write a report on every student at the end of the term, but I always feel like I don't have enough meaningful data about my students' progress. I know this is important because our coordinator uses our assessments in reporting progress under our federal grant. I need to find ways to conduct meaningful and reliable assessments in class.

Assessment Issue	Teacher Concerns
Standardized tests	Learners don't have experience with testing. Don't know if I should work on test-taking skills in class.

The concerns of these teachers are echoed throughout the adult ESL community. What teachers really want to know is: *Are my students learning and are my classroom practices helping them learn?* Many teachers question the need to spend significant amounts of class time on assessment. Many new teachers (and experienced ones, for that matter) do not feel that they have the expertise to design tasks and tools that measure progress, nor do they appreciate the need to assess learning on a continual basis. As Diane highlights, capturing progress is important for accountability to funders, but who else is concerned with those results? Students, teachers, program staff, and other stakeholders, such as employers or family members, are concerned about how learners are progressing. Assessment results let learners know how they are progressing in relation to personal and program goals. Teachers use results to examine the effectiveness of their teaching. Program administrators place learners and shape curricula based on assessment results (Wrigley and Guth 1992). Programs need to employ a variety of processes that, in combination, provide all of these different stakeholders with the information they need.

Do you need to be an expert in assessment to measure learner progress in ways that are helpful for all stakeholders? The answer is no, otherwise few of us would be equipped to conduct the kinds of assessments covered in this chapter.

9.1.2 Clarifying Terms

One thing that makes the topic of assessment daunting for many teachers is the complexity of assessment terms and concepts. In this section, I pose some common questions and follow them with brief explanations. There are a number of resources available for those interested in a more in-depth study of test construction and assessment overall (see Recommended Reading section).

1 *What is the difference between* ***testing, assessment,*** *and* ***evaluation?***

Testing typically refers to those times when "we administer a prepared instrument to students for the purpose of measuring their language competence" (Brown 2001:384). **Assessment** is a broader term that encompasses day-to-day observations as well as a variety of alternative assessment tools that will be explored later. **Evaluation** entails an in-depth study of assessment results to determine the effectiveness of programs.

2 *What do I need to know about practicality, reliability, and validity in assessing students in my classes?*

Practicality refers to the feasibility of implementing a particular assessment or test. Conducting one-on-one interviews of learners at the end of class may be practical if you have 15 students, but not if you have 40. Is the tool you are using reliable? **Reliability** means that the assessment tool would result in consistent outcomes if administered more than one time or if rated by more than one assessor. What is the **validity** of the test results? Does the tool assess what it is intended to assess? A benchmark reading test used in public schools where I live used a text about Twinkies®, this in a district where more than 40% of the learners come from non-English-speaking homes (Wong Fillmore 2002). Failure on that test may have little to do with reading ability and everything to do with a lack of prior knowledge about the subject area. Does the test correspond to what was taught and what learners can reasonably be expected to know?

3 *How are placement, diagnostic, achievement, and proficiency testing different?*

Look at Table 9.1 for a summary of these types of tests.

TABLE 9.1 Test Types and Purposes

Placement testing	Where should a learner be placed in a program? Placement testing is conducted for the purpose of identifying the level most suitable for a learner. While most programs use a standardized test such as the BEST/BEST Plus or CASAS for this purpose, placement testing may also include interviews, surveys, or an in-house placement test that adequately differentiates learner levels.
Diagnostic testing	What do learners already know and what do they need to learn in relation to course outcomes? A diagnostic test reveals a learner's competence in relation to the outcomes of a particular class. In a class that focuses on speaking and pronunciation, the diagnostic test assesses oral skills; in a VESL class, the test assesses strengths and weaknesses for that particular work setting. Teachers employ a variety of tasks for the purpose of diagnosing learner needs, including interactive tasks, role-plays, writing samples, and observation by the teacher.
Achievement testing	What have learners gained through a unit or course? In many programs, standardized pre- and post-tests such as CASAS are given to ascertain achievement. This can be appropriate in cases where the program outcomes are strongly tied to CASAS (or other standardized test) outcomes. Alternative assessments are commonly used to determine achievement.
Proficiency testing	What is the learner's overall competence? A proficiency test is not designed for a specific course or set of outcomes. It may be used to determine someone's readiness for academic work, for example, the TOEFL (Test of English as a Foreign Language), which is given to thousands of students throughout the world hoping to enter universities in the U.S. (Brown 2001).

9.1.3 Standardized Tests

First of all, it is important to understand what standardized tests can do and what they cannot do. Standardized tests are typically used to differentiate among learners at different levels in order to determine the most appropriate level for them within a program, or to determine whether or not they have made progress in relation to a norm or criterion. Standardized tests are said to be **norm-referenced,** which means that scores reflect a comparison to a group (or norm) or **criterion-referenced,** which means that scores reflect a comparison to a set of outcomes (or criteria). They are administered and scored using procedures that are uniform and consistent (Holt and Van Duzer 2000). As a result, test scores can give a broad and consistent view of learner progress within and across levels, programs, and states. Results can depict progress in relation to the skills and competencies that the test covers. Federally funded programs often require performance measures on standardized tests along with teacher reports of learner progress, as one Adult Basic Education state director explains:

> I expect that our state and federally funded Adult Basic Education programs will use adult-appropriate, standardized tests to measure pre- and post-academic progress. Since the National Reporting System (NRS) is mandated for use in all of our programs funded through my office, we place high importance on the measurement of level change through the use of standardized tests. At present, the CASAS and BEST tests are the most popular for measuring ESL learner level change.
>
> *Dr. Barry Shaffer ◆ MN State Director of Adult Education*
> *Minnesota Department of Education*

Now let's consider what standardized tests cannot do. When used for placement, they cannot tell us what individual learners want and need as they enter programs. Because of a lack of test-taking experience, a learner's score may not reflect his or her real strengths and prior knowledge. When used to measure level change, unless the test mirrors program outcomes, it cannot provide us with learner progress and achievement in relation to unique learner or program goals. Nor can it depict learner achievement of more elusive skills, for example, increased use of learning strategies, or reading daily to a child. That is why standardized tests must be only one of many assessment tools used in adult ESL.

There are a number of standardized tests commonly used in adult ESL programs, which are outlined in Table 9.2.

TABLE 9.2 Standardized Tests Commonly Used in Adult ESL

BEST (Basic English Skills Test)	Intended for new immigrants with very limited English. Includes listening, speaking, reading, and writing. Can be used with pre-literate students, and those with little or no spoken English, through tasks that require only pointing to a picture. Includes an individual oral interview which requires training to administer. The test contains simulated real-life listening comprehension and speaking tasks such as counting money to buy items or telling time. Elementary reading and writing tasks are used for learners identified as having at least minimal literacy and includes tasks such as reading labels or writing a check. Two variations are available: BEST Oral and BEST Written and the just-released BEST Plus, which is a computer-administered version.
CASAS (The Comprehensive Adult Student Assessment System)	Has an array of standardized tests for placement and achievement for reading, writing, listening, and life skills. Different forms of the tests are available for different levels. Requires at least minimal literacy. Oral interview tests are available. CASAS has a strong focus on life skills competencies, for example, calling in sick to work. The CASAS Employability Competency System includes common workplace competencies (reading schedules, manuals, safety instructions). Easy to administer and score.
NYSPLACE (New York State Test)	Screens for basic literacy and includes an oral interview.
C.E.L.S.A. (Combined English Language Skills Assessment)	Includes reading, vocabulary, and grammar through the use of cloze and multiple-choice items. Commonly used in community college settings. Not suitable for nonliterate learners; contains no oral test.
TABE (Tests of Adult Basic Education)	Assesses English, math, and reading in Adult Basic Education programs. While intended for native-English speakers, it is sometimes used in advanced ESL and transition programs to determine learner readiness for university, GED, or adult diploma programs.

In reviewing the tests, it becomes evident that different standardized tests emphasize different skill areas. Some are more appropriate for literacy or beginning-level learners. As a classroom teacher, chances are you will not be the one selecting or administering the test, however, it is beneficial to have a general understanding of what learner test scores represent. Also, in cases where standardized tests are used throughout the program to measure learning gains, there are some things that can be done that do not require 'teaching to the test'.

- Carefully examine the content of tests used and check to see when and where test items correspond to course outcomes and learner goals.
- When you cover a particular competency in class, tell your students that this is something they may encounter on the test.
- Use multiple-choice activities in reading and listening lessons periodically to get learners used to that format (not as a test item per se).

Standardized tests need to be chosen carefully so that the outcomes assessed correspond at least partially to learner and program goals. Standardized test results provide only a partial view of learner ability and achievement. There are alternative means of capturing learner progress and achievement that engage learners in ways that more closely mirror instruction, many of which are more meaningful to teachers and students alike. These assessments that do not entail a formal paper-pencil test or standardized test fall under the umbrella of **alternative assessment.** A variety of alternative assessment techniques are described in the next section, including observation, performance assessment, learner self-assessment, and dialogue journals, among others.

9.1.4 ALTERNATIVE ASSESSMENT

Alternative assessment aligns with many of the principles of learner-centered teaching:

- It is program-based and reflects the content/context of the course in which it is used.
- It mirrors the approach to teaching used in the classroom, meaning it is likely to be more comfortable for learners.
- It allows learners to demonstrate accomplishments in ways that reflect natural use of language.
- It captures ongoing, continuous progress.
- Many alternative assessment techniques (performance assessment, dialogue journals, group projects) involve interaction among learners or between teacher and learner in communicative ways.

Before reading about alternative assessment techniques, complete the following task.

Task 9.2

Read the description of Annick's lesson and answer the questions that follow:

Annick has just finished the lesson on telephoning outlined in Chapter 3 (see page 58). The learners completed listening activities, took messages, practiced using semiscripted conversations, role-played several telephone exchanges, and gathered names and phone numbers. At the end of the lesson, Annick also had them make phone calls in class in preparation for the homework assignment, which was to make phone calls outside of class and to bring the information they gathered back to class the next day.

1 Think of two ways that Annick can assess that learning took place in her lesson.

2 Think of two ways the learners could assess their own progress.

Follow-up Now see if your own ideas are among the suggestions offered in the sections below.

OBSERVATION Ongoing assessment entails a process of observation, reflection about learner progress, and adjustments to teaching so that learners can find the best means of learning (Isserlis 1992). It is a way to capture learning in the moment, not from the beginning to the end of an entire term. It also allows us to notice those times when a learner makes gains and then backslides, a normal part of learning, and hopefully allows us to notice what approaches to teaching and learning promote the most success for learners. Teachers observe learning every day, but are they always assessing learning in the process? A teacher may report that the class did very well on an activity, but is not able to report specifically what went well, who was engaged and successful in the lesson, and who wasn't. For **observation** to be a valid assessment tool, the teacher needs to have a clear idea of what she or he is *looking for* in the classroom. This starts with articulating clear objectives in a lesson and observing for evidence that learners are moving toward meeting those objectives, then noting what happens in class in relation to those objectives either during or after the lesson. Is it only language that should be assessed? Assessing a learner's ability to use and interpret nonverbals, employ learning strategies, and meet employment or personal goals are equally important. The sample observation tool in Figure 9.1 consists of a simple teacher-made grid with the day's objectives and space for recording progress. This example corresponds to Annick's lesson on telephoning.

FIGURE 9.1 Sample Observation Tool

Lesson Objectives	Evidence of Progress
Students will be able to make telephone calls for a variety of everyday purposes: calling for hours and information, leaving a message.	Every student made at least one phone call. All but two students recorded and reported the information from the call. Nguyen made three calls—in the follow-up he reported store hours and copied down directions to the mall. He was so much more confident this time.
Students will alphabetize names.	Only two of the 20 students had trouble putting names in the right place in the phone directories we made, Mira and Yang.
Students will listen for and record phone numbers.	Most of the students were able to record numbers from the taped messages after one or two listenings; Ana confused 17/70 and 18/80; I need to work on those numbers more with this group.

While it may be unrealistic to maintain records like these on a daily basis, doing so even weekly or bi-weekly allows a teacher to analyze in more detail the learning that is going on in class. The same can be achieved on a more immediate, smaller scale. Teachers can add Post-its™ or notes in the margins of handouts and lesson plans on learner success and teaching effectiveness. This daily documentation and reflection can feed into the planning of subsequent lessons. A practical benefit of observation and ongoing assessment is that the job of writing progress reports at the end of the term is far easier and far more meaningful as a teacher draws on data collected during the term.

PERFORMANCE ASSESSMENT

Performance assessment involves learners demonstrating their ability to perform a real-life task, for example, calling in sick to work, reading a bill and writing a check for the correct amount, or writing a note regarding a child's absence from school. Central to performance assessment is the development of a **rubric** for evaluating learner outcomes on the task. What criteria should

I use for evaluating performance? What language forms, functions, and vocabulary are needed to perform the task successfully? What extralinguistic features of language (tone, nonverbals) should learners make use of to be intelligible? Figure 9.2 illustrates what Annick would look for in a successful performance of calling in sick to work, which learners practiced the day after the initial lesson on telephoning.

FIGURE 9.2 Performance Assessment Rubric

Assessment Rubric **1** needs improvement **2** adequately conveys information **3** very clearly conveys information; pronunciation is intelligible; uses appropriate intonation	**Competency: Calling in sick to work**			
	1	**2**	**3**	**Comments**
Uses appropriate opening				
Makes request appropriately				
Gives reason for missing work				
Gives expected length of absence				
Uses appropriate closing				

(Lanning and Parrish 1999)

In order for performance assessment to be a meaningful measure of learner competence, the task learners perform needs to be as authentic as possible. This can be a challenge when conducted within the four walls of a classroom.

- When possible, use authentic materials such as real bills, work documents.
- Use realia for role-plays (real receipts, foods, telephones).
- Use a native-English speaker volunteer as a partner in order to replicate what learners may encounter outside of class.
- In workplace programs, observe and assess learners performing tasks on the job.

Conducting frequent performance assessments may not be the most practical form of assessment in a large class. There is an alternative that is learner directed and provides the same kind of feedback for teachers and learners (Savage and Howard 1991). When conducting role-plays in class, create groups of three and have one learner act as an observer, who completes a rubric like the one above. Each group member takes the role of observer in turn as the other two members repeat the role-play.

OTHER FORMS OF ALTERNATIVE ASSESSMENT

There are a number of other means of assessing learning on an ongoing basis.

Dialogue journals: oral and written Dialogue journals provide a vivid record of learner progress as well as an ongoing sense of growth for the learner, making them an ideal vehicle for ongoing assessment. Taped oral journals can be used in much the same way written journals are used through an ongoing spoken dialogue between a teacher and learner. When I used taped dialogue journals in an advanced speaking/pronunciation class, I responded first to the content of what the learners told me, then provided language feedback for those areas where word choice or pronunciation affected intelligibility. At the end of term, the learners had the satisfaction of hearing themselves at the beginning and end of the class. This form of assessment may have limited practicality in very large classes, but could become more so with the help of volunteers.

Videotape/audiotape at intervals It is difficult for teachers and learners to perceive progress in oral proficiency; most of the products we keep are written or depicted with pictures or drawings. While we may have a sense that a learner is more fluent, creating records of that progress is easy to do. You can occasionally audiotape or videotape learners performing a role-play, performing a short conversation, or telling a story. Tape a class periodically on one videotape, and review it with learners so that they can recognize their development and growth.

Portfolio assessment A portfolio is a collection of learner work (selected by the students) that is representative of accomplishments made in a class or during a term of study. It may include writing samples, written exercises, projects, videotaped presentations, audiotaped stories, drawings, readings, and accompanying activities completed, learning logs, or even letters from teachers or employers. Planning for the portfolio can become an activity by having learners brainstorm and discuss what they would like to include. This is also a time for the teacher to clarify the purposes and benefits of creating a portfolio.

Work samples/group projects Evaluating group projects can provide insights into learners' ability to distribute tasks, work on a team, and present information clearly, either through a final written product or presentation. As with performance assessment, a teacher can create a rubric for assessing the final project, which can be completed by the teacher, the learners, and the audience who sees the final product.

KWL Charts: What do I know? What do I want to learn? What did I learn? This strategy is used for multiple purposes: to activate prior knowledge on a topic, to set learning goals, and to assess learning. At the start of a unit, learners work in small groups and brainstorm everything they know and everything they want to learn about the topic. Their responses are compiled to create a group chart on the board, overhead, or wall chart. At the end of the unit, learners go back to the chart and assess what they learned and compare those outcomes to their learning goals.

FIGURE 9.3 KWL Chart

What do I know?	What do I want to learn?	What did I learn?

9.1.5 LEARNERS ASSESSING THEIR LEARNING

Learner self-assessment should be an integral part of an ESL class. The benefits are numerous:

- It allows students to reevaluate the goals they have set for themselves, to recognize their progress in relation to those goals, and to identify new goals revealed as they progress.
- It heightens their awareness of the goals and outcomes of the program and allows them to identify their strengths and needs in relation to those outcomes.
- It helps them identify how they learn best; reflect on what they can do as learners (not just what the teacher does as a teacher).
- It develops a skill common in many workplaces, but that is new for many immigrants.
- It gives learners a voice in their education and in shaping the curriculum; they can see themselves as one of the many stakeholders.

Self-assessment needs to be a daily routine that can start with something as simple as asking learners to reflect on that day's lesson:

> What is one thing you learned that was new for you and particularly helpful?
>
> How will what you learned help you in your daily life, at home, work, in the community?

During review the following day, ask learners if they used anything from the previous lesson outside of class. Did they notice any of the new words they learned on signs, on the news, or anywhere in their community?

At the end of a unit, learners can reflect on what they learned as well as how they learned best. The teacher can develop a simple task like this one from Annick's lesson on telephoning:

FIGURE 9.4 **Lesson Self-assessment**

Looking Back

Think about your learning. Complete this form and tell the class your ideas.

1 The most useful thing I learned in this lesson was ______________________.

2 I still want to learn ______________________.

3 I learned the most by working:

____ with the teacher and class ____ alone ____ with a partner

4 The activity I liked best was:

____ listening to phone calls and completing activities
____ making calls on the cell phone
____ practicing phone calls with my partner (role-play)
____ practicing dialogues
____ making a phone book

(Adapted from unit reflection tasks used in Collaborations, *Heinle and Heinle)*

In order to highlight learner achievement in relation to the specific language outcomes in a lesson or unit, students complete a **learning log** or checklist of what they have accomplished.

This example from *Stand Out* assesses learning that took place during a unit of study.

FIGURE 9.5 **Sample Learner Log**

LEARNER LOG

Circle what you learned and write the page number where you learned it.

1. I can identify buildings.
   Yes Maybe No Page ____
2. I can read maps.
   Yes Maybe No Page ____
3. I can follow directions.
   Yes Maybe No Page ____
4. I can give directions.
   Yes Maybe No Page ____
5. I can read a directory.
   Yes Maybe No Page ____
6. I can use prepositions.
   Yes Maybe No Page ____
7. I can write a letter.
   Yes Maybe No Page ____
8. I can use the simple present and present continuous.
   Yes Maybe No Page ____

Did you answer *No* to any questions? Review the information with a partner.

Rank what you like to do best from 1 to 6. 1 is your favorite activity. Your teacher will help you.

☐ practice listening

☐ practice speaking

☐ practice reading

☐ practice writing

☐ learn new words (vocabulary)

☐ learn grammar

In the next unit I want to practice more

______________________.

(From Jenkins, R. and Sabbagh, S. (2003:100), Stand Out Level 1, *Heinle and Heinle)*

9.1.6 Using Assessment Results for Accountability Purposes

The assessment techniques and tools outlined above provide fairly immediate results to those stakeholders in the classroom, i.e., learners and teachers. But what about those stakeholder who are outside of the classroom? What information do they need and what are the means of gathering that information and reporting it to them? In a discussion of **accountability,** it is crucial that classroom teachers hear from stakeholders that are outside of their classrooms. I asked a state adult ESL specialist as well as a program director to reflect on the following questions:

- What are the signs of a successful program?
- What **performance indicators** are the most important to you (e.g., gains on tests, employment, increased involvement in child's school, or GED completion)?

Their responses give classroom teachers insight into the kind of data they need to gather about learner progress.

Task 9.3

First reflect on this question: In your opinion, what are the signs of a successful program?

Now read excerpts from the administrators' responses and identify what they say about program success and performance indicators:

> The signs of successful programs and the most important performance indicators are one and the same: meet the goals the students have established for themselves and a successful program will result. My experience has shown me that if one structures ESL classes around the stated goals of students, then all other measures of program accountability (NRS requirements, demonstrated gains, etc.) will fall into place. ESL programs that focus on learner goals will have significantly higher retention rates, which will improve student performance, which will please the NRS people; bottom line, everybody will go home a winner.
>
> *James Douglas ◆ Program Specialist V*
> *State contact for EL/Civics programs in Texas*
> *Adult and Community Education*
> *Texas Education Agency*

> The first thing that comes to mind is the program rate of student retention. Critical to retention is the personal connection they make with the teacher and their classmates. If they believe that the teacher is providing appropriate instruction and ensuring support to succeed, they will stay. Of course, other indicators of a successful program need to be measured in more concrete ways: CASAS tests provide us a way to benchmark progress and apply some numbers to track and record a process that is

very "squishy" and hard to get your hands around. Any student that learns enough English to get a job and keep a job is a success. Any parent in our program that can help their family successfully adjust to a new life, become a partner in their child's education, become true members of their community. . . is a success.

Ellen Lowry ◆ Program Director
Adult Options/Minnesota

	What are the signs of a successful program?
James	
Ellen	

Follow-up Both James and Ellen identify learner involvement and attainment of personal goals as signs of a successful program. While Ellen refers to measuring progress through standardized testing, it is clear that other means of assessment need to be used to capture gains such as employment, cultural adjustment, or attainment of personal goals. You have already learned about numerous means of assessing learning and teaching, all of which can be used to gather data that provides all stakeholders with evidence of learner achievement and suitability of programming.

Task 9.4

Look at five examples of learner outcomes that need to be assessed and reported. What do you think would be the most suitable assessment technique (e.g., performance assessment, dialogue journals) for measuring achievement of each outcome?

You need to . . .	What assessment tool could you use?
capture gains in writing ability throughout the term.	
know if the learner achieved employment goals.	
know if students can comfortably perform tasks such as making a doctor's appointment or calling in sick to work.	
capture improved intelligibility in pronunciation over time.	

find out if learners are doing independent reading or reading to their children more frequently.	

The best assessment tools are those that are compatible with the content of instruction, or the outcomes being assessed, as well as the approach to learning and teaching used in your class. This means that you need to use multiple means of gathering data to capture the breadth of learning that occurs in a class. Table 9.3 reviews assessment tools and techniques and describes how they can be used for accountability purposes. See if any of your ideas from Task 9.4 are included in the table.

TABLE 9.3 Tools for gathering data for reporting progress

Portfolios	Make learners aware of program standards and accountability expectations. Have them collect work for their portfolios that corresponds to the standards and accountability requirements of your program. This includes in-class work as well as achievement of employment and other personal or educational goals (e.g., job retention, citizenship).
Performance assessments	Conduct performance assessments that align with program outcomes and standards and keep rubrics as a record of learner achievement. This technique is particularly useful for assessing outcomes of competencies such as reporting an accident at work or calling in sick.
Taped samples	Audio/videotape performance assessments or speech samples periodically to capture progress over time. If you are looking for improvement in intelligibility of pronunciation, recorded speech samples are crucial.
Learner journal entries collected over time	As with taped samples, writing samples gathered over time are a powerful means of capturing development in writing ability.
Projects	Collect projects and identify the standards covered through the development of the project. Document outcomes using checklists or rubrics that delineate the standards.
KWL Charts What do I know? What do I want to learn? What did I learn?	Save KWL charts as a record of learning goals and achievement of those goals.
Reading logs	Both for personal reading and books read to children, record titles, brief summaries, and feelings about the books.
Learner folders	Keep a folder for each student with all test scores, learner goals, and any information gathered using the techniques above.

Checklists of learner achievement of program outcomes are commonplace in adult ESL programs. Sometimes they are developed by the program and used program wide, and other times the teacher and learners develop checklists themselves. A teacher can assess achievement throughout the class, not only at the end of the term, through both observation and simple tasks. Figure 9.6 is an excerpt from a Level 1 class checklist used in a large ABE/ESL program in Minneapolis.

FIGURE 9.6 **Checklist of Learner Outcomes**

Teacher Checklist: Level 1

Sample learner outcomes		Means of assessing outcomes
____ I can say the sounds of all the consonants. ____ I can write the big and small letters of the alphabet. ____ I can put the letters of the alphabet in order.		Have student write the alphabet, both big and small letters. Ask them to say the alphabet. Point to a letter and say it; have them do the same with other letters. Give learners letters on flash-cards and have them order them. In class, check by giving learners a name tag and asking them to stand in alphabetical order.
____ I can do what the teacher asks me to do in class.		Use TPR to check understanding of classroom routines: Open your book. Come to the board. Write your name. Circle your last name.
I know some words for:		Give learners flashcards with words and pictures of things from each category and have them match the vocabulary to the category:
____ food	____ clothes	
____ numbers	____ money	Food: meat, milk, vegetables
____ time	____ the months	Time: AM, PM, 6:00 o'clock
____ weather	____ school	Give them blank cards and have them add two other words they know to each category.
____ home	____ family	
____ health	____ work	Ask the students two questions from each category. This can be done as a group activity and observed by the teacher.
____ I can use these words when I talk to people.		

(based on Lynne Dotzenroth as cited in Easter and Wilson 2002)

The same checklist is used for learner self-assessment, allowing students to assess themselves in relation to program outcomes. This can be done individually or as a small group activity, reflecting on learner progress as well as achievement of common class goals. Questionnaires and checklists that focus on personal, professional, and academic goals, such as reading to a child, setting up a job interview, getting a library card, or enrolling in a computer class, are no less important than language goals, and need to be included in goal setting, record keeping, and self-assessment during a course. Figure 9.7 includes a number of these types of goals.

FIGURE 9.7 Sample Learner Checklist

I can do something new!

Name: ______________________ Teacher: ______________________ Date: ____________________

Can you do something new because you are studying English? What can you do?
Circle YES if you can do it.
Circle YES if you did it.

1 Yes I got a job.
2 Yes I kept my job.
3 Yes I got a better job.
4 Yes I applied for U.S. citizenship.
5 Yes I got my U.S. citizenship.
6 Yes I registered to vote, or I voted for the first time.
7 Yes I got off welfare.
8 Yes I read more to my children at home.
9 Yes I am talking more to my children.
10 Yes I am talking more to my children's teachers.
11 Yes I am talking more to my boss or my co-workers.
12 Yes I am speaking English more in public.
13 Yes I can read and write the English alphabet.
14 Yes I can write my name and address.
15 Yes I took the GED exam.
16 Yes I ______________________.

Congratulations! You can do something new!

(Maryland State Department of Education)

9.1.7 ASSESSMENT RESULTS INFORMING LEARNING AND TEACHING

Far too often teachers fail to make use of the information and data they gather through the assessment processes outlined in this section. Sharing the results of standardized tests, alternative assessments, and learner self-assessments with learners allows them to see the benefits of testing and assessment. In programs that allow time for teacher collaboration, sharing results with colleagues provides a means of building cohesion among classes in the program, as well as a means of identifying common strengths and weaknesses of instructional practices.

- Inform students of their successes on tests and alternative assessments as well as the areas in which they need improvement.
- Show them the link between their results and subsequent instruction. The outcomes of a performance assessment on returning items to the store indicate that the class needs more work on this competency. Show them those results and the ways the new lesson will help them to improve in this area.

- Collect and use the results of learner self-assessment. Show them the link between those assessments and subsequent instruction so that they see the ways in which they have an impact on instruction.
- Compare the outcomes of assessment with other teachers in the program. Also share the assessment tools themselves so that the processes used throughout the program become more consistent.

CONCLUSION In this section, I have explored the place of standardized tests and alternative assessment tools commonly used in adult ESL programs. A fair assessment reflects what students have learned and is conducted in ways that are familiar to students. Developing valid means of capturing learner performance and achievement is paramount, not only for the benefit of teachers, program administrators, and funders, but most importantly for learners. Seeing progress motivates students; observing and recording learner outcomes has a positive impact on teaching.

Part II ◆ Assessing Teaching Effectiveness

9.2.1 INTRODUCTION

One of the primary goals of assessment is to determine the extent to which instructional practices meet the needs of learners. An observant teacher modifies content, activities, and techniques as she or he observes and reflects on learner outcomes in their lessons. Teachers also need to be deliberate about their growth and professional development; effective change takes intentional and purposeful reflection. In this section, we explore processes for teacher reflection and personal development, including peer and self-observation, learning logs, journals, and mentoring.

Task 9.5

Discuss these questions with a partner or write answers in your journal if you are on your own:

How do you assess the effectiveness of the work you do (as a teacher or as a professional in another setting)?

How do you continue to grow in your professional life?

How do you collaborate with others to work on issues you face in your class or at your job?

9.2.2 PEER OBSERVATION

One of the most valuable resources for teacher development is communication with other teachers. Heavy teaching schedules, busy lives, and little preparation time are all obstacles to cooperative development among teachers, but finding a colleague for peer observations is well worth the effort. Recognizing the strength of this process, some administrators give release time once a term (or more in a few cases) to conduct peer observations. If this is not an option, find a peer with a different work schedule than yours and arrange to visit one another periodically.

Just as with any form of observation, having a clear task and focus can make the experience richer. The task can be a set of questions that your peer wants you to respond to, questions you have about your own teaching, or a rubric or set of questions that delves into a specific area of learning and teaching. The task below was designed for students to use while observing peers during their practicum, but would work equally well for teachers observing one another in their own classrooms.

SAMPLE OBSERVATION TASK

Your task during this lesson is to look at the language that the teacher and the students use. Overarching questions are: Is the language authentic? Do students have adequate opportunities to practice the language? Are they engaged in real communication?

Remember that some of the characteristics of real communication are that:

- there is a gap in information or opinion.
- language is used for a real-life purpose and is meaningful (students use true information—everyone doesn't repeat, "I have blond hair").

As you watch the lesson, note examples of how the activities support this type of language.

Info/opinion gap	
Real-life purpose	
Meaningful	
More than one answer	

Possible questions for follow-up conversation with teacher:

1 Share the information you gathered through the observation task about communicative activities. How well does the teacher feel his or her activities supported communicative language? Brainstorm some ways to work with activities so that they become more communicative.

2 How much of the lesson was devoted to having students practice the language by actually using it? Does this seem like an adequate amount of time? Brainstorm ways in which the lesson might be modified to give students more practice.

3 In what ways was the students' language incorporated into the lesson? For example, look at the board: is the language teacher-generated or student-generated? Whose language is used for examples?

(Reimer 1999)

9.2.3 Self-Assessment

There are a number of ways a teacher can assess him or herself, including observation, journaling, or learning logs. Videotaping a class and conducting a self-observation is one of the most powerful means of identifying strengths and weaknesses in our teaching. It can also be very intimidating for new teachers (or veterans, for that matter), so it is important to have a focus when observing yourself, one that allows you to observe purposefully and as objectively as possible.

Videotape a lesson and. . .

- Complete an observation task like the one on page 275.
- Use a grid with the lesson objectives and watch and listen for evidence of learner progress.
- Observe how learners interact with one another.
- Listen for the way you use key interactions: introductions, transitions, directions to activities, or checking questions (audiotaping for this purpose works equally well).

Think of two more possibilities.

____

____

Lesson Analysis

To observe learners' comfort and success with different teaching strategies and activities, a record like the following can be kept. Figure 9.8 includes some of the activities and teaching strategies used in Annick's telephoning lesson (p. 264).

Figure 9.8 Assessing effectiveness of teaching strategies

Activities/techniques	Learner comfort/involvement
Role-play	I need to give them more time to practice language they need for the role-play. My cards weren't clear enough; couldn't tell who was supposed to be the caller.
Making calls on cell phones from class	Seemed to enjoy this; lots of laughter. All but two pairs finished making their calls. Maybe I can have them finish at home next time.
Selective listening	So many of the students wanted to write down everything from the taped messages. I really need to work on helping them see the value of listening only for the info they need outside of class.

Notice how the teacher identifies aspects of her lesson that need adjusting; she's not just observing learner outcomes, but also teaching effectiveness.

9.2.4 Journals and Learning Logs

I never kept a journal until I was asked to do so as a requirement in my teaching practicum in 1982. Journaling allowed me to process what had happened each day, to pose questions for myself or to ask my mentor. Looking back over my entries allowed me to see development in my thought processes about teaching and learning. Journaling does not need to be a solo endeavor. Teachers can work cooperatively with a peer or mentor using dialogue journals. Pairs or groups of teachers commonly create online bulletin boards for this purpose. An alternative to keeping a journal is to maintain a learning log in which the teacher records observations, reflections, insights, or questions about the teaching and learning that occur in a lesson.

> I wonder what would happen if I tried. . .
>
> The language experience activity worked well today; need to use that more often.
>
> I was uncomfortable with Souling's questions about my colleague. I need to think of ways to handle situations like that.

Capturing these thoughts and reflections immediately after teaching is important, otherwise they tend to vanish from our memory.

Another way to interact with colleagues is through the formation of cooperative development groups, which are small groups of teachers devoting time to support one another through active listening and exploration of issues and concerns they are having in their teaching (Edge 1992). My colleague and I set aside time for this purpose—sometimes weekly and sometimes much less frequently. The important thing is that I know she is always there to listen when I am grappling with an issue in my teaching. We start by having one of us talk through an issue while the other listens actively, not interpreting, judging, or interjecting anything into the dialogue. We may paraphrase to check our understanding or clarify what we have heard. Afterward, we mirror back what we heard, allowing each of us time to hear our problem or issue as we stated it, which then often leads to more clarity and self-discovery of possible solutions. Try this technique with a teaching colleague, family member, or friend.

9.2.5 Action Research

All of the processes above can lead to deeper exploration of your teaching through **action research,** which involves teachers identifying problems or issues in their teaching, gathering data or information about what is happening, researching the topic, and taking action in their classes. "Research is designed, conducted, and implemented by the teachers themselves to improve teaching in their own classrooms" (Johnson 1993). This kind of exploration, which is situated in the teachers' classrooms, is a powerful tool for ongoing personal development. Nunan (1992) and others propose the following steps for conducting action research:

- **Identify an issue:** What is something that you are struggling with as a teacher? Is there an approach or strategy that you want to experiment with in your class? Any of the teacher development ideas outlined above, as well as the outcomes of the ongoing assessment tools described in Part I of this chapter can provide possible topics for action research.
- **Gather information about the issue:** There are many ways to gather information about any area of teaching: read, conduct online research, talk to other teachers, observe others.
- **Use that information to design changes in classroom procedure:** Design activities, implement specific strategies that apply what you have learned through your research.
- **Implement this procedure:** Now try the procedure out in your classroom over a period of time.
- **Observe changes this implementation brought about in the classroom:** Observation takes planning; use observation grids/checklists, journals, video/audiotaping, learning logs, and self-assessment to capture the changes that occurred as a result of the action research.
- **Reflect on the outcomes and implications of the process:** Keep a log or journal and share your findings with colleagues.

Action research can be as simple or complex as a teacher wants it to be. It is a common tool in teacher training programs, allowing teachers to apply the principles they are learning about to their classes. For those of you already teaching, it can be away for you to apply principles you are learning about right now. The next section includes a description of an action research project by one of the teachers in a mentoring project I conducted this year.

MENTORING

Over the past year, I engaged in a mentoring project with ESL teachers in the community with the aim of helping novice and experienced teachers reflect on the extent to which their teaching practices are truly learner-centered. The goal of the project was to heighten teacher awareness of the impact their practices have on learner involvement, encourage ongoing teacher development and action research, and improve learner outcomes. The project consisted of a mentoring cycle, beginning with observations and personal assessments to identify areas for growth. In the second stage the teachers conducted action research around the identified growth areas and I provided targeted mentoring sessions on topics that arose through the observation process. The third stage consisted of follow-up observations and discussions of the effects changes in teaching practices had on learner involvement.

All of the processes the teachers and I engaged in could be utilized between peers, with a mentor and new teacher, or even individually as a means of observing and reflecting on one's own teaching. All of the teachers began the cycle by completing this task:

MENTORING PRE-ACTIVITY

Provide examples of what learners and you are doing in your classroom that correspond to each of these characteristics of the learner-centered classroom (see checklist on page 7 in Chapter 1). In what areas are you most responsive to your learners' needs? What are some areas that would benefit from further research and experimentation in your classroom? We will use the outcomes of this initial assignment to determine the areas for focus during the first observation. From there, you will develop targeted observation tasks for me to complete as I observe the learners in your class, and for you to complete after your lesson.

Celeste was particularly concerned that quieter students in her class were not participating enough and that if provided the opportunity to do so, they would. She incorporated two familiar teaching techniques that had not yet become routine: think-pair-share and the language of turn-taking. She taught her students the language of turn-taking (*It's your turn. Do you have something to add? What do you think?*) explicitly and asked her students to use it consistently. In previous lessons on adverbs, she adhered closely to the textbook. See how she implemented the strategies above in a lesson on adverbs and job routines to make her lesson more participatory and learner-centered:

- Learners moved to tables based on their type of job (here or in their country): retail, housekeeping, food service, education, office. This grouping strategy promoted a fair amount of communication among students as they determined which table was the best fit for them.
- Next she used think-pair-share: Think of activities you do on the job and work together to create a list of at least five items. Each member needs to add at least one thing. (She directed them to the turn-taking phases on the wall that they could use to elicit information from one another.)
- Groups shared ideas as Celeste wrote activities on the board. Now Celeste asked what a good day or bad day on the job would be like, first modeling for herself:

  On a good day, I plan carefully.

  On a bad day, I speak too quickly.

Again, groups worked together to create good day/bad day lists. As an observer, I recorded which learners contributed at my table and how frequently. The result was that two of the typically quiet students were among the most involved in the activities. Celeste and I continued the process over several weeks, each time focusing on different aspect of learning and teaching. Celeste revisited the preactivity at the end of the cycle, and the following is a sample of how the process affected her teaching:

> **The learners control direction of the activities.** With the group-work language, students are politely and appropriately communicating with one another, encouraging participation of quieter students, developing English confidence, and learning great skills for outside of the classroom. Looking back at group work just a couple months ago and now, there is a great improvement.

All of the processes for teacher development outlined in this section take intentional effort on the part of teachers, but none is terribly time-consuming. Taking time to truly reflect on what we do is actually very energizing and allows us to collaborate with colleagues in new and meaningful ways.

9.2.6 LEARNERS ASSESSING INSTRUCTION

The processes of assessment discussed throughout this chapter provide us with rich data about the effectiveness of learning and teaching, but there is one more important piece to the assessment puzzle: What do learners feel about instruction? How do students evaluate the effectiveness of our teaching? As with all forms of assessment, teachers need to gather ongoing and meaningful input from their learners, but this can be difficult for both linguistic and cultural reasons:

Language Obstacles Learners may not have enough language to talk about instruction. Use bilingual aids or interpreters, or develop strategies by which learners can show or demonstrate their feelings through visuals.

Cultural Obstacles Understand that in many cultures, students would never be asked to evaluate their teachers. Develop means of evaluation that allow learners to provide meaningful feedback in nonthreatening ways. Assure them that feedback does not affect their standing in the program. Use consensus activities, which give a group opinion rather than a personal opinion.

Students may have an easier time talking about activities and content as opposed to the teacher and teaching. The following evaluation activity can be conducted on a regularly basis (weekly, monthly) as well as at the end of a term as a final evaluation. In either case, it is imperative that learners recognize that their input will make a difference. List typical activities: role-plays, reading short articles, writing exercises, grammar exercises, listening activities with tapes/video, and content covered: health, shopping, using the telephone. Have the students complete sentences like these:

I liked doing ______________________________

I didn't like ______________________________

I liked learning about ______________________________

I didn't like learning about ______________________________

Next week/term I want to ______________________________

To elicit group feedback, have small groups of students answer these two questions:

What have you learned (this week, month, in this class)?

What helped you learn best?

Invite a group representative to write their answers on the board, compile the lists, and ask the class to identify the five most common responses to the two questions. The outcomes of this activity provide the teacher with feedback about which activities had the most impact and which instructional strategies were the most beneficial for this particular group. In cases where the learners will continue on in the program, the teacher needs to inform them that these results will help shape the instruction in the next class, whether with the same teacher or with another teacher.

CONCLUSION

Many forms of assessment have been examined in this chapter, including standardized tests, alternative assessment, as well as teacher assessment. All of these processes take careful consideration and planning. The information gathered allows teachers, program administrators, and students to monitor and adjust the strategies they employ to make learning and teaching as productive as possible. Assessment results are also used to inform funders about program effectiveness and learner successes.

KEY TERMS

CHECKLIST OF KEY TERMS	On your own, or with a partner, provide an example or brief definition for each concept.
practicality	
reliability	
placement test	
diagnostic test	
validity	
achievement test	
proficiency test	
standardized tests	
BEST	
CASAS	
alternative assessment	
performance assessment	
KWL chart	

learner logs	
action research	

Applying What You Learned

1 Program Intake

Every program uses different processes at intake to place students in the most suitable class. **If you are already teaching. . .** find out what processes your program uses. What placement test do they use (a standardized test or their own)? What other processes do they use at intake? Reflect on the following:

What do the test scores and any other intake procedures tell you about your learners?

Describe two things you do once students are with you to have a more complete picture of their level and needs.

If you're not teaching yet. . . visit a site and ask the intake coordinator, an administrator, or a teacher what process they use for placement. If possible, look at copies of their intake forms. Reflect on the following:

What would the test scores and intake process tell you about students?

Describe two more things you would do at the beginning of a course to have a more complete picture of their level and needs.

2 Developing Performance Assessments

If you are already teaching. . . choose an upcoming unit for which you have not developed an assessment tool before. Identify a competency that is covered in that unit and develop a performance assessment you can use to measure learner achievement. Describe the task you will ask learners to perform (e.g., a role-play, a real-life written task) and develop a rubric that you could use to assess learner performance with this competency.

If you are not teaching. . . choose a unit from an ESL textbook and do the same thing.

3 Learner Self-assessment

Look at three ESL textbooks and find out if they include any kind of learner self-assessment at the end of the units or periodically throughout the book. Choose one unit from a textbook and develop a learner log and a reflective task that would allow learners to identify what they accomplished.

4 Action Research (for those already teaching)

Identify an issue that you want to work on in your teaching.

- Gather information about the issue (read, talk to other teachers, observe others).
- Use that information to develop a procedure (technique, activity) that is new for you.
- Implement this procedure.
- Observe changes this implementation brought about in the classroom, particularly, what impact does that change have on student learning.
- Reflect on the outcomes and implications of the process with a colleague.

Recommended Reading

Bailey, K. 1998. *Learning about language assessment.* Boston, MA: Heinle and Heinle.

This text outlines the principles of second language assessment through three sections, beginning with authentic dilemmas from practicing teachers, followed by principles of assessment, and ending with inquiry-based activities.

Brown, J.D. 1996. *Testing in language programs.* Upper Saddle River, NJ: Prentice Hall Regents.

This book provides teachers with tools for developing good tests, analyzing and interpreting test results, and improving tests so that they are fair and accurate measures of learner achievement.

Cohen, A. 1994. *Assessing language ability in the classroom* (2nd ed.). Boston, MA: Heinle and Heinle.

This text provides an overview of assessment theory and practice, including examples of various types of assessment, including performance assessment, self-assessment, and portfolio assessment.

Genesee, F., and **J. Upshar.** 1996. *Classroom-based evaluation in second language education.* New York, NY: Cambridge University Press.

This book presents numerous formal and informal classroom-based assessment techniques and tools.

Holt, D., and **C. Van Duzer** (eds.) 2000. *Assessing success in family literacy and adult ESL.* Washington, DC and McHenry, IL: National Center for ESL Literacy Education and Delta Systems.

This text provides an overview of assessment issues in adult ESL with guidelines for developing an assessment plan in general English, workforce programs, and family literacy programs. It includes numerous examples of assessment tools.

Teacher Development

Richards, J., and **C. Lockhart.** 1994. *Reflective teaching in second language classrooms.* New York, NY: Cambridge University Press.

This text provides teachers with tools for critically reflecting on their teaching practice in meaningful and substantive ways through self-observation and self-evaluation.

Waynryb, R. 1992. *Classroom observation tasks.* Cambridge: Cambridge University Press.

This text provides practicing teachers with observation tasks and tools that they can use for self-assessment or peer assessment.

Online Resources

Adventures in Assessment

http://www.sabes.org/resources/adventures/

This site is an online journal that provides a forum for adult literacy practitioners to reflect critically upon a range of issues and experiences pertaining to alternative assessment.

Focus on Basics

http://www.gse.harvard.edu/~ncsall/fob/1999/fobv3ic.htm

Vol. 3, Issue B June 1999 is dedicated to issues of assessment and accountability.

Practical Assessment, Research and Evaluation

http://ericae.net/pare/Home.htm

This is an online journal devoted to research and practice in assessment and evaluation. While it is not written specifically for adult ESL educators, there are many useful and relevant articles for ESL educators.

For teacher development, consider joining **TESOL,** the professional organization **Teachers to Speakers of Other Languages.**

http://www.tesol.org/

Here you can find a database of TESOL members; links to state, local, and international affiliates; advocacy information; and information about TESOL membership, publications, and services such as its placement/career services.

Standardized Tests and Contact Information

BEST (Basic English Skills Test)
Center for Applied Linguistics
4646 40th Street NW,
Washington, DC 20016–1859
http://www.cal.org/BEST/

CASAS (Comprehensive Adult Student Assessment System)
8910 Clairemont Mesa Boulevard
San Diego, CA 92123
http://www.casas.org

NYSPlace (New York State Placement Test for Adult ESL Students)
City School District of Albany
Albany Educational TV
27 Western Avenue,
Albany, NY 12203

CELSA (Combined English Language Skills Assessment)
1187 Coast Village Rd., Suite 1 #378
Montecito, CA 93108
http://www.cappassoc.com/actt/actt.htm

TABE (Tests of Adult Basic Education)
CTB/McGraw-Hill
20 Ryan Ranch Road
Monterey, CA 93940-5703

10 Standards and Accountability

10.1 Introduction

This book has focused on principles and practices of learner-centered teaching. Much, if not all, of what ESL teachers do each day could not happen without resources and funding from state and federal agencies. What are funders' expectations? Are they radically different from those of learners, classroom teachers, and program administrators? What **standards** do state and federal funders hold programs to and how do they measure that those standards have been met? What do ESL teachers need to know about those standards, and how can they align instruction to meet them in ways that are consistent with learner goals and their own practice? While accountability and standards may seem daunting, being accountable for what you do in an ESL classroom is simply one of the responsibilities of the job; accountability and standards provide a means of capturing the achievement of students as well as the effectiveness of instruction.

Getting Started

Thinking back to Diane Pecoraro's reflections in Chapter 9, she raises the following questions about accountability and standards:

What are the funding sources for our programs?
What are the accountability requirements?
What standards drive practice?
What national initiatives drive practice and policy?
How can teachers reconcile learner goals with program goals that don't appear compatible?

Task 10.1

Before reading, discuss the following questions with a partner, or write answers if you are on your own.

Why is it important for teachers to know about accountability and standards?

Checklist

After reading this chapter and completing the activities, you should be able to

- describe the purpose of standards and accountability systems.
- find out what standards and accountability systems are in place in programs where you teach.
- identify learner needs and find places where they align with program standards and outcomes.

How will answers to Diane's questions help you as a classroom teacher?

A key purpose of this chapter is to demystify standards and accountability. Many teachers lack knowledge about what guides decisions that come from on high. However, understanding these larger systems allows us to have a better understanding of what guides policy decisions. Knowledge of these systems also gives us the language we need to advocate for the learners in our programs. We begin with an overview of current federal requirements for adult ESL education. It must be noted that adult education laws and policies change, and what is current practice may look very different ten years down the road.

10.2 Reporting Results to Funders

> The accountability system for our programs is somewhat complex because of the great variability of learner levels, goals and types of programs. Nevertheless, reporting and accountability is an essential factor in the funding for our Adult Basic Education system, and the state has an expectation that programs be in compliance with these policies in order to ensure the public that tax dollars are used wisely and that positive results are being attained.
>
> *Dr. Barry Shaffer ◆ MN State Director of Adult Education*
> *Minnesota Department of Education*

Barry underscores the importance of reporting and accountability in adult ESL. This reflects the current trend throughout education, which is that funders want to know what they get for the dollars they spend. For the majority of adult ESL programs, state departments of education receive funding from the federal government, and then they disperse those funds to individual programs. Some funding is earmarked for specific types of programming, for example, workplace ESL, citizenship, or family literacy. In both instances, programs need to apply for funds through their state department of education, usually through a competitive grant process.

Under current law[1], states gather learner data from programs, and each state is required to report levels of performance with the U.S. Department of Education for three core indicators. To facilitate this process, the U.S. Department of Education developed the **National Reporting System (NRS),** an accountability system used to measure the effectiveness of federally funded adult education programs (Van Duzer 2002). In keeping with federal requirements, the NRS consists of three types of **core measures** (U.S. Department of Education), and programs have the responsibility of gathering data in all of these areas:

- Outcome measures, which include educational gains (level change, test scores), gaining or retaining employment, receipt of secondary school diploma or GED, and placement in postsecondary education or training.

[1] Current law falls under the Adult Education and Family Literacy Act (Title II of the Workforce Investment Act (WIA) of 1998). The WIA is under reauthorization in 2003.

- Descriptive measures, including student demographics (e.g., immigration status, nationality), reasons for attending, and student status (full-time, part-time).
- Measures of participation: contact hours received and enrollment in instructional programs for special populations or topics (such as family literacy or workplace literacy).

The NRS also includes optional secondary measures that states *are not required* to collect and that are not to be used in assessing state performance under federal law. These measures correspond to the outcomes in many content-specific grants such as EL civics and workplace or family literacy (Diane Pecoraro, personal communication). The **secondary measures** are in the areas of employment, community, and family, for example, achievement of citizenship skills, voting behavior, general involvement in community activities, or involvement in children's education.

While federal rules require programs to report measurable progress by learners and effective programming, the Department of Education leaves it up to each state or program to determine which standards are most suitable for the learners they serve and to choose the most appropriate tools, be it tests or checklists, to gather data (Van Duzer 2002). Particular sets of standards have evolved through which educators measure and report on learner progress.

10.3 STANDARDS

So what are teachers' responsibilities within this larger accountability system? I asked a classroom teacher, Elizabeth, what she thought:

> What do you see as your responsibilities regarding program accountability?
>
> *That's easy...to teach, teach, teach! Keep good records and monitor improvement in language.*

Elizabeth recognizes her dual role: she needs to teach and gather evidence of learning. A variety of tools and techniques for assessing learner achievement and progress are presented in Chapter 9. But what are teachers measuring learner progress against? What standards and/or outcomes guide their curricula? Here is what Elizabeth said about that question:

> What program standards guide your curriculum?
>
> *I agree with and use our program mission statement as a guide. Material is relevant, meaningful, authentic, based on everyday experiences and encounters. I give students an opportunity to use language in a variety of ways and situations. Topics are student generated. Providing an optimal learning environment helps our students to ultimately achieve economic independence and become productive citizens in the community.*

When I asked other teachers if their program's curricula adhere to any particular set of standards, more often than not they were not sure, other than to tell me what standardized test their program uses. A number of the teachers replied that CASAS competencies guided their curricula. These responses reveal the confusion many teachers have about standards and program outcomes. In this section we look at:

- common standards in adult ESL;
- how these standards can shape teaching and learning practices; and
- how these standards relate to accountability.

Standards-based education has grown out of the expressed need for programs to be held accountable for the work they do. Standards "make explicit what the goals of instruction should be and therefore provide a way to align curriculum, instruction, assessment, and accountability" (National Institute for Literacy 2003). Standards are a broad set of desired outcomes for learners from which programs develop their curricula. **Content standards** represent what students are expected to know and be able to do as a result of instruction, and **performance standards** indicate what learners need to do to *demonstrate* their proficiency within the content standards (TESOL 1998 as cited in Florez 2002). There are standards that have evolved through national initiatives: **EFF, SCANS, CASAS** (a competency-based accountability system), and **state standards,** which vary from state to state.

10.4 Equipped for the Future (EFF)

The goal of instruction, regardless of the approach we take as ESL teachers, is to help diverse groups of learners acquire the tools they need to thrive in society as parents/family members, citizens/community members, and workers. These roles are the foundation of a standards-based adult education initiative that has identified necessary roles, activities, and skills for adult learners and programs: Equipped for the Future (EFF)[2]. EFF was developed in response to the question: What do adults need to know and be able to do in order to carry out their roles and responsibilities as workers, parents and family members, and citizens and community members? (Stein 2000). The framework outlines the knowledge and skills adults need in order to fulfill these responsibilities and it can be used for a multitude of purposes, including:

- a means for adult learners to assess their own personal and professional goals;
- a means of connecting curriculum and instruction to real-world outcomes; and
- a means of defining results for accountability.

---

[2] EFF is a project of the National Institute for Literacy.

TABLE 10.1

Content Framework for the EFF Standards

In order to fulfill responsibilities as parents/family members, citizens/community members, and workers, adults must be able to:

Meet These Four Purposes	Accomplish These Common Activities	Demonstrate These Skills
Access To access information so adults can orient themselves in the world **Voice** To be able to express ideas and opinions with the confidence they will be heard and taken into account **Independent Action** To be able to solve problems and make decisions on one's own, acting independently, without having to rely on others **Bridge to the Future** Learn how to learn so adults can keep up with the world as it changes	• Gather, Analyze, and Use Information • Manage Resources • Work within the Big Picture • Work Together • Provide Leadership • Guide and Support Others • Seek Guidance and Support from Others • Develop and Express Sense of Self • Respect Others and Value Diversity • Exercise Rights and Responsibilities • Create and Pursue Vision and Goals • Use Technology and Other Tools to Accomplish Goals • Keep Pace with Change	**Communication Skills** • Read with Understanding • Convey Ideas in Writing • Speak So Others Can Understand • Listen Actively • Observe Critically **Decision-making Skills** • Use Math to Solve Problems and Communicate • Solve Problems and Make Decisions • Plan **Interpersonal Skills** • Cooperate with Others • Advocate and Influence • Resolve Conflict and Negotiate • Guide Others **Lifelong Learning Skills** • Take Responsibility for Learning • Reflect and Evaluate • Learn through Research • Use Information and Communications Technology

(From EFF site http://www.nifl.gov/lincs/collections/eff/eff_framework.html)

The EFF framework views learning as activities that extend far beyond the classroom. Acquiring skills needed to act independently, cooperate with others, or resolve problems are no less important than language competence and communication skills. At present, many programs use the EFF framework to shape and plan learning and teaching.

10.5 SECRETARY OF LABOR'S COMMISSION ON ACHIEVING NECESSARY SKILLS (SCANS)

In 1992 the **Secretary of Labor's Commission on Achieving Necessary Skills (SCANS),** in collaboration with business and educational leaders, identified skills essential to success in the workplace. The SCANS framework includes workplace competencies, including managing resources, information, systems, and technology, as well as basic language skills, thinking skills, and personal qualities. Table 10.2 provides examples from three areas.

TABLE 10.2

Sample SCANS Standards
Managing Resources/Allocates Time Selects relevant, goal-related activities, ranks them in order of importance, allocates time to activities, and understands, prepares, and follows schedules.
Foundation Skill/ Reading Locates, understands, and interprets written information in prose and documents—including manuals, graphs, and schedules—to perform tasks; learns from text by determining the main idea or essential message; identifies relevant details, facts, and specifications; infers or locates the meaning of unknown or technical vocabulary; and judges the accuracy, appropriateness, style, and plausibility of reports, proposals, or theories of other writers.
Foundation Skill/ Speaking Organizes ideas and communicates oral messages appropriate to listeners and situations; participates in conversation, discussion, and group presentations; selects an appropriate medium for conveying a message; uses verbal language and other cues such as body language appropriate in style, tone, and level of complexity to the audience and the occasion; speaks clearly and communicates a message; understands and responds to listener feedback; and asks questions when needed.

(A complete list of SCANS competencies is available at: http://wdr.doleta.gov/opr/FULLTEXT/1999_35.pdf)

The SCANS framework is commonly used for planning integrated vocational and basic skills instruction (Johns Hopkins University 2000). SCANS outcomes may be included in checklists for accountability purposes in vocational programs.

10.6 COMPREHENSIVE ADULT STUDENT ASSESSMENT SYSTEM (CASAS)

While many teachers refer to CASAS competencies as standards, standards and outcomes on a standardized test are not the same. CASAS, or the Comprehensive Adult Student Assessment System, is an assessment system that contains tools for assessing learner outcomes, instruction, and program evaluation. The CASAS standardized tests are used in a variety of adult ESL settings, including life skills, EL civics, or workplace ESL. CASAS delineates literally hundreds of suggested competencies that are often used as the desired outcomes of programs. Because of the broad range of outcomes provided by CASAS, as well as the fact that many programs use CASAS standardized tests for placement and achievement, many programs use the competencies as their program outcomes. In other words, CASAS becomes the driving force behind the curriculum and teachers develop lessons to address the competencies. The competencies are highly specific, as illustrated in the following sample:

CASAS Outcome 2.2

2.2 Understand how to locate and use different types of transportation and interpret related travel information

2.2.1 Ask for, give, follow, or clarify directions (see also 1.1.3, 1.9.4, 2.2.5)

2.2.2 Recognize and use signs related to transportation (see also 1.9.1)

2.2.4 Interpret transportation schedules and fares

2.2.5 Use maps relating to travel needs (see also 1.1.3, 1.9.4, 2.2.1)

(Go to http://www.casas.org/01AboutCasas/01Competencies.html for the complete list of competencies.)

Because most states require standardized test scores in reporting, many programs using different standards (state or other) may choose to use CASAS for testing purposes without developing the curriculum around CASAS competencies.

10.7 STATE STANDARDS

Many states have developed standards through collaboration with ESL professionals, including teachers, program coordinators, state administrators, and researchers. These standards can take on very different forms, as demonstrated by the standards for two states that serve large numbers of ESL learners: Massachusetts and Florida. In the case of Massachusetts, standards are broad and serve to provide a framework to help teachers and programs develop varying curricula in a wide range of settings.

> This framework articulates the knowledge and skills adult ESOL learners need in order to communicate effectively and confidently in English so that they can meet their needs; advocate for themselves, their families and their communities; and participate more fully in U.S. society (Mass DOE 1999).

The Massachusetts framework begins with broad strands, under which standards are articulated. Examples of performance indicators for each standard are provided, but the assumption is that each program develops outcomes that correspond to the strengths and needs of each class.

Example from Framework for Adult ESOL in the Commonwealth of Massachusetts

Strands:

- Oral and Written Communication
- Language Structure and Mechanics
- Intercultural Knowledge and Skills
- Navigating Systems

Within each strand is a set of standards as depicted below for the strand **"Oral and Written Communication."**

Standard: *Learners will become increasingly able to express themselves orally in English for social, functional and self-expressive purposes.*

Sample performance indicators:

- telling one's life story,
- describing how to do something or get somewhere,
- advocating for oneself and others,
- using set conversational phrases (such as those used for agreement and dissent, offering suggestions, polite interruptions, etc.).

To view the complete framework go to: http://www.doe.mass.edu/acls/frameworks/

(Massachusetts Department of Education 1999)

Sample Standards from Florida

V. INTENDED OUTCOMES: After successfully completing the appropriate level for each Literacy Completion Point (LCP) of this program, the students will be able to:

LITERACY COMPLETION POINT A — Literacy/Foundations — 450 hours

LIFE SKILLS

0.50 Demonstrate English skills necessary for effective interpersonal communication.

0.60 Demonstrate English skills necessary for effective telephone communication.

0.70 Demonstrate English skills necessary to communicate effectively on health and nutrition topics.

For a complete list of standards, go to http://www.firn.edu/doe/dwdframe/ad/pdf/3201030a.pdf

(Florida Department of Education, Tallahassee, FL 2001)

The Florida standards are connected to specific levels (Literacy Completion Points or LCPs). Programs are expected to teach to and assess learning in relation to these standards; however, the contexts for instruction and activities vary depending on the needs of students and program mandate.

10.8 Standards in the Classroom

How does all of this play out in the ESL classroom? Recall the words of James Douglas in Chapter 9:

> My experience has shown me that if one structures ESL classes around the stated goals of students, then all other measures of program accountability (NRS requirements, demonstrated gains, etc.) will fall into place.

Standards should guide curricula; they should not dictate everything that happens in the classroom. The teacher's job is to guide learners to articulate their goals, and then look for overlaps among those goals and program or state outcomes and standards by which learners will be assessed. Teachers also select materials that respond to both learner needs and program standards.

Choosing Standards-based Textbooks

One way for programs to align instruction to standards is by adopting a **standards-based textbook series.** The scope and sequence excerpt from *Taking Off* (Fesler and Newman 2003), a beginning-level standards-based text, illustrates what such a curriculum looks like. The scope and sequence chart aligns EFF, SCANS standards, and CASAS outcomes to the topics and languages skills covered in each unit (Figure 10.1).

Many publishers provide correlations to standards of states with extremely large ESL populations, for example California, Florida, Texas, and New York. While these correlations to standards are very useful, an important question to ask continually is: *Does the text align with learner goals as well as the program standards?* One can assure a measure of alignment between learner and program goals by providing ample opportunities for learners to reflect on what they've learned in a lesson and, more importantly, articulate how what they have learned can help them in their lives (see 9.1.5 for ideas on learner self-assessment).

Figure 10.1

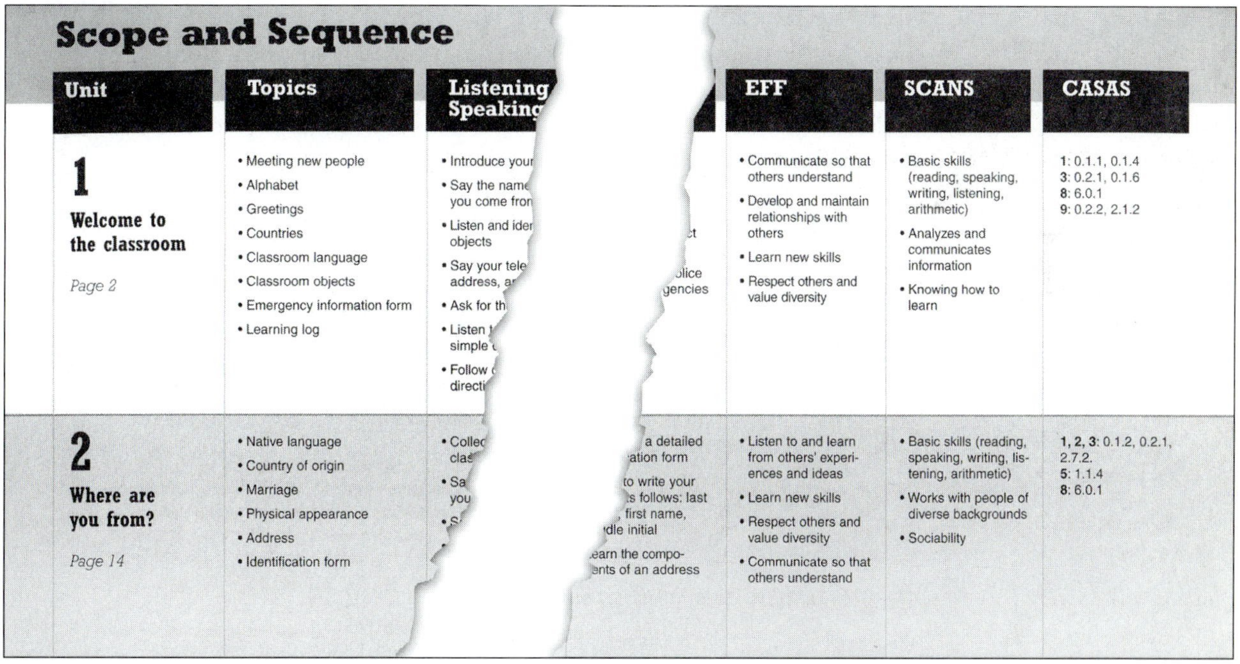

Scope and Sequence

Unit	Topics	Listening Speaking		EFF	SCANS	CASAS
1 Welcome to the classroom *Page 2*	• Meeting new people • Alphabet • Greetings • Countries • Classroom language • Classroom objects • Emergency information form • Learning log	• Introduce your • Say the name you come fron • Listen and ider objects • Say your tele address, a • Ask for th • Listen simple • Follow directi	ct olice gencies	• Communicate so that others understand • Develop and maintain relationships with others • Learn new skills • Respect others and value diversity	• Basic skills (reading, speaking, writing, listening, arithmetic) • Analyzes and communicates information • Knowing how to learn	1: 0.1.1, 0.1.4 3: 0.2.1, 0.1.6 8: 6.0.1 9: 0.2.2, 2.1.2
2 Where are you from? *Page 14*	• Native language • Country of origin • Marriage • Physical appearance • Address • Identification form	• Collec clas • Sa you • S	a detailed ation form to write your s follows: last , first name, dle initial earn the components of an address	• Listen to and learn from others' experiences and ideas • Learn new skills • Respect others and value diversity • Communicate so that others understand	• Basic skills (reading, speaking, writing, listening, arithmetic) • Works with people of diverse backgrounds • Sociability	1, 2, 3: 0.1.2, 0.2.1, 2.7.2. 5: 1.1.4 8: 6.0.1

Emergent Curricula and Standards: Two Cases in Point

Many programs, even those using a core series for instruction, utilize practices that allow the curriculum to emerge from learners' lives and needs, for example, project-based learning or participatory problem posing. How do teachers reconcile the issues and concerns that emerge through these approaches with the standards and accountability systems that may be in place in their programs? The following cases illustrate how a teacher can align learner needs with different standards or outcomes.

Case 1 Aligning learner needs to different standards In a recent visit to an adult ESL class, learners shared a number of challenges they had encountered over the previous few weeks. The teacher was concerned that the issues raised did not fit the program curriculum. As I analyzed the learner challenges, I was able to identify specific language needs that are common to many sets of standards.

As you read the learner challenges, see if you can identify the language skills Diana and Chae need to develop in English.

Learner challenge 1 Diana wrote a check from her account for \$500.00. She wrote \$500.00 numerically, but inadvertently wrote five thousand in longhand. When she cashed the check, the cashier gave her \$500.00. The next week she was told she had an overdraft. She found that \$5000.00 had been withdrawn from her account. She couldn't figure out what had happened and didn't know how to explain that she had received only \$500.00. Fortunately, the bank found that \$500.00 had been printed electronically on the back of the check and they realized what had happened. She was unable to straighten out the problem on her first few visits to the bank, but she finally resolved it with the help of a friend.

Learner challenge 2 Chae tried to call school to report his daughter's illness. He couldn't navigate the voicemail system so he gave up. Not surprisingly, his daughter's teacher called him at mid-morning to find out where his daughter was. This student was highly motivated to learn the skills of calling school and using voicemail systems.

Learner challenge 3 Diana found that she had unknowingly purchased a very expensive service contract for her car. When she realized it, she had tremendous difficulty canceling the policy. She couldn't understand all of the options on the voicemail system when she called the dealership. She finally gave up and kept the contract.

I identified the following language needs. Diana and Chae need to. . .

- explain that there is a problem so that the others can understand.
- verify information during interactions like the one at the bank.
- be able to understand voicemail systems that offer multiple options.
- understand how and when to leave a message.
- read contracts, conventions of service contracts.
- learn how to recognize offers and refuse offers.

Now let's see in Table 10.3 how some of the learner needs align with various standards from the Equipped for the Future framework, California Model Standards, and Florida standards.

TABLE 10.3 Aligning Learner Needs to Standards

Learners need to. . .	EFF Purposes and Standards	California Model Standards	Florida Standards
• describe a problem so that the others (e.g., bank teller, clerks, employers) understand.	***Purpose*** ***Voice*** To be able to express ideas and opinions with the confidence they will be heard and taken into account.		**59.02** Demonstrate understanding of banking problems.
	Standard ***Speak so Others Can Understand:*** Organize and relay information to effectively serve the purpose, context, and listener.		
• verify information during interactions such as the one at the bank or car dealership.	**Standard** ***Speak so Others Can Understand:*** Organize and relay information to effectively serve the purpose, context, and listener.	Demonstrate strategies to check for understanding—clarifying by attempting to reproduce what has been heard, for example.	
• understand voicemail systems that offer multiple options. • understand how and when to leave a message.		Demonstrate understanding of non-face-to-face speech in familiar contexts, such as simple phone conversations and routine announcements.	**Lifeskills 07.0** Demonstrate English skills necessary for effective telephone communication. **Lifeskills 23.02** Use appropriate telephone greeting, leave oral message, and take written message.

The needs expressed by Chae, Diana, and others in their class are real and immediate. These learner challenges can now provide rich contexts for instruction that are relevant to the learners, while at the same time help the students meet standards like the ones above.

Case 2 Linking project outcomes to CASAS outcomes A teacher recently asked me how project-based learning could possibly prepare his students for CASAS tests, which are administered every eight weeks in his program. I shared with him a class project on learning about the neighborhood, and identified some of the CASAS outcomes addressed in the project. I have correlated outcomes in CASAS 2.2 to the activities that emerged through the project in Figure 10.2.

CASAS Outcome 2.2

2.2 Understand how to locate and use different types of transportation and interpret related travel information

2.2.1 Ask for, give, follow, or clarify directions (see also 1.1.3, 1.9.4, 2.2.5)

2.2.2 Recognize and use signs related to transportation (see also 1.9.1)

2.2.4 Interpret transportation schedules and fares

2.2.5 Use maps relating to travel needs (see also 1.1.3, 1.9.4, 2.2.1)

See Figure 10.2 below.

Not only does the project in Figure 10.2 provide instruction and practice in all of the outcomes in CASAS 2.2, it takes learners into the community, introduces them to neighborhood resources, and gives them an opportunity to present what they have learned to others.

FIGURE 10.2

Civics education: Learning about our neighborhood
Project objective: Create a booklet for class and other members of the school who live in this community.

Materials and resources needed: Internet, neighborhood association, film and/or disposable cameras, maps.

Sample Unit Activities

1 In-class practice of asking for directions; role-plays (CASAS 2.2.1)

2 During computer class, find maps and information about services in the neighborhood on Internet (2.2.5).

3 Functional reading task: following directions on neighborhood maps (2.2.5).

4 Scavenger Hunts:
Group A: Students gather information about stores and services in neighborhood. With disposal cameras from school, take photos of locations (2.2.1).
Group B: Locate bus stops, bus routes, and schedules (2.2.2; 2.2.4).
Group C: Parents in class identify parks, playgrounds, and free/low-cost after-school activities for children.

5 Language Experience Activity: Group text about the experience with scavenger hunt. Multiple reading activities conducted using class-generated text.

6 Guest speaker from neighborhood association; Prepare for visit with prelistening activities; provide listening tasks at time of visit.

7 Present booklet at all-school event.

The two cases in this section illustrate how learner input provides the content and context for instruction that is compatible with a variety of standards, and in many cases multiple standards. Here is a checklist of important reminders:

- Provide ongoing opportunities for learners to articulate their goals.
- Find out what standards your program uses for accountability purposes and to guide the curriculum, and look for places where learner goals align with them.

- Use textbooks that correspond as closely as possible to outcomes and standards that address both learner and program needs and expectations.
- Use learner strengths, needs, wants, and dilemmas as the starting point of instruction.
- Develop assessment tools that capture learning in these areas.

Standards need not be a noose around teachers' and learners' necks; use standards to guide, shape, and help you in the process of developing lessons that are, first and foremost, responsive to learners.

CONCLUSION

I began this book with an examination of the unique strengths and challenges adult learners bring to ESL classrooms, and I have ended with a look at the larger picture of adult ESL standards and accountability. These topics, along with everything in between, should be seen as interconnected with the learner at the center, and each element in the adult ESL system should inform the others.

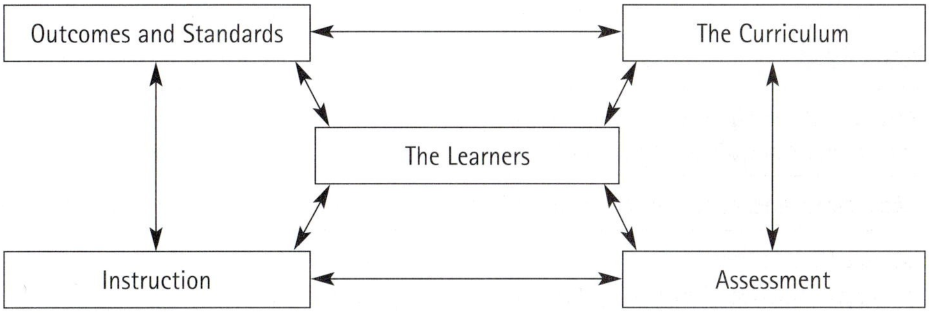

Our primary responsibilities as ESL teachers are to the learners. Standards and accountability systems should be viewed as one means of providing and maintaining quality instruction. They should be connected to the lives and needs of the learners, while at the time satisfying the needs of other stakeholders. I have argued, along with many other professionals in the field, that the most suitable approaches for working with adult ESL learners within this system are those that are truly learner-centered. It is my hope that the principles and practices in this text will get you started on the road to teaching in a variety of settings, with diverse groups of learners, and in keeping with your own beliefs and strengths as a teacher.

KEY TERMS

CHECKLIST OF KEY TERMS	On your own, or with a partner, provide an example or brief definition for each concept.
standards	
accountability	
National Reporting System	
performance indicators	
Equipped For the Future	
SCANS	
CASAS	
standards-based textbook series	

APPLYING WHAT YOU LEARNED

1 Standards in Your State

If you are already teaching. . . answer as many of these questions as you can. Then do research to answer those you were not sure about, or to add to your current understanding:

a What are the accountability requirements of my program and/or state?

b What standards guide my program?

c To whom is my program accountable and for what purposes?

d How can I align program standards with learner goals?

If you are not teaching. . . answer questions a, b, and c by calling the adult education office of your state, conducting online research, or by interviewing an ESL teacher or program coordinator. For question d, describe two things you would do in an ESL class to align learner goals and program standards.

2 Developing an Accountability Tool

If you are already teaching. . . identify and describe three standards or outcomes for which learners need to be assessed in your program. Describe what you believe would be the best means of gathering data to capture evidence of achievement of that standard or outcome (Recall ideas from Chapter 9: a performance assessment, collection of journal entries, KWL charts, etc.).

If you are not teaching. . . ask a teacher from your state to share three outcomes or standards from a class she or he teaches or find a list of the standards for your state and choose three for this activity. Describe what you believe would be the best means of gathering data to capture evidence of achievement of that standard or outcome (a performance assessment, collection of journal entries, KWL charts, etc.).

3 Aligning Learner Goals to Standards

If you are already teaching. . . identify three standards or outcomes from your state or program that you believe overlap with learner goals you have elicited. Describe two ways you would connect the program standard to your learners' goals.

If you are not teaching. . . find a list of the standards for your state (ask an ESL teacher or do an online search) and look for places where the *Learner Challenges* in section 10.8 on pages 294–295 overlap with those standards.

POST-TASK

Looking back. . .

Go back to the statements you reflected on at the beginning of this book. With a partner or on your own, complete these statements again with your current beliefs about teaching and learning in adult ESL contexts. Afterward, discuss the ways in which your views have evolved or changed through the course of working through this book, completing the activities, and working with others to develop your knowledge and skills as an ESL teacher.

1 Strengths and challenges adult learners bring to the ESL classroom are. . .

2 Some common purposes for learning English are. . .

3 Learning a second language involves. . .

4 If I walked into an adult ESL classroom, I'd like to see. . .

5 Learners' roles and responsibilities in class are. . .

6 My responsibilities as an ESL teacher are. . .

Recommended Reading

A Selection of Standards

(from Florez 2002)

California Department of Education, Adult Education Unit. 1992. Sacramento, CA: Author. http://www.otan.dni.us/webfarm/emailproject/standard.pdf

California's standards for adult ESL have three sections: (1) separate program, curriculum, instruction, and student assessment standards with accompanying examples; (2) descriptions and exit criteria for seven levels of English proficiency (beginning literacy to advanced); and (3) standards for ESL testing and a bibliography of tests and testing references.

Comprehensive Adult Student Assessment System. *CASAS competency list.*

This site contains a complete list of CASAS competencies. http://www.casas.org/01AboutCasas/01Competencies.html

Florida Department of Education. 2001. Tallahassee, FL: Author. http://www.firn.edu/doe/dwdframe/ad/pdf/3201030a.pdf

The adult ESL standards for Florida describe skills for workplace, life, and academic contexts at six proficiency levels (literacy to advanced). A summary of the general standards for each level is offered first, with specific performance indicators for each standard provided in the following section.

Massachusetts Department of Education. 1999. http://www.doe.mass.edu/acls/curriculum_frameworks.htm

The framework begins with the principles that guided this statewide effort and describes the primary components of the document: five strands (specific areas of learning and instruction that relate to all learners' needs, skill levels, or goals) and learning standards for each strand. Examples of performance indicators for each standard are included. Case-study-like learner profiles, anecdotal vignettes from practitioners, and five essays on topics that cut across strands and standards provide additional context.

New York State Education Department. 1997. *Adult education resource guide and learning standards.* Albany, NY: Author. http://www.hudrivctr.org/adedres.pdf

This document, addressing adult education in general in New York, includes a section on goals and standards for adult ESL. Nine broad standards (goals) with accompanying objectives and supporting performance task examples are presented. Descriptions of exit criteria or competencies for three proficiency levels, and suggestions of content areas and contexts in which the standards can be incorporated, are provided to help practitioners contextualize the standards as they develop curricula and assessment plans.

Stein, S. 2000. *Equipped for the Future (EFF) content standards: What adults need to know and be able to do in the 21st century.* Washington, DC: National Institute for Literacy. http://www.nifl.gov/lincs/collections/eff/standards_guide.pdf

This publication documents the development of EFF, a national effort to establish content standards for adult education. Sixteen standards define the knowledge and skills adults need to carry out their roles in three categories, or role maps: worker, citizen/community member, and parent/family member. Also provided are insights from field research on using the standards and a discussion of standards-based education reform.

TESOL. 2002. *Standards for Adult Education ESL Programs.*

TESOL's standards for adult education ESL. Programs define quality components from a national perspective. Using program indicators in eight distinct areas, the standards can be used to review an existing program or as a guide in setting up a new ESOL program.

U.S. Department of Labor. 1991. *Secretary's Commission on Achieving Necessary Skills.*

This report outlines the SCANS framework and contains a complete list of SCANS competencies.
http://wdr.doleta.gov/opr/FULLTEXT/1999_35.pdf

Useful Websites and Online Resources

Office of Vocational and Adult Education

http://www.ed.gov/offices/OVAE/AdultEd/index.html

This site provides updates on federal policies and laws. It contains links to *OVAE Review,* the biweekly update from the Office of the Assistant Secretary at the Office of Vocational and Adult Education, as well as links to statistics and information about the National Reporting System (NRS).

Alegre, Mary Kay. 2002. *A busy teacher's guide to EFF lesson planning.* Arlington, VA: Arlington Education and Employment Program.

This practical guide illustrates the ways in which a teacher can apply the EFF framework in lesson planning and implementation.
http://www.aelweb.vcu.edu/publications/teacher_guide/

National Reporting System Website

This site provides adult education teachers, administrators and others interested in the adult education program reference material and training related to the guidelines of the National Reporting System.
http://www.nrsweb.org/

Focus on Basics

Vol. 3, Issue B June 1999 is dedicated to issues of assessment and accountability, and Vol. 3, Issue C September 1999 is dedicated to standards-based education.
http://www.gse.harvard.edu/~ncsall/fob/1999/fobv3ic.htm

Glossary

accommodations allowances made for students with learning disabilities or physical handicaps that allow them equal access to all aspects of programs.

accountability being answerable to program administrators and funders for instruction and learner outcomes.

acculturation understanding of the beliefs, emotions, and behaviors of the dominant culture, without letting go of the first culture.

achievement test measures what learners have gained through a lesson, unit, or course.

acquisition vs. learning acquisition refers to natural, unconscious processes that children go through as they acquire their first language; learning refers to consciously learning the rules and patterns of the language.

action research a process of teachers identifying problems or issues in their teaching, gathering data or information about what is happening, researching the topic, and taking action in their classes.

affective filter hypothesis Krashen's term for emotional barriers to learning, for example, high stress or embarrassment.

alternative assessment refers to tools to assess learning that are typically classroom based and ongoing, and reflect the outcomes of a particular course. Examples include performance assessment, observation, self-assessment, or portfolio assessment.

assimilation is the complete absorption of the second culture practices, beliefs, and norms.

balanced literacy approach an approach to literacy development that draws on the principles of Whole Language teaching as well as more form-focused activities.

BICS Basic Interpersonal Communication Skills.

basic skills refers to everyday life skills needed to navigate in a new culture.

behaviorism refers to a theory that human beings learn new behaviors through a stimulus and response cycle.

BEST (Basic English Skills Test) intended for new immigrants with very limited English. Includes listening, speaking, reading, and writing.

bottom-up processing involves attempts to decode and understand a language word-for-word.

CALL Computer-assisted language learning is any means of enhancing instruction through the use of computer-based activities including software, the Internet, e-mail, or basic word processing.

CALP Cognitive Academic Language Proficiency.

CASAS (Comprehensive Adult Student Assessment System) an assessment system that includes an array of standardized tests for placement and achievement for reading, writing, listening, and life skills.

chain drills begin by a teacher or learner asking a question, another answers and asks the next question, in a chain fashion until all learners have practiced the language.

checking questions used so that learners *demonstrate* their understanding of new concepts (content, vocabulary, grammar, functions, or competencies).

communicability the ability to meet communicative demands.

communicative competence the ability to use language in a variety of settings (at work, at a store, at home) with varying degrees of formality (with a friend *vs.* with a boss).

Communicative Language Teaching (CLT) an approach to teaching that focuses on developing fluency and communicative competence through extensive interaction and use of authentic materials.

competencies real-life tasks learners need to complete at home, in their communities, or workplace, for example, calling in sick to work or completing a permission form for child's teacher.

competency-based education (CBE) an approach to education whereby language competencies become the basis for instruction.

Language functions, grammar, vocabulary, and skills are taught to assist learners in achieving the competencies.

comprehensible input Krashen's term for language input that is understandable to learners. Language is made comprehensible through gestures, visual support, repetition, or prior knowledge.

content standards refers to what students are expected *to know* and be able to do as a result of instruction.

content words those words that are stressed within a sentence; those that carry the most meaning, for example, nouns, verbs, or adjectives.

content-based instruction (CBI) curricula which have a content area as the focus of instruction, for example citizenship, math, social studies, or global studies. Often used in pre-academic programs.

contextualized language lessons focus on a particular language competency, function, grammar, or set of vocabulary used in real-world contexts.

core series consists of a sequence of books for beginning through high-intermediate or advanced-level learners that integrate instruction in all skill areas as well as grammar, functions, and competencies.

criterion-referenced test a test for which the scores reflect a comparison to a set of outcomes (or criteria).

critical period the stage when one is best able to acquire a second language, thought to be from around three years of age to just before puberty.

cultural competence understanding cultural norms and practices.

curricular routines daily or weekly classroom routines that make instruction consistent and predictable for learners.

diagnostic test a test or assessment tool that determines what learners do and do not know in relation to the course objectives.

dialogue journals learner journals that include an ongoing reader (usually the teacher) response.

discourse chains a controlled practice activity whereby learners are provided with the steps in a conversation (greet, request information, provide information) to complete with a partner.

discrimination task a listening task used in pronunciation instruction whereby learners demonstrate their ability to discriminate between different sounds or different stress or intonation patterns.

display questions questions for which one already knows the answer.

distance learning instruction where there is a separation of place and/or time between the learner(s) and the instructor, conducted through one or more media, for example, video or online learning.

dominant culture the majority and long-established culture of a society.

echoing a teacher repeating verbatim what learners say in class, either correctly or incorrectly.

EL civics programs that promote active citizenship and participation in all aspects of the community including voting and civic involvement, involvement in neighborhood programs, and active participation in children's schooling.

emergent curriculum a curriculum that develops around learners' expressed wants and needs.

environmental print print that is found in the community or workplace such as street signs, billboards, warning signs, or store names.

Equipped for the Future (EFF) a national initiative in adult education intended to help diverse groups of learners acquire the tools they need to thrive in society as parents/family members, citizens/community members, and workers.

family/intergenerational literacy these programs promote connections between homes and schools by promoting literacy among adults and their children in order that children reach their highest academic potential.

fluency the ease with which one is able to communicate in a second language, even without accuracy in the language.

function words the words that are typically unstressed within a sentence.

functional texts reading texts that are used for an everyday, functional purpose, such as menus, phone books, or labels.

functions of language represent the ways we use language forms and phrases in social interactions, for example, greetings and introductions, making invitations, making polite requests, or complaints and apologies.

graphic literacy the ability to use and understand pictorial symbols to convey meaning.

graphic organizers any means to visually organize information, for example, Venn diagrams, word webs, or charts.

i + 1 is Krashen's terms for input that is just beyond a learner's current level. This kind of input challenges yet is accessible to learners.

independent field trips are field trips that are completed by individual students outside of class time.

information-gap activity refers to an activity that requires a genuine exchange of information in order for learners to complete the task.

integrated-skills general English programs that serve a broad population of learners without specific vocational or academic outcomes. All four skills and all areas of language are integrated into the curriulum.

integrated-skills texts provide practice in all four skills areas and typically integrate grammar, language functions, and competencies.

intelligibility pronunciation that is understandable by the listener and does not interfere with communication.

interactionism a view that second language acquisition requires interaction between speakers. Language is made comprehensible through modifications or comprehension checks by both the speaker and listener.

intergenerational tension struggles that emerge among generations in immigrant families as a result of conflicting values, beliefs, and norms between the first culture and the new culture.

interpersonal dialogue dialogue for the purpose of communicating with others for personal reasons, for example, making small talk with a co-worker or talking to a friend about a concern at home.

jigsaw reading (or listening) refers to a reading or listening activity that involves different groups of learners reading or listening to different texts related to one theme, and then grouping with others in class to exchange the information they learned about in their text.

KWL chart is a means of activating background knowledge, setting learning goals, and reflecting on learning. The chart contains three sections: What do I know? What do I want to learn? What did I learn?

L1 an individual's first language.

Language Experience Approach (LEA) an approach that starts with a class recounting a shared experience, which is transcribed by the teacher. The class-generated text becomes the basis for literacy instruction.

language learning strategies tools learners employ to help them learn better, remember or organize information, or compensate for lacks in their language.

language skills the four language modes: listening, speaking, reading, and writing.

learner-centered instruction that puts the learners' backgrounds, expectations, strengths, wants, and needs at the center of curricular choices and classroom practices.

learning disability refers to any of a group of disorders manifested by significant difficulties in the acquisition and use of listening, speaking, reading, writing, reasoning, or mathematical abilities, presumed to be due to central nervous system dysfunction.

learning styles a person's preference for understanding and processing information.

linguistic competence refers to the ability to use and understand language forms, including grammar, spelling, and pronunciation.

literacy-level texts are intended for emergent readers who may have extremely limited literacy skills in their first language.

managed enrollment refers to a practice of admitting students only at particular times in a program, be it once a week or once every six weeks. It is an alternative to open enrollment, whereby learners enter programs on an ongoing basis.

meaningful practice involves activities in which learners talk about information that is truthful and relevant to their lives.

mechanical practice helps learners reinforce forms without necessarily creating meaningful utterances.

minimal pair pairs of words that have only one phonemic difference, for example, *bat* and *vat*: /b/ and /v/.

minority cultures groups that arrived in a country more recently than the dominant culture and make up a minority of the population.

monitor hypothesis Krashen's term for learned language acts as a monitor that edits and corrects language.

multiple intelligences Howard Gardner's term for at least seven *intelligences* that learners draw on to process and understand the world: verbal/linguistic, musical, logical/mathematical, spatial/visual, bodily/kinesthetic, intrapersonal, natural/environmental.

National Reporting System (NRS) an accountability system used to measure the effectiveness of federally funded adult education programs.

Natural Approach an approach to teaching that starts with providing abundant comprehensible input to learners, much in the way children acquire their first language.

nonliterate refers to students who speak a language which has a written form, but the students don't read or write that language themselves.

norm-referenced test a test for which the scores reflect a comparison to a group.

objectives what learners will be able to do at the completion of a lesson. Objectives should be observable and/or measurable.

open enrollment refers to allowing learners to enter programs at any time during a course or term.

outcomes the desired results of instruction.

parallel writing a guided writing activity that starts with a text that learners follow as a model for their own writing.

participatory approach drawn from Freire's work, a teaching that derives from learners' lives and personal issues within their social context so that they can take action to improve their lives.

performance assessment an assessment tool whereby learners perform language tasks to demonstrate their competency with language. The assessor uses a rubric with specific criteria in order to determine learner achievement.

performance indicators various means of providing evidence that learners are meeting program standards or outcomes, e.g., gains on test scores, achievement of personal goals, employment.

performance standards represent what learners need to do *to demonstrate* their proficiency within content standards.

phonics is a view that literacy development is a linear process whereby learners first acquire sound/letter correspondences with which they create words and then sentences.

placement test is used to determine the most suitable level for a learner within a program.

practicality the extent to which an assessment tool is practical to administer.

pre-academic ESL programs that prepare ESL learners to enter academic settings.

prelistening activities that serve to activate learner prior knowledge about a theme before listening to a passage and completing listening activities.

preliterate refers to students who speak a language that does not have a written form, or has a form that is rare or has developed very recently (e.g., Hmong).

prewriting activities that prepare a learner to write, for example, brainstorming ideas and organizing ideas.

problem posing a process in participatory education whereby learners identify problems that are affecting their lives. These issues and concerns become the basis of further activities.

process-oriented approach a multistep approach to writing that includes pre-writing, on-going feedback, and multiple drafts.

productive skills speaking and writing skills.

product-oriented writing focuses on the finished product rather than the process of writing.

proficiency test measures a learner's overall competence.

realia real objects brought into class for demonstration or practice.

receptive skills listening and reading skills.

reformulation responding to learner errors by naturally restating learner language correctly.

reliability refers to tests that provide consistent results.

scaffolded writing writing tasks whereby learners complete a sample text with key information left out.

scanning reading a text only for specific information.

SCANS (Secretary's Commission on Achieving Necessary Skills) refers to the *soft* skills needed to perform adequately in the workplace, for example, asking for help, working in teams, managing resources.

schema theory suggests that prior knowledge shapes our expectations and understanding of what we hear; the closer our schema is to the content of what we hear or read, the easier it will be for us to understand.

semiliterate refers to students who have some formal education or are able to read and write but only at an elementary level.

semiscripted dialogue dialogues that have some of the words provided and learners must fill in the missing portions to complete the dialogue with a partner.

sentence stress refers to the words that are stressed within a sentence.

silent period Krashen's term for the initial period of language acquisition when a learner understands some language but is not able to produce it.

skimming reading for the main idea or gist of a text.

sound/letter correspondences the correlation between written symbols (letters) and the sounds they represent in a language.

standardized tests administered and scored using procedures that are uniform and consistent; typically used to differentiate among learners at different levels for placement purposes.

standards-based textbooks those texts that are aligned to a particular set (or sets) of standards, either state or national.

target language 1) the second language learners are working to acquire; 2) the language focus of a particular lesson, for example, returning something to a store or the simple present tense.

think-pair-share a classroom routine whereby learners think of an answer or brainstorm ideas, then talk about it with a partner before sharing with the whole class.

top-down processing involves making educated guesses about content based on prior knowledge and visual clues (facial expressions, context, etc).

Total Physical Response (TPR) a teaching method whereby learners respond physically to teacher commands and eventually commands from other learners.

transactional dialogue dialogue that serves to transmit factual information.

transition programs programs offered in adult education that are the most advanced and aim to develop academic skills.

validity refers to tests or assessment tools that test what they are intended to test.

vocational English as a second language (VESL) VESL refers to courses that provide instruction in English needed for a particular vocation, for example, nursing or carpentry.

virtual field trips 'field trips' that are completed through online searches, typically around a particular theme with particular tasks to complete.

Whole Language an overall philosophy to learning, which views language as something that should be taught in its entirety, not broken up into small pieces to be decoded.

word stress refers to the syllable that is stressed within a multi-syllable word.

wait time the time provided for a learner to think of and respond to teacher questions.

word web a visual presentation of how words or concepts are interconnected, with a key word in the center and related words branching out from there.

workplace ESL programs ESL programs offered at the workplace.

work readiness programs ESL programs that prepare learners for a variety of work settings.

References

Adams. L. and **V. Ferlet.** 2002. Adult pre-literacy and low literacy: Classroom theme-based teaching and learning ideas. Paper presented at the Midwest TESOL Conference, St. Paul, MN.

Auerbach, E. 1992. *Making meaning, making change: A participatory curriculum development for adult ESL literacy.* Washington, DC and McHenry, IL: Center for Applied Linguistics and Delta Systems.

Auerbach, E. 1995. From deficit to strength: Changing perspectives on family literacy. In *Immigrant learners and their families.* Weinstein-Shr, G., and E. Quintero, (eds.) Washington, DC and McHenry, IL: Center for Applied Linguistics and Delta Systems.

Auerbach, E. and **D. Burgess.** 1985. The hidden curriculum of survival ESL. *TESOL Quarterly* 19 (3): 475-495.

Auerbach, E. and **N. Wallerstein.** 1987. *ESL for action.* Reading, MA: Addison Wesley.

Azar, B. 2000. *Chartbook*, 3rd Edition. White Plains, NY: Prentice Hall Regents.

Baca, L., and **H.T. Cervantes.** 1991. Bilingual special education. *ERIC Digest.* Reston, VA: Clearinghouse on Disabilities and Gifted Education (ED No. 333 618).

Bakin, B. 2003. Lessons for the one-computer classroom. *Language Magazine.* April pp. 38-40.

Balliro, L. 1997. Multiple levels, multiple responsibilities. *Focus on Basics*, Volume 1, Issue C. http://www.gse.harvard.edu/~ncsall/fob/1997/balliro.htm

Barton, D. and **M. Hamilton.** 2000. Literacy practices. In Barton, D., M. Hamilton, and R. Ivanic (eds.) *Situated literacies: Reading and writing in context.* London: Routledge.

Becker, A. and **M. Lindt.** 1996. U.S. citizenship and ESL: The pivotal role of ESL instructors. *TESOL Matters*, 7, (1), p. 16.

Bell, J. 1991. *Teaching multilevel classes in ESL.* Carlsbad, CA: Dominie Press.

Bello, T. 1999. New avenues to choosing and using videos. *TESOL Matters*, 9(4), 20.

Blanton, L. 2002. *Idea exchange.* Boston, MA: Heinle and Heinle.

Brinton, D.M., M.A. Snow, and **M.B. Wesche.** 1989. *Content-based second language instruction.* New York: Newbury House Publishers.

Brod, S. 1990. Recruiting and retaining language minority students in adult literacy programs. *ERIC Digest.* Washington, DC: National Clearinghouse for ESL Literacy Education (ED 321 621).

Brod, S. 1999. Focus on reading: Seven easy pieces. *Focus on Basics*, Volume 3, Issue D. http://www.gse.harvard.edu/~ncsall/fob/1999/brod'sarticle.html

Bronz, C., and **L. Dorwaldt.** 2001. Vermont students win resources and action. In Nash, A. (ed.) *Civic participation and community action sourcebook.* Boston, MA: New England Literacy Resources Center.

Brown, H.D. 2001. *Teaching by principles: An interactive approach to language pedagogy.* New York: Longman.

Burt, M. 1999. Using video with adult English language learners. *ERIC Digest.* Washington, DC: National Center for ESL Literacy Education (EDO-LE-99-03).

Byrd, P. 2001. Textbooks: Evaluation for selection and analysis for implementation. In *Teaching English as a second or foreign language.* Celce-Murcia, M. (ed.) Boston, MA: Heinle and Heinle.

Canadian Centre for Victims of Torture. Torture and second language acquisition. http://www.icomm.ca/ccvt/intro.html.

Celce-Murcia, M., D. Brinton, and **J. Goodwin.** 1996. *Teaching pronunciation.* Cambridge: Cambridge University Press.

Chomsky, N. 1959. Review of *Verbal behavior* by B.F. Skinner. *Language* 35/1: 26-58.

Crandall, J., and **J. Peyton.** (eds.) 1993. *Approaches to adult literacy instruction.* Washington, DC and McHenry, IL: Center for Applied Linguistics and Delta Systems.

Crawford, J. 1999. Re: LD - Disability or difference? Posting to NIFL LD listserve (NIFL-LD:2408) http://www.nifl.gov/nifl-ld/1999/1034.html.

Cummins, J. 1979. Cognitive/academic language proficiency, linguistic interdependence, the optimum age questions, and some other matters. *Working Papers in Bilingualism* 19, 121-129.

Dyck, S.V., E. Battell, J. Isserlis, and **K. Nonesuch.** 1996. Women and work. In *Making connections: A literacy and EAL curriculum from a feminist perspective.* Toronto: Canadian Congress for Learning Opportunities for Women.

Easter, B. and **L. Wilson.** 2002. ESL from A to Z: Orienting new teachers to your adult ESL program. Paper presented at Midwest TESOL Conference. Bloomington, MN.

Edge, J. 1992. *Cooperative development.* Harlow, UK: Longman.

EEOC. 1995. Daly vs. U.S. Postal Service, 96 FEOR 3008. U.S. Equal Opportunity Employment Commission.

Ferguson, P. 1998. The politics of adult ESL literacy: Becoming politically visible. In Trudy Smoke (ed.): *Adult ESL: Politics, pedagogy and participation in classroom and community programs.* Mahwah, NJ: Lawrence Erlbaum Associates.

Fitzgerald, N. 1994. ESL instruction in adult education: Findings from a national evaluation. *ERIC Digest.* Washington, DC: National Clearinghouse for ESL Literacy Education (ED385171).

Flege, J. 1981. The phonological basis of foreign accent: A hypothesis. *TESOL Quarterly,* 15(4), 443-455.

Florez, M.C. 2000, June/July. Native languages in the beginning adult ESL classroom: To use or not to use. *WATESOL News,* 30(4), 1, 10.

Florez, M.C. 2002. An annotated bibliography of content standards for adult ESL. Washington, DC: National Center for ESL Literacy Education.

Gaer, S. 1998a. Using software in the adult ESL classroom. *ERIC Digest.* Washington, DC: National Center for ESL Literacy Education (EDRS No. ED 418 607).

Gaer, S. 1998b. Integrating computer skills into low level ESL. *Literacy Links* Vol. 3, No. 2, Section A College Station Texas: Texas Center for Adult Literacy and Learning.

Gaer, S. 1998c. Project-based learning. *Focus on Basics,* Volume 2, Issue D. http://www.gse.harvard.edu/~ncsall/fob/1998/gaer.htm

Gardner, H. 1993. *Frames of mind: The theory of multiple intelligences* (10th anniversary ed). New York: Basic Books.

Gilbert, J. 1993. *Clear speech.* New York: Cambridge University Press.

Graves, K. 2000. *Designing language courses.* Boston, MA: Heinle and Heinle.

Grognet, A. 1997. Integrating employment skills in adult ESL instruction. *ERIC Q and A.* Washington, DC: National Center for ESL Literacy Education.

Hacker, E. and **M. Capehart.** 1999. *Surfing for substance.* New York, NY: Literacy Assistance Center. http://hub1.worlded.org/docs/surfing/

Hamilton, M. 1999. Ethnography for classrooms: Constructing a reflective curriculum for literacy. *Curriculum Studies,* Volume 7, Number 3.

Harmer, J. 2000. *The practice of English language teaching.* Harlow, UK: Longman.

Haverson, W.W., and **J.L. Haynes.** 1982. ESL/literacy for adult readers. *Language in education: Theory and practice* No. 49. Washington, DC: Center for Applied Linguistics (*ERIC Digest* No. 217-703).

Healey, D. and **N. Johnson.** 2002. A place to start in selecting software. *CAELL Journal* 8:1, Winter 1997/98; last updated May 2002. http://www.onid.orst.edu/~healeyd/table2.html

Holt, D. and **C. Van Duzer.** (eds). 2000. *Assessing success in family literacy and adult ESL.* Washington, DC and McHenry, IL: Center for Applied Linguistics and Delta Systems.

Holt, G., and **D. Holt.** 1995. Literacy program design: Reflections from California in Weinstein-Shr, G., and E. Quintero (eds.). *Immigrant learners and their families.* Washington, DC and McHenry, IL: Center for Applied Linguistics and Delta Systems.

Huizenga, J. and **J. Bernard-Johnston.** (1995). *Collaborations.* Boston, MA: Heinle and Heinle.

Isserlis, J. 1992. What you see: Ongoing assessment in the ESL/literacy classroom. *Adventures in Assessment,* Volume 2. SABES/World Education, Boston, MA.

Isserlis, J. 1996a. Women at the centre of the curriculum. In K. Nonesuch (ed.), *Making connections: Literacy and EAL curriculum from a feminist perspective* (pp. 13-14). Toronto, Canada: Canadian Congress for Learning Opportunities for Women.

Isserlis, J. 1996b. Dialogue journal writing as part of a learner-centered curriculum. In (eds) Peyton, J.K. and J. Staton, *Writing our lives.* Washington, DC and McHenry, IL: Center for Applied Linguistics and Delta Systems.

Isserlis, J. 2000. Trauma and the adult English language learner. *ERIC Digest.* Washington, DC: National Clearinghouse for ESL Literacy Education (EDO-LE-00-02).

Jacobs, B. 1988. Neurobiological differentiation of primary and secondary language acquisition. *Studies in Second Language Acquisition,* 10, 303-337.

Johnson, B. 1993. Teacher-as-researcher. *ERIC Clearinghouse on Teacher Education.* Washington DC (ED355205). http://www.ericfacility.net/ericdigests/ed355205.html.

Kenworthy, J. 1987. *Teaching English pronunciation.* London: Longman.

Kramsch, C. 1996. Proficiency plus: The next step. *ERIC Clearinghouse on Languages and Linguistics.* (ED402789).

Krashen, S. 1982. *Principles and practice in second language acquisition.* Oxford: Pergamon.

Krashen, S. 1985. *The input hypothesis.* London: Longman.

Krashen, S. and **T. Terrell.** 1983. *The natural approach: Language acquisition in the classroom.* Oxford: Pergamon Press.

Kress, G. and **T. Van Leeuwen.** 1996. *Reading images: The grammar of visual design.* London: Routledge.

Ladousse, G.P. 1987. *Role play.* Oxford: Oxford University Press.

Lanning, K. and **B. Parrish.** 2000. Authentic assessment in adult ESL classes. Presentation at the Spring ELL/Bilingual Education Conference. St. Paul, MN.

Levis, J. 1999. Intonation in theory and practice, revisited. *TESOL Quarterly* 33:1, pp. 37-63.

Lightbown, P. and **N. Spada.** 1999. *How languages are learned.* Oxford: Oxford Univerity Press.

Long, M. 1983. Native speaker/non-native speaker conversation and the negotiation of comprehensible input. *Applied Linguistics* 4:126-41.

Lowry, C. 1990. Teaching adults with learning disabilities. ERIC Clearinghouse on Adult Career and Vocational Education. Columbus, OH (ED321156).

MacDonald, B. 1997. The impact of content-based instruction. *Focus on Basics,* Volume 1, Issue D.

McKay, H. and **H. Tom.** 1999. *Teaching adult second language learners.* Cambridge: Cambridge University Press.

Morley, J. 1991. The pronunciation component in teaching English to speakers of other languages. *TESOL Quarterly* 25:3, pp. 481-518.

Mulhern, M., F. Rodriguez-Brown, and **T. Shanahan.** 1994. Family literacy for language minority families: Issues for program implementation. *NCBE Program Information Guide Series,* Number 17, Summer 1994.

Nash, A. 2001. *Civic participation and community action sourcebook.* Boston, MA: New England Literacy Resources Center.

National Institute for Literacy. 2000. How states are implementing distance education for adult learners. NIFL policy update based on survey by Tracy-Mumford.

National Joint Committee on Learning Disabilities. 1994. Collective perspectives on issues affecting learning disabilities. Austin, TX: Pro-ed.

New England Literacy Resource Center. 2002. New England ABE-to-college transition project. http://www.nelrc.org/abe.htm.

Nixon-Ponder, S. 1994. Teacher to teacher: Using problem-posing dialogue in adult literacy education. Ohio Literacy Resource Center Lincs. http://literacy.kent.edu/Oasis/Pubs/0300-8.htm

Nunan, D. 1991. *Language teaching methodology: A textbook for teachers.* New York: Prentice Hall International.

Nunan, D. 1992. *Research methods in language learning* Cambridge: Cambridge University Press.

Nunan, D. 1999. Approaches to teaching listening in the language classroom. *Proceedings of the 1997 Korea TESOL Conference.*

Olsen, L. 1988. *Crossing the schoolhouse border: Immigrant students and the California public schools.* Oakland, CA: A California Tomorrow Report.

O'Malley, J.M. and **A. Chamot.** 1990. *Learning strategies in second language acquisition.* Cambridge: Cambridge University Press.

Oxford, R. 1990. *Language learning strategies: What every teacher should know.* New York: Newbury House.

Parrino, A. 2001. The politics of pronunciation and the adult learner. In Trudy Smoke (ed.): *Adult ESL: Politics, pedagogy and participation in classroom and community programs.* Mahwah, NJ: Lawrence Erlbaum Associates.

Parrish, B. and **D. Pecoraro.** 2002. EL civics: Taking learning outside of the classroom. Presentation at *Minnesota ABE Summer Intensive.* Breezy Point. Brainerd, MN.

Peyton, J. 1993. Listening to students' voices: Publishing students' writing for other students to read. In Crandall, J. and J. Peyton, (eds.) *Approaches to adult ESL literacy.* Washington, DC and McHenry, IL: Center for Applied Linguistics and Delta Systems.

Peyton, J. and **J. Staton.** (eds.) 1996. *Writing our lives.* Washington, DC and McHenry, IL: Center for Applied Linguistics and Delta Systems.

Pienemann, M., M. Johnston and **G. Brindley.** 1988. Constructing an acquisition-based procedure for second language assessment. *Studies in Second Language Acquisition* 10/2:217-43.

Price-Machado, D. 1998. *Success in English.* Cambridge: Cambridge University Press.

Raimes, A. 1984. Anguish as a second language? Remedies for composition teachers. In S. McKay (ed.) *Composing in a second language.* Rowley, MA: Newbury House.

Ramirez, S. 2001. Noncredit ESL managed enrollment pilot. MiraCosta College report. http://www.miracosta.cc.ca.us/conted/esl/enrollment.htm

Rance-Roney, J. 1995. Transitioning adult ESL learners to academic programs. Washington DC: National Clearinghouse on ESL Literacy Education (ERIC no. EDO-LE-95-05).

Reimer, J. 1999. Learner to observe learning: The role of peer interaction in a practicum. Unpublished MA Project. Vermont: School for International Training.

Richards, J. and **T.S. Rodgers.** 1986. *Approaches and methods in language teaching.* Cambridge: Cambridge University Press.

Rivera, K. 1999. Native language literacy and adult ESL instruction. *ERIC Digest.* Washington, DC: National Center for ESL Literacy Education (EDO-LE-99-04).

Salehi, N. 2000. Using the Internet in ESL instruction. Presentation for the *TEFL Certificate Program.* St. Paul, MN: Hamline University.

Savage, K.L. 1993. Literacy through a competency-based educational approach. In *Approaches to adult literacy instruction.* Crandall, J. and J. Peyton, (eds.) Washington, DC and McHenry, IL: Center for Applied Linguistics and Delta Systems.

Savage, K.L. 1984. Teaching strategies for developing literacy skills in non-native speakers of English. Unpublished manuscript (ERIC Document Reproduction Service No. ED 240 296).

Savage, K.L., and **L. Howard.** 1992. *Teacher training through videos: ESL techniques.* White Plains, NY: Longman.

Scarcella, R. 1990. *Teaching language minority students in the multicultural classroom.* Upper Saddle River, NJ: Prentice Hall.

Scarcella, R. 1992. Providing culturally sensitive feedback. In Richard-Amato, P. and M. Snow, (eds.) *The multicultural classroom.* Reading, MA: Addison-Wesley.

School Services of California. 2002. Report from the Superintendent to the Governor's Board. http://www.regional.org/execreport/2002/03.pdf

Schumann, J. 1986. Research on the acculturation model for second language acquisition. *Journal of Multilingual and Multicultural Development.* 7, 379-392.

Scogins, J. and **S. Knell.** 2001. Observations in adult ESL classrooms: What is really going on? Final report to Illinois State Board of Education. http://www.ilrdc.org/COR.pdf.

Scrivener, J. 1994. *Learning teaching.* Hampshire, UK: Macmillan Heinemann.

Shank, C. and **L. Terrill.** 1997. Multilevel literacy planning and development. *Focus on Basics* Volume 1, Issue C. http://www.gse.harvard.edu/~ncsall/fob/1997/shank.htm.

Simons, A. 1999. Teaching ESL among adults with learning disabilities. Training materials for facilitators and participants *CAEPA Conference Fall 1999.* http://www.swadulted.com/workshops/ld/esl-ld.html.

Skinner, B.F. 1957. *Verbal learning.* New York, NY: Appleton-Century-Crofts.

Spener, D. 1993. The Freirean approach to adult literacy education. In *Approaches to adult literacy instruction.* Crandall, J. and J. Peyton, (eds.) Washington, DC and McHenry, IL: Center for Applied Linguistics and Delta Systems.

Stein, S. 2003. *Equipped for the future content standards.* Washington, DC: National Institute for Literacy.

Sticht, Tom 1997. The theory behind content-based instruction. *Focus on Basics,* Volume 1, Issue D.

Taggart, K. 1996. Preparing ESL workers to work in teams. *The Connector,* 4, 2-3. http://www.cal.org/Archive/projects/Mellon.htm#NEWS

Tarone, E. and **B. Parrish.** 1994. Task related variation in interlanguage: The case for articles. In H.D. Brown and S. Gonzo (eds.) *Readings on second language acquisition,* Englwood Cliffs, NJ: Prentice Hall.

Taylor, M. 1993. The language experience approach. In Crandall, J. and J. Peyton, (eds.) *Approaches to adult ESL literacy.* Washington, DC and McHenry, IL: Center for Applied Linguistics and Delta Systems.

University of Kansas Center for Research on Learning 1998. Accomodating adults with disabilities in adult education programs. Lawrence, KS: University of Kansas Center for Research on Learning.

Van Duzer, C. 1999. Reading and the adult ESL learner. National Center for ESL Literacy Education (EDO-LE-99-02).

Van Duzer, C. 2002. Issues in accountability and assessment for adult ESL instruction. National Center for ESL Literacy Education (NCLE) http://www.cal.org/ncle/digests/accountQA.htm

Vinogradov, P. 2001. A look at ESL instruction for literacy-level adults. *MinneTESOL/WITESOL Journal,* Vol. 18:23-41.

Weinstein, C.E. 1988. Assessment and training of student learning strategies. In R. Schmeck, (ed.). *Learning strategies and learning styles* (pp 275-290). New York: Plenum Press.

Weinstein, G. (ed.). 1999. *Learners' lives as curriculum.* Washington DC and McHenry, IL: Delta Systems and Center for Applied Linguistics.

Whetzel, D. 1992. The Secretary of Labor's Commission on Achieving Necessary Skills. ERIC Clearinghouse on Tests Measurement and Evaluation Washington DC. *ERIC Digest* (ED339749).

Wilberg, P. 1988. *One to one: A teachers' handbook.* London: Language Teaching Publications.

Wong Fillmore, L. 2002. Language for learning and testing: How do English language learners acquire it? Plenary talk at the Spring ELL/Bilingual Education Conference. St. Paul, MN.

Woodward, T. and **S. Lindstromberg.** 1995. *Planning from lesson to lesson.* Essex: Pilgrims.

Wrigley, H.S. 1998. Knowledge in action: The promise of project-based learning. *Focus on Basics,* Volume 2, Issue D.

Wrigley, H. and **G. Guth.** 1992. *Bringing literacy to life: Issues and options in adult ESL literacy.* San Mateo, CA: Aguirre International.

Index

D

E

F

G

H

I

J

K

L

[redacted]

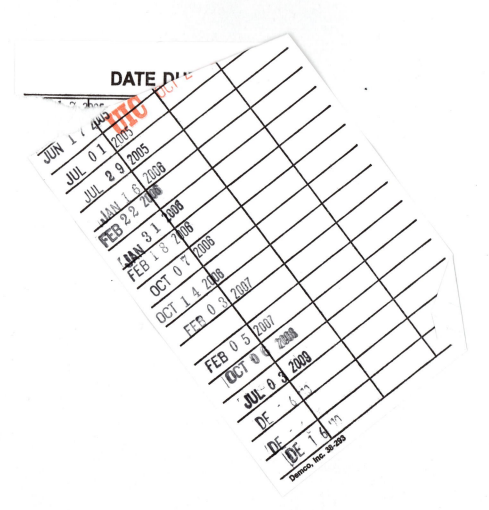